A COLLECTORS IDENTIFICATION AND VALUE GUIDE

LUCKEY'S
HŬMMEL
FIGURINES & PLATES
9th Edition
Carl F. Luckey

*For
Rue Du Mann
with highest
regards Carl
June '92*

BOOKS AMERICANA
INC

ISBN 0-89689-091-0

Cover photo courtesy
Royal Dutch Collectables and Roz.
Nashville, Tennessee

i

For Mary Frances – my light, love and life.

For Dan - in friendship, with much respect and gratitude; naturally for the last fourteen years but the forty years before as well.

ACKNOWLEDGEMENTS

It is never possible to acknowledge all who contribute to works of this sort. There are always so many helpful and cooperative people in on an endeavor such as this that to thank them all in print would be impractical. To those of you who worked so hard on my behalf, I proffer my heartfelt thanks. I hope the finished work meets with your approval.

Without photographs the book would be unfinished at best, so many thanks to the following for their cordial hospitality and permission to photograph their collections: Rue Dee, Judy and Kim Marker, Mrs. James E. Anderson, Jr., Mr. and Mrs. William J. Donley, Mr. and Mrs. Erich H. Sigle, George W. Terrell, Jr., and Mr. and Mrs. Ed F. Hodges.

Extra special thanks to Rue Dee and Judy Marker and Pat and Carol Arbenz, for their kindness and patience, and more thanks to Mr. and Mrs. Robert L. Miller, Don Stevens, Eileen Grande, Mr. and Mrs. Irving Dunckelman, Helen L. Jacobs, and Mr. and Mrs. Tibor Kovesdy for their invaluable contributions.

AUTHOR'S NOTE

Now that I have written the ninth edition of this book, you might think that the note in the first paragraph of the **Author's Note** in the first eight editions is redundant. Not so. It still applies, hence: ''It must be emphasized that the current market value information presented herein is for the most part an approximation. It is meant to be a guide only and not the final, authoritative word.'' Indeed it would be most presumptious for me or any other author to claim he could do so. I can only say that the value information you will find here is the result of a conscientious effort to find the fair secondary market values for each object. The values are not inflated or deflated for anyone's advantage. They are not ''crystal gazing'' nor are they guesses. They are simply the reflection of secondary market trading. The pieces listed herein are those which are **known** to exist either by personal observation or substantiated by trusted dealers and collectors. There may be others but their existence can only be conjecture at this point in time.

It is incumbent upon an author of *any* price guide to point out they are all, *without exception,* out of date the day of publication. This phenomenon is unavoidable due to the inherent delays in the preparation of the manuscript, typesetting, layout, printing, proof reading corrections, binding and, finally publication and distribution. *Use the value information while keeping in mind the above* and that because of the delays, the statistical data used to derive the value information is from a period of time ending roughly February, 1992. See page 15 for a more detailed discussion of pricing.

As for the sizes, anyone who has ever tried to categorize by actual size knows what a tremendous task it is. There are few lists, if any, which agree with each other, including factory published lists from one release to the next. If one had at his disposal all variations in size, color and model of every single piece ever produced, he could compile an accurate size listing. This is the only way an accurate cataloging as to size could be accomplished. Wouldn't we all like to have a collection such as that!?

As has been my habit in my other books, I invite any or all of you with additional information, constructive criticisms and, especially, suggestions as to how I might improve the book to write me direct. Because the book is not absolutely complete, I particularly welcome any new information and photographs you may choose to send. Because there are so many diverse opinions about certain areas, I do not apologize if I have disagreed with someone's particular point of view; however, if it can be successfully demonstrated that I am wrong in some area, I will gladly correct it in the next edition.

I have, over the years, received thousands of letters from Hummel collectors, dealers and those who discover that they have a Hummel item or two as a result of seeing my book. As a result I have been able to uncover new (old) pieces and add much good new data to my bulging research files making a better book for the collector in the subsequent editions. **The greatest majority of these letters however, are not about original M.I. Hummel pieces at all but, are from folks who think they have a rare item because it bears the Goebel trademark and does not correspond with the piece pictured in the book even though it appears to have the same mold number; or the item they have bears a number I list as a Closed Number. In every case they had one of the many non-Hummel items produced by Goebel. So, before writing to me, please be sure to study the section entitled "Non-Hummel Items Made by Goebel" beginning on page 5.**

Please do not ask me to appraise lists or answer questions regarding your collection. Time no longer allows me that luxury.

If you choose to write me I can't promise to acknowledge

every single letter, but I will attempt to do so in time, as number allows. **Please, no telephone calls** and do remember to enclose a self-addressed, stamped envelope with your letter. That will go a long way toward helping to assure a response.

Happy Collecting!

Carl F. Luckey
Lingerlost
Route 4, Box 301
Killen, Alabama 35645

INTRODUCTION
TO THE NINTH EDITION

There is continuing and unprecedented interest in Hummel figurines with every passing year. Of course there have been many, many collectors in Germany around 1934-35, but there has been an incredibly enormous surge in their popularity over the past fifteen years. Because of this increased interest, there is a growing need for accurate information concerning their identification and worth and periodic updating of that data.

That need is being fulfilled by various periodicals, books and other publications, some good and a few not so good ones.

Values have skyrocketed in the past but have settled down more or less in the last few years to a less spectacular but still mostly positive rate. Indeed some values have decreased, but these are the exception rather than the rule. Now that Hummel figurines and related articles have become so popular and so valuable alas, there have appeared not a few scurrilous individuals who take advantage of the situation and attempt to reproduce the figures, alter trademarks or pass off poor copies as the original genuine article to unsuspecting and uninitiated buyers. This possibility is increasing; therefore, it behooves any potential purchaser to arm himself with an arsenal of information. This is not to say that there are no honest dealers, quite the contrary. There are hundreds and hundreds of fine, upstanding and trustworthy firms and individuals in the country, and ninety-nine times out of a hundred there is no problem. It must be emphasized, however, that this phenomenon has followed every type of work of art or collectible that has ever become as popular, as valuable, and as widely sought as Hummel figurines have. It is particularly prevalent in areas where the objects are as numerous as are Hummel figurines and other related Hummel articles.

The task of identification and evaluation is complicated simply by the sheer number of figures and objects which have been produced, as well as the lack of good production records and quality control in the early years. It is further complicated by the inherent changes in design, size, coloration, complex system of trademarks and size designator markings, wrought by the changing times, and the normal changes present in the growth of any large firm such as the W. Goebel firm. They, like any other company, did not begin producing the figures with any knowledge that they would become so popularly collected and therefore did not realize the future need for a set of controls and simple system of marking. Over the years they have realized this need and, for their own protection and for that of the collector, have developed (about 1960) the technology of production and control to a point where the sizes are somewhat standard and markings more representative.

This book is for anyone who has an interest in Hummel figurines; the dealer, the collector, or anyone owning just one or two figures or who may be contemplating beginning a collection. It is important to restate that it is not an absolute authority, for that is impossible to do at this time. There is not enough known by any one individual to present the unquestionable, authoritative book just yet. There are too many diverse opinions, too many unknown circumstances surrounding the history of production and marketing of the objects, too many pieces not yet uncovered, too many variations in pieces already known and new variations being constantly discovered and, last but not least, unquestionably genuine figures showing up, never believed to have existed before.

This is a collector's guide, just that, a *guide,* to be used in conjunction with every other bit of information the collector may be able to obtain.

The information in this book was obtained from the same sources the dealer and collector presently have available. It is a compendium of information gleaned from the historians, pamphlets, brochures, the dealers and collectors themselves, shows and conventions, the distributors, the manufacturers, the writers, which has all been drawn together for their use.

There are a few other books and some specialists and experts on this subject in the world, some of which are listed elsewhere in this volume. The book also contains a brief history of the figures, the factory, and Sister Maria Innocentia Hummel (the artist from whose work virtually all Hummel figurine designs are taken); an explanation of the markings found on the objects; a glossary of terms; a brief description of productions techniques and most important of all, a comprehensive listing of the figurines and objects themselves. In this ninth edition the listing has been expanded considerably and is the most comprehensive and accurate possible. It includes sizes, color and mold variations, current production status, a detailed description, the Hummel mold number, a picture and current market evaluation, where either or both were available, and other remarks of interest concerning each of the pieces.

The pieces listed in the book are those produced with

trademarks, from the first Crown trademarks through the current trademark being used by the company.

Since this book was released in first edition fourteen years ago there have been other books by other authors to follow. In addition to them there have been many articles written in various publications. As a result of this there are several different methods of indicating the particular trademark associated with the Hummel pieces discussed. In the interest of helping to alleviate the confusion sometimes resulting, the trademark nomenclature coming into the most popular usage as abbreviation will be presented in chart form here and scattered throughout the Hummel Collection Listing. It consists simply of assigning a number for each of the trademarks found on Hummel pieces chronologically in their order of appearance beginning with the Crown Mark, Trademark Number One abbreviated "TMK 1."

Crown	CM	TMK-1	1934-1950
Full Bee	FB	TMK-2	1940-1959
Stylized Bee	Sty Bee	TMK-3	1958-1972
Three Line Mark	3-Line	TMK-4	1964-1972
Last Bee Mark	LB	TMK-5	1970-1980
Missing Bee Mark	MB	TMK-6	1979-1991
Hummel Mark (Current)	HM	TMK-7	1991-Present

CONTENTS

SECTION I
W. GOEBEL PORZELLANFABRIK
A Short History of the Factory

The factory is W. Goebel Porzellanfabrik, located in Rodental, Germany. The factory began production of china and porcelain soon after being founded by Franz Detlev Goebel in 1871. An independent operation, Schmid Brothers, Inc. of Boston, Massachusetts is also authorized by Goebel to distribute Hummel pieces in the United States and Canada.

In 1934 Franz Goebel conceived the idea of fashioning figurines based on drawings of Sister Hummel and secured permission from her and her convent to begin production. The first figurines were produced in 1935 and introduced at the Leipzig Trade Fair. There were a total of 46 different figures issued during the year and each of them bore the Crown WG mark sometimes known as the Wide Crown (TMK-1).

During the war years production of Hummel figurines and other related articles slowly diminished due to Nazi government policies and by the end of the war their production had ceased altogether. During the American occupation, the United States Military Occupation Goverment allowed the firm to resume production. During this period of time the figures became quite popular among U.S. servicemen and upon returning to the States their interest in them engendered a new popularity for the pieces. Figures produced during the Occupation (1946-48) were marked "U.S. ZONE, GERMANY" or U.S. Zone", in addition to the trademarks in use at the time, i.e., the Crown and the Full Bee (see pages 31 and 32).

Today the firm maintains a large complex of factories in Rodental, manufacturing, among other things, Hummel figurines and related articles.

SISTER MARIA INNOCENTIA
(BERTA HUMMEL)
1909-1946

Sister of the Third Order of Saint Francis. Siessen Convent, Saulgau, Germany, in the Swabian Alps.

In a way of a brief history of the life of Sister Maria Innocentia Hummel, reprinted below are a few paragraphs officially issued by the Siessen Convent as the only "Story of the Hummel figures":

The story of the Hummel Figures is very unique and full of interest for all lovers of the arts.

The charming but simple figurines of little boys and girls capture the hearts of all who love children. In them we are, perhaps, our girl or boy, or even ourselves when we were racing along the path of happy childhood. These endearing figurines will take you back to your school days so vividly sculptured in the "Schoolboy" or "Schoolgirl" to the time when you perhaps stole your first apple from a tree in the neighbor's garden and were promptly set upon by his dog, as shown in the "Apple Thief" figure (now known as "Culprits").

You will delight in the beauty of the "Flower Madonna" or the "Little Shepherd". Yes, you will love them all with their little round faces and big, questioning eyes. You will want to collect them. Then, you might ask yourself, who is this artist, the creator of beauty and simplicity?

Her name is Berta Hummel, and she was a Franciscan nun called Sister Maria Innocentia.

Berta Hummel was born on May 21, 1909, at Massing in Bavaria, about thirty miles southeast of Munich and twenty miles north of Oberammergau. She grew up among a family of two brothers and three sisters in a home where music and art were a part of everyday life. Is is, therefore, easy to assume that her talent for drawing and coloring was nourished and fostered by her parents.

The years between 1916 and 1921 were spent at a Primary School in Massing and we note that her imagination was vivid even at this early age. She painted delightful little cards and printed verses for family celebrations, birthdays, anniversaries and Christmas. The subjects of her art were always the simple objects with which she was so familiar: flowers, birds, animals and her little school friends. In this child world in which she lived, Berta Hummel could see only the beautiful things around her. After that, however, it was necessary to give her great talent a wider scope for development.

In 1921 she joined the Girls' Finishing School at Simbach. Here again her drawing and coloring found such acclaim that a further cultivation was found advisable. There was only one place in which her talent and, by now, her desire for art and its translation into everyday life, could be satisfied. It was Munich, the town of arts on the Isar.

In 1927, after completing her elementary and secondary education, Berta Hummel, now a budding artist, moved to Munich, where she entered the Academy of Fine Arts. There she lived the life of the artist of her day, made friends, and painted her heart's content. Here she acquired full mastery of art theory and method and it is here that she met two Franciscan sisters who, like her, attended the school for Industrial Arts.

It is an old adage that art and religion go together. In Berta Hummel's case this was no exception. Her desire to serve humanity became so great that she decided to join the two sisters in their pilgrimage for art and God. So we find her for a time dividing her talent for drawing and her great love for her fellow men between hours of devotion and worship. The first step into a new life, a life of sacrifice and love, was taken. For Berta Hummel, there was no turning back. After completing her Novitiate, she took her vows in the Convent of Siessen on August 30, 1934.

While Berta Hummel, now Sister M. Innocentia, gave her life unselfishly to an idea which she thought greater than anything else, the world became the recipient of her great works. Within the walls and beautiful surroundings of this centuries-old Cloister she created the pictures which were to make her name famous throughout the world. Within this sacred confine, she could give her desire unbounded impetus. There she made the sketches for the "Hummel Cards" and "Hummel Figures". These little images were, after all, her childhood friends as she remembered them and one by one they appeared before her eyes until she had immortalized those who made her early life "Heaven on Earth".

Little did her superiors dream that this modest blue-eyed artist, who had joined their community, would someday win world-wide renown and realize enough from her art work to give her beloved convent a telling financial assistance.

However, in 1945, after the French had occupied the region, the noble minded artist's state of health was broken. On November 6, 1946, despite all the self-sacrificing care taken of her, God summoned her to His eternal home, leaving in deep mourning all her fellow nuns.

Today her figurines are once again reaching the public and her royalties continue to support her Order and its principally charitable works.

3

SECTION II
HOW TO USE THIS BOOK

This book is quite easy to use without any specific directions but made more simple if one understands how it is organized.

The introductory pages, glossary, and various sections dealing with history, marks, etc., are self-explanatory and the actual listing of the pieces is organized so as to facilitate quick location of a particular figure in the book. The expanded listings are arranged in ascending numerical order according to the Hummel mold number assigned to each piece by the factory. It begins with Puppy Love (Hummel Mold No. 1) on page 98.

Because of occasional variations in resulting translations from the original German names to English, one may encounter different names for some of the figures. You may find the name of a piece in the alphabetical list, ascertain the Hummel Mold number, and locate the piece in the expanded numerical listing beginning on page 98. There is also a comprehensive index in the back of the book for your convenience, and a large glossery of terms and phrases specific to the collecting of Hummel figurines.

NOTES FOR THE COLLECTOR
AND WOULD-BE COLLECTOR
Where to Find Hummel Figurines

The first thing one may say is "How do I find Hummel figurines?" In today's market there are many, many sources, some quite productive, others not so productive. The best way to start or to expand a collection (after you have learned all you can about them) is to subscribe to various collectors' periodicals (see page 81-82). Most will have a section of classified advertisements where dealers and collectors alike advertise Hummel figurines and related pieces such as plates, etc., as being available for sale or trade (rarely). This would be the most practical source of available pieces. The most productive source, insofar as a large selection is concerned, is one of the large annual gatherings of dealers at shows held periodically around the country. Naturally the pieces are found variously in gift shops, antique shops, jewelry stores, galleries and shops specializing in collectibles, but almost all of these sources inventory the recent production pieces from the factory for the most part. There are a few who stock pieces bearing the old trademarks along with those having the latest trademark however, so don't overlook this possible source for the older pieces. With the increased awareness of Hummel figurines it is very unlikely, but still possible that some smaller, uninformed shops could have a few pieces bearing the old trademarks, bought some years ago but as yet unsold and marked for sale at whatever the current retail price is for the newer pieces.

By far the best sources for bargains in old pieces are flea markets, junk shops, attics, basements, relatives, friends, acquaintances and neighbors. In short, anywhere one might find curios, old gifts, cast-aways, etc. As a good example, a few years ago, I discovered that one of my neighbors had eight or ten old figures, including a relatively uncommon Hummel lamp, "Out of Danger" (44/B), all bearing the Full Bee trademark.

These engaging little figures have for many years now been considered a wonderful gift or souvenir for all of the motifs, one can almost always find a figure to fit a friend's or relative's particular personality or profession. Until recent years they were also relatively inexpensive gifts. So, "bone up" and start looking and asking. You may find a real treasure!

Non-Hummel Items Made By Goebel

The W. Goebel Company, like many other companies producing collectibles, produces fine porcelains and ceramics other than those objects fashioned after original designs of M. I. Hummel. If you are a collector of Hummel only, be very sure that what you obtain is indeed Hummel art.

The various identifying characteristics specific to M. I. Hummel figurines and other related objects will be covered in depth later. For now you must understand some of the ways Goebel marks their other fine products.

The factory usually places a one, two or three letter prefix along with mold number identifying the item. They do occasionally use letters with the Hummel item mold numbers, but these are almost invariably placed **after** the incised number and not preceding it as the other Goebel products.

(cont.)

A non-Hummel figurine made by Goebel. Base markings: "FF 124/1 with a Full Bee trademark and Black Germany.

A non-Hummel figurine made by Goebel. Base markings: Crown and Full Bee trademarks, "FF 124/1 B"

A few examples of the many prefix letters and what they mean follows:

KF -Whimsical Figurine
Rob -Taken from designs by Janet Robson
MH -Madonna
HX -Religious Figurines
Byj -Taken from designs by Charlot Byj
FF -Free standing figurine
Spo -Taken from designs by Maria Spotl
Rock-Taken from designs by Norman Rockwell

There are many more than listed here, and the pieces that they are used on are just as well made as are the Hummel pieces, and are themselves eminently collectible. They are not Hummel art, however, so be sure before you buy.

There seems to be a secondary market in the infancy of development in some of the non-Hummel Goebel products such as the Charlot BYJ design figurines and the Little Monk or "Friar Tuck" pieces and there is a definite market for the discontinued Rockwell pieces and the Walt Disney characters, but none of the above are Hummel. **The collector must understand this:** No matter the amount of material written pointing this out, the confusion continues to exist. The one rule the collector can rely on almost always is that *the M.I. Hummel signature must appear on the pieces somewhere.* There is the very rare exception but the occurence is so rare that it is inconsequential.

Collectors should be aware that from 1871, when the company was founded, until 1991, Goebel used the same trademark system on just about all of its products, therefore the existence of one of the familiar trademarks is not an indication that the item with it is a Hummel design. In 1991 Goebel changed the mark for the first time since 1979. This new mark will be found only on Hummel items in the future. Another will be used on the non-Hummel designs. For more information with regard to the new mark or backstamp turn to the section on history and explanation of the trademarks.

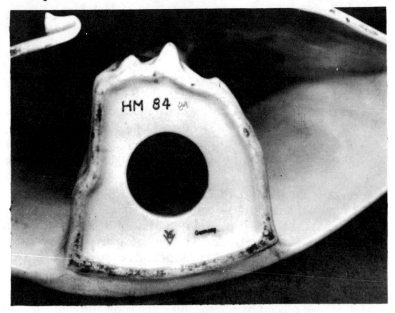

Base marking found on a non-Hummel Madonna made by Goebel. Note the "HM" letter prefix (enhanced for reproduction with pen and ink).

GLOSSARY

The following pages contain an alphabetical listing of terms and phrases you will encounter in this book, as well as other related books and literature during the course of collecting the figures. They are specific to Hummel figurine collecting and, in some cases, will apply to other porcelain, ceramic and earthenware products. Refer to this glossary whenever you don't understand something you read or hear. Frequent use of it will enable you to become well versed in collecting Hummel figurines and other related articles.

Air Holes – Small holes under the arms or other unobtrusive locations to vent the hollow figures during the firing stage of production to prevent them from exploding as the air expands due to intense heat. Many pieces have these tiny little holes, but often they are very difficult to locate.

Anniversary Plate – In 1975 a 10'' plate bearing the Stormy Weather motif was released. Subsequent anniversary plates were released at 5 year intervals. 1985 saw the 3rd and last in the series released.

Annual Plate – Beginning in 1971 the W. Goebel firm began producing an annual Hummel plate. Each plate contains a bas-relief reproducing one of the Hummel motifs. The first was originally released to the Goebel factory workers in 1971, commemorating the hundredth anniversary of the firm. This original release was inscribed, thanking the workers (see page 294).

Ars Sacra – The trademark sometimes found on the gold label of a New York firm which produced Hummel-like figures during the World War II period when Hummel figurines were not being produced. The firm is now in Germany and engaged in the authorized production of Hummel art cards, prints and other related items in two-dimensional renderings.

Artist's Mark – Could be called the artist's signature. This mark is the mark placed by the master artist indicating approval of the actual figure painter's work. The master artist mixes all the colors for the other artists to ensure uniformity. The other marks, small numbers, X's, etc. are apparently for internal production use only and, at this point, it is generally felt they are of no use in determining value or age. Beginning with the introduction of a new trademark in 1979 the date of finishing decoration of the figure is added by the artist.

8

Baby Bee – Describes the trademark of the factory used in 1958. A small bee flying in a V.

Basic Size – The term, *as used in this book only*, is generally synonymous with STANDARD SIZE. However, because the sizes listed in this book are not substantiated initial factory released sizes, it was felt that it would be misleading to label them "STANDARD". BASIC SIZE was chosen to denote only an *approximate* standard size.

Bas-relief – A raised or sculpted design as on the Annual Bells and the Annual Plates, as opposed to a two-dimensional painted design.

Bee – A symbol used since about 1940, in various forms, as a part of or along with the factory trademark on Hummel pieces until 1979 when the Bee was dropped.

Bisque – A fired but unglazed condition. Usually white but sometimes colored.

Black Germany – Term used to describe one of the various wordings found along with the Hummel trademarks on the underside of the pieces. It refers to the color used to stamp the word 'Germany'. There have been many colors used for the trademarks and associated marks, but black generally indicates the figure is an older mode; however, this is not a reliable indicator.

Candle Holder – Some Hummel figurines have bene produced with provisions to place candles in them.

Candy Bowl – See CANDY BOX, CANDY DISH

Candy Box – Small covered cylindrical box with a Hummel figurine on the top. There have been design changes in the shape of the box or bowl over the years, as well as the manner in which the cover rests upon the bowl. See individual listings.

Candy Dish – See CANDY BOX

CE (Closed Edition) – A term used by the Goebel factory to indicate that a particular item is no longer produced and will not be placed in production again.

CN (Closed Number) – A term used by the Goebel factory to indicate that a particular number in the Hummel Mold Number sequence has never been used to identify an item and never will be used. A caution here: Several unquestionably genuine pieces have been found recently bearing these so-called Closed Numbers.

Collector's Plaque – Same as the Dealer Plaque except it does not state "authorized dealer", as most later Dealer Plaques do. Frequently used for display with private collections (see DEALER PLAQUE).

Crown Mark – One of the early W. Goebel firm trademarks. Has not been used on Hummel figurines and related pieces since sometime around 1949-50 (see page 25).

Current Mark – This is the name used until recently when referring to the trademark currently in use by the factory. A newer mark is now being used that is similar but does not have the traditional Vee Bee (see page 28). The name that the majority of collectors and dealers have adopted is "The Missing Bee", but "Current Use Mark" still persists.

Current Production – Term describing figurines, plates, candy boxes, etc. supposedly being produced at the present time. They are not necessarily readily available, because the factory maintains the molds but doesn't always produce the figure with regularity.

Dealer Plaque – A plaque made and distributed by the Goebel firm to retailers for the purpose of advertising the fact that they are dealers in Hummel figurines. Always has the "Merry Wanderer" incorporated into it. Earlier models had a Bumblebee perched on the top edge (see COLLECTOR'S PLAQUE).

Display Plaque – see COLLECTOR'S PLAQUE & DEALER PLAQUE

Donut Base – Describes a type of base used with some figures. Looking at the bottom of the base, the outer margin of the oval base forms a circle or oval, and a smaller circle or oval within makes the base appear donut-like.

Donut Halo – The only figures on which these appear are the Madonnas. They are formed as a solid cap type, or molded so that the figure's hair protrudes through slightly. The latter are called Donut Halos.

Double Crown – From 1934 to 1938 there were many figures produced with two Crown WG marks. This is known as the Double Crown. One of the crowns may be a stamped crown and the other incised. Pieces have been found with both trademarks incised (see page 25). Thereafter only a single Crown Mark is found.

Embossed – An erroneous term used to describe INCISED (see INCISED below).

Font – A number of pieces have been produced with a provision for holding a small portion of holy water. They can be hung on the wall. Often referred to as Holy Water Fonts.

Full Bee – About 1940 the W. Goebel firm began using a Bee as part of their trademark. The FULL BEE trademark has been found along with the Crown trademark. The FULL BEE is the first and largest bee to be utilized. There were many versions of the Full Bee trademark. The first Full Bee is sometimes found with (R) stamped somewhere on the base.

Full Blown Bee – See FULL BEE.

Germany (W. GERMANY, West Germany, Western Germany) – All have appeared with the trademark in several different colors.

Goebel Bee – See BEE on page 9.

Goebelite – This is the name the Goebel firm gives to the patented mixture of materials used to form the slip used in the pouring and fashioning the earthenware Hummel figurines and other related Hummel pieces. Not often heard.

High Bee – A variation of the early Bee trademarks wherein the Bee is smaller than the original Bee used in the mark and flies with its wings slightly higher than the top of the V (see page 27).

Hollow Base – A base variation. Some bases for figures are solid and some are hollowed out and open into a hollow figure.

Hollow Mold – An erroneous term actually meaning Hollow Base, as above. All Hummel pieces are at least partially hollow in finished form (see X-Ray on page 18).

Holy Water Font – See FONT above.

Hummel Number or Mold Number – A number or numbers incised into the base or bottom of the piece, used to identify the mold motif and sometimes the size of the figure or article. This designation is sometimes inadvertently omitted, but rarely. (See page 33 for an in-depth discussion.)

Incised – Describes a mark or wording which has actually been pressed into the piece rather than printed or stamped on the surface.

Indented – See INCISED above.

Jumbo – Sometimes used to describe the few Hummel figurines which have been produced in a substantially larger size than the normal range. Usually around 30″. (See Hum Nos. 7, 141, 142.)

Light Stamp – (See M.I. HUMMEL below) It is thought that every Hummel figurine has Sister M. I. Hummel's signature stamped somewhere on it; however, some apparently have no signature. In some cases the signature may have been stamped so lightly that in subsequent painting and glazing all but unidentifiable traces are obliterated. In other cases the signature may have been omitted altogether. The latter case is rare. The same may happen to the mold number.

M.I. Hummel (Maria Innocentia Hummel) – This signature, illustrated below, is supposed to be applied to every Hummel article produced. However, as in LIGHT STAMP above, it may not be evident. It is also reasonable to assume that because of the design of a particular piece or its extreme small size, it may not have been practical to place it on the piece. In these cases a small sticker is used in its place. It is possible that these stickers become loose and are lost over the years. The signature has been found painted on in some instances but rarely. It is also possible to find the signature in decal form, brown in color. Around the late 1950's to early 1960's Goebel experimented with placing the signature on the figurines by the decal method but abandoned the idea. A few of the pieces they tried it on somehow found their way into the market.

Collectors should also take note of the fact that sometimes the signature appears as "Hummel" without the initials.

M.J. Hümmnl

Missing Bee Mark – See CURRENT MARK.

Model Number – The official Hummel Mold Number designating each figure or motif used (see page 33).

Mold Growth – There have been many theories in the past to explain the differences in sizes of figurines marked the same and with no significant differences other than size. The explanation from Goebel is that in the earlier years of molding, the molds were made of plaster of paris and had a tendency to wash out and erode with use. Therefore successive use would produce pieces each being slightly larger than the last. Another possible explanation is that the firm has been known to use more than one mold simultaneously in the production of the same figure and marketing them with the same mold number. The company developed a synthetic resin to use instead of plaster of paris in 1954. While this is a vast improvement, the new material still has the same tendencies but to a significantly smaller degree.

Mold Induction Date (MID) – The actual year the original mold was made. Often the mold is made but figures are not produced for several years afterward. The MID is sometimes found along with other marks, on older pieces but not always. All pieces currently being produced bear an MID.

Mold Number – See HUMMEL NUMBER.

Narrow Crown – Trademark used by the W. Goebel firm from 1937 to the early 1940's. To date this trademark has never been found on an original Hummel piece (see page 26).

One-Line Mark – See STYLIZED BEE.

O.E. (Open Edition) – Designates the Hummel figurines presently in production or in planning. It does not mean all are in production, only that it is 'open' for production, not necessarily available.

O.M. – Abbreviation sometimes meaning Old Mark (other than the current trademark).

O.N. (Open Number) – A number in the numerical sequence of factory designators HUMMEL MODEL NUMBER which has not been used to identify a piece but may be used when a new design is released.

O.P. (Out of Current Production) – A confusing term sometimes used to indicate a piece is no longer being produced. It could be construed to mean no longer produced but, due to the Goebel factory's policy of placing some pieces that have not been produced for many years back in production, it has little meaning.

Oversize – A term sometimes used to describe a Hummel piece which is larger than the size indicated by the designator on the bottom. It is also used to describe a piece which is larger than that which is currently being produced. These variations could be due to mold growth (see MOLD GROWTH).

PFE (Possible Future Edition) –A term applied to a Hummel mold design that does exist, but is not yet released.

Red Line – A red line around the outside edge of the base of a figurine means that the piece once served as the model for the painters.

Size Designator – Method of identifying the size of a figure. It is found in conjunction with Hummel Mold Number on the bottom of the figure (see page 33).

Slash-Marked – From time to time a figure or a piece will be found with a slash or cut through the trademark. There are two theories as to their origin. One, that it is used to indicate a figure with some flaw or imperfection, but several have appeared with a slash mark which are, upon close examination, found to be in excellent, unflawed condition. The other theory is that some are slash-marked to indicate that the piece was given to or sold at a bargain price to factory workers, and marked so to prevent resale.

Small Bee – A variation of the early Full Bee trademark wherein the Bee is about one-half the size of the original Bee (see page 27).

Stamped – A method of placing marks on the bottom of a figure wherein the data is placed on the surface rather than pressed into it (see INCISED).

Standard Size – As pointed out in the section on Size Designators, this is a general term used to describe the size of the first figure to be produced, when there are more sizes of the same figure to be found. It is not the largest nor the smallest, only the first. Over the years, as a result of mold design changes and, possibly, mold growth, all figures marked as standard are not necessarily the same size (see BASIC SIZE above).

Stylized Bee – About 1955 the traditional BEE design in the trademark was changed to reflect a more modern "stylized" version. Also called the "One-Line Mark."

Terra Cotta – Literally translated from the Latin it means "baked earth." A naturally brownish-orange earthenware.

Three Line Mark – A trademark variation used in the 1960's and 1970's (see page 28).

U.S. Zone (U.S. Zone Germany) – During the American occupation after World War II the W. Goebel firm was required to apply these words, in various forms, to all articles produced. Some were not so marked, but most were. The various configurations in which these words are found are illustrated on page 32.

Vee Bee – Around the late 1950's the traditional BEE mark was changed slightly so that the Bee had its wings in a V-like configuration (see page 28).

White Overglaze – When a figure is formed and fired a white glaze is applied rather than paint and clear glaze. It results in an all-white, shiny figure.

Wide Crown – When the first Hummel figurines were produced, this was the trademark being used at the time (see pages 25-26).

THE PRICE TO PAY

The province of this book is primarily Hummel figurines and related articles which bear trademarks other than the one currently being used by the factory and produced by Goebel. It is always nice to have a retail price list of those items in current production. They are readily available from your nearest dealer.

The collector should be aware of some factors which influence the actual selling price of the newly produced pieces.

The suggested retail price list released by the factory periodically is for those pieces bearing the current production trademark. Each time the list is released it reflects changes in prices from the factory. These changes (usually increases) are due primarily to the basic principle embodied in the law of supply and demand, economic influences of the world money market, ever increasing material and production costs, the expanding numbers of collectors in the United States and, last but certainly not least, a much greater interest in the pieces on the European market.

These suggested retail price lists do not necessarily reflect the actual price you may have to pay. The expanding popularity and limited supply can drive these prices quite a bit higher. In some parts of the country one may encounter a price up to 50% higher than that found on the most recently released list of suggested retail prices. Some of the less popular items in the collection may even sell for less than suggested retail.

The value of Hummel figurines, plates, and other related Hummel pieces bearing trademarks other than the current use trademark is influenced by some of the same factors discussed above, to a greater or lesser extent. The law of supply and demand comes into even more important light with reference to pieces bearing the older trademarks, simply because articles bearing the older trademarks are no longer produced. Since they are no longer being produced, there is a fixed number of them available that could be far less than the number of collectors desiring to possess them. Generally speaking, the older the trademark the more valuable the piece, but one must recognize the possibility of a larger number available of a particular figure bearing one of the older marks than one bearing a later mark. If the latter is a more desirable figure and is in much shorter supply, it is perfectly reasonable to assume it is the more valuable.

There is another important factor which *may* influence the value of a few specific pieces to experience a fall in price. The re-issue of some older pieces, previously thought by collectors to be permanently out of production, will obviously increase the number of those specific pieces available. Many collectors wish to possess a particular piece because they simply like it and have no real interest in an older trademark. These collectors will buy the new release rather than the older because they can buy it for less. It follows that demand for an older trademarked piece will be less.

If this happens at all, it will probably be a temporary situation; for, after all, the ranks of collectors are expanding and there is still a finite number of older trademarked pieces available, regardless of current production status. See page 52 for a list of pieces which have been, or are slated to be, reissued.

You may find surprising the fact that many of the values in the listings are actually less than the Suggested Retail Price List from Goebel. One must realize that most serious collectors have little interest in the price of, or the collecting of the pieces currently being produced. That is not to say they are not valuable, only that time must pass before those pieces produced in the past few recent years will begin to make their way into the secondary market. Make no bones about it, with the recent change of trademark will come the logical step into the secondary market eventually. The principal market for the recent and new pieces is found in the general public, not the seasoned collector. The heaviest trading in the collector market recently has been in the Crown and Full Bee trade-marked pieces and values of the Stylized & Three-line mark pieces are remaining stable presently.

16

PITFALLS YOU MAY ENCOUNTER

Be ever alert to the trademarks found on the pieces and how to interpret them (see pages 25-32). It is a complicated and sometimes confusing system and you must know how they are used and what they mean in order to know what you are buying.

Variations are rampant (see individual listings) in both size, coloration and mold variations, and you may think you are buying one thing and you'll be getting something quite different.

Concerning the value of broken but expertly restored pieces, they are generally worth one-half or less than the going current value of the unbroken, "mint" ones. This value is entirely dependent upon the availability of other "mint" pieces bearing the same mold number, size designator, and trademark. In the case of a rare piece, however, many times it is worth almost as much as the mint piece, if expertly restored, due simply to its scarcity. (See page 48-49 for a list of some restorers).

Detecting Restored Pieces

Even the most expertly restored Hummel figures or articles are detectable, but it is sometimes difficult or impossible for the average collector. The two most reliable methods are examination by (1) *long-wave* ultraviolet light and (2) examination by X-ray. Until very recently one could rely almost 100% on ultraviolet light examination, but some restorative techniques have been developed in the past few years, that are undetectable except by X-ray examination.

Examination by X-ray.

Access to X-ray equipment may prove difficult, but if you have a good friend who is a doctor or dentist, you might convince him to help you occasionally for his expenses. The best way to explain how you can detect is to show you. Please refer to the accompanying illustration showing an X-ray of a damaged and professionally restored figurine. Although the restoration is not apparent to the naked eye, the X-ray clearly shows where the head was broken off. It is a safe assumption that it has been broken and restored. This type of restoration represents the present state of the art.

Examination by Long-wave Ultraviolet Light

When an undamaged piece is exposed to this light, it will appear uniformly light purple in color, the value of the purple will varying with color on the piece. A crack or fracture with glue in it will appear a lighter color (usually orange or pink), patches will appear almost white, and most new paint will appear a much, much darker purple.

Fakes and Forgeries

As far as I have been able to determine, there are not yet many blatant forgeries on the market, but, as noted earlier, we must be ever aware of their possibility and their nature.

Unfortunately there have been a few rather obvious alterations to the trademarks and to the figurines themselves to make them appear older or different from the norm therefore more valuable. There have been additions or deletions of small pieces (i.e. birds, flowers, etc.) to a figure and worse, one or two unscrupulous individuals have been reglazing colored figurines and other articles with a white overglaze to make them appear to be the relatively uncommon to rare, all-white pieces. These can be detected but it is best left to the experts. Should you purchase a piece that is ultimately proven to be one of these, I know of no reputable dealer who wouldn't replace your figure if possible. At the very least, he would refund your money.

Imitations and Reproductions of Original Hummel Pieces

There are many reproductions and imitations of the original Hummel pieces, some better than others, but so far all are easily detectable upon the most casual examination if one is reasonably knowledgeable about what constitutes an original.

The most common of these imitations are those produced in Japan, similar in design motif but obviously not original when one applies the simplest of rules. (See discussion of Trademarks and other markings found on original pieces, pages 25-32).

Pictured below are examples of some imitations showing the full figure and the base.

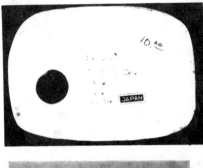

On the base appears a sticker indicating the article was made in Japan and a German name in signature form. The figure is very Hummel-like but not a replica of any known original M.I. Hummel design.

Left. Plastic imitation of Hum 201. Made in Hong Kong it appears as if the mold for this plastic piece was taken from the genuine Hummel figurine.

Pictured here is a reproduction of Hum 201, Retreat To Safety. To look at the picture is disconcerting in that it appears to be so real. However when you look at the figure and hold it, it is decidedly inferior and made of plastic. Beneath the base is the phrase "Made in Hong Kong." The author purchased this particular piece at a truck stop in a midwestern state, June of 1979, for $3.95. It was probably worth about 50 cents; an interesting adjunct to any collection.

I have seen many other figurines and articles which are obvious attempts at copying the exact design, but every single one I have seen was immediately detectable as being made of materials and paints severely inferior to the quality of a genuine article. Almost all have been manufactured from a material similar to the plaster-like substance used in the manufacture of the various prizes one wins at the carnival game booth. Some of these I have seen actually bore a sticker proclaiming it a genuine, authentic or original Hummel piece. See following pictures.

A very crude attempt at copying a Hummel figurine.

Markings found on base of figurine at right. "Two Chicks SH1D"

(cont.)

Same figures as in photo at top of next page. Shows sticker on bottome. States: "Deutschland".

Copies of Hum 63, Singing Lesson and Hum 74, Little Gardner. Both made in Japan.

Same figures as in photo above. Shows "Japan" stamped on base.

German made copies of
Hum 86, Happiness and
Hum 47, Goose Girl.

A Hummel Imitation of
unknown origin.

THE DUBLER FIGURES

There was one instance of the production of figurines which are very much like the original designs where there is some indication, albeit very cloudy, that they might have been authorized properly. These pieces are known as the DUBLER FIGURES. They are pieces from a small collection produced during the World War II years when the Goebel factory was not in production. The manufacturer was in the United States (Herbert Dubler, Inc. New York) and has a sticker label applied to the bottom as drawn here:

AUTHENTIC
HUMMEL FIGURE
PRODUCED BY ARS SACRA
MADE IN USA

The Dubler
"SKIER"

The Dubler
"LITTLE SWEEPER"

The Dubler figures were produced in a chalk-like substance and are definitely much like the original designs, but still easily observed as not being an original M.I. Hummel piece produced by the W. Goebel firm.

The Herbert Dubler firm is still in business but is in Germany. It is associated with the production of some two-dimensional Hummel art on paper.

A HISTORY AND EXPLANATION
OF THE PROGRESSION OF TRADEMARKS
FOUND ON HUMMEL FIGURINES

There has been since 1935, a series of changes in the trademarks used by the W. Goebel firm for trademarking Hummel figurines. In most cases each new trademark replaced the previous one. Occasionally the new trademark design has been used in addition to the one it is to replace for a time. The following is an illustrated guide to the major trademarks and their evolution to the present marks used. There are many variations not illustrated or explained; however, the ones listed and illustrated are subtle ones and easily recognizable as being a variation of one or the other trademarks included here. The dates are approximate, but are as close to the actual as could be determined. There are also a number of wordings found associated with the various trademarks (see pages 25-32). These wordings can help to establish the time of production, though not always reliable. They can also have an influence on a particular figure's value.

Note: It is very important that the collector know the various trademarks illustrated and discussed here are used by Goebel on all of their products and not limited to Hummel items alone, until about mid-1991 when a new mark for exclusive use on Hummel items was developed.

THE CROWN MARK
1934-1950

THE CROWN MARK (TMK-1) - The Crown WG illustrated above is the earliest mark found on Hummel figures and articles. It is the mark which was in use by the Goebel firm in 1935 when the first Hummel figurines were produced. Variations are found, but the basic design shown above is easily recognizable. It is found both incised and stamped and many times wording is found in conjunction with the mark – most commonly ''Germany''. The ''W G'' under the crown stands for W. Goebel. This mark is frequently referred to as the ''Crown W G'' and sometimes ''Wide Crown'' mark. Some sources refer to a ''Narrow Crown'' trademark and for the readers' information this mark is illustrated below. The Narrow Crown Trademark is not known to have ever been found on a Hummel piece.

THE NARROW CROWN

The Narrow Crown. To date this particular trademark has never been found on an original M.I. Hummel piece, but is encountered on some products made by the W. Goebel firm.

Often the Crown trademark may appear twice on the same piece, more often one being incised and the other stamped on. There have been some pieces found with two incised Crown marks. When two Crown marks are found on the same piece, it is referred to as the "Double Crown". Some Crown marked pieces are found bearing the Full Bee in addition. These pieces represent the transition period from one mark to a newer design. This mark was used in various forms until about 1949. At about that time there occasionally appeared a small WG monogram crammed in with the M.I. Hummel signature, usually found at the edge of the base. It is illustrated below.

The U.S. ZONE GERMANY or U.S. ZONE mark is mentioned here because at this point in the evolution of trademarks this marking appeared. It was required by the United States Military Occupation Government to be added to the trademark when the Occupation forces allowed the W. Goebel firm to resume production around 1946. The Occupation marks which the wording has been found are illustrated in the section entitled "Miscellaneous Notes About The Trademarks", beginning on page 29.

THE FULL BEE (TMK-2) - Sometimes called the FULL BLOWN BEE – was introduced about 1950 and is illustrated below. The bumblebee part of the mark is thought to have been derived from a childhood nickname of Sister M.I. Hummel, meaning

26

bumblebee. The bee flying in a 'V' was used in various forms from then until mid 1979 when it was eliminated as part of the current factory trademark. Until 1960 this mark remained basically the same. There were several changes in it over the years, the major variations being illustrated on the next two pages.

THE FULL BEE
1940-1956

THE SMALL BEE – note the wing tips are exactly aligned with the top of the 'V'. About 1956.

THE HIGH BEE – Note the bee flies higher in the V with the wings extending above the top. About 1957.

THE BABY BEE – A smaller bee flying well within the confines of the V. About 1958.

THE VEE BEE – Around 1959 the bee was changed slightly. The wings are more angular and form a definite V by themselves.

All of the BEE marks have appeared both stamped and incised. The stamped trademarks appear mostly in blue or black, but some have been found in green or a reddish color. The incised BEE trademarks bear no color at all.

THE STYLIZED BEE (TMK-3) – In the mid 1950's (probably 1955) the trademark was changed to reflect a more simplified modern version. The bee was stylized as in the following illustrations and flies completely within the confines of the V. It appears in black and blue color. There have been three variations of this Stylized Bee trademark and were used until about 1965.

1. The **LARGE STYLIZED BEE** was used from 1960 to 1963.

2. The **SMALL STYLIZED BEE** was in use simultaneously with the LARGE STYLIZED BEE from about 1960, but continued in use until 1972. This trademark is sometimes referred to as the One-Line Mark.

3. The **THREE—LINE MARK** (TMK-4) – utilized the same stylized bee in a V, but included three lines of wording to the right, as illustrated here. The years of use are 1964-1972. This major change appeared in blue color, some but not many being accompanied by additional wording. (See pages 50-51 for a list of figures which bear only this or a later trademark.)

THE GOEBEL BEE or THE LAST BEE MARK (TMK-5) - Goebel made a major design change in the trademark in 1970. This trademark is known by some collectors as the "Last Bee" mark because the next change in the mark no longer incorporated any rendition of the "V" and "Bee". The mark was used until about mid-1979 when they began to phase it out completing the transition in 1980. There are three minor variations in the mark as illustrated below.

THE MISSING BEE MARK (TMK-6) - In mid-1980 Goebel changed the trademark by removing the stylized "Vee" and "Bee" from its position between and above the b and the e in the word "Goebel". Many collectors and dealers lament the passing of the traditional "Bee" and have described this new current-use trademark as the "Missing Bee". In addition to this change, the company has instituted the practice of having the artist to add the date of finishing the painting of the piece in conjunction with the artist's mark beneath the base. Because the white overglaze pieces are not painted, it can be reasonably assumed that this date may not appear on those. The Missing Bee mark is illustrated here.

THE HUMMEL MARK or THE CURRENT USE MARK

(TMK-7) - 1991 saw another change of the mark, this time of historical import. For many years the trademark has incorporated the words "West Germany". With the reunification of Germany Goebel felt a change was in order, that should reflect this change. Hence, the design illustrated below. Another very significant fact is that for the first time, the trademark will be exclusive to items made from the paintings and drawings of M.I. Hummel. Other Goebel products will bear a different mark than that used on Hummel pieces.

MISCELLANEOUS NOTES ABOUT THE TRADEMARKS
Why is the V and Bee Missing?

In the 1970's Goebel observed that many people were equating the V and Bee with Hummel pieces only and, not realizing that the trademark was used throughout their very extensive line of other products. After some experimentation it was decided to drop the V and Bee completely beginning in 1979. This was disappointing to many collectors for they thought that to drop it was to drop a tradition. Collectors widely believed that the Bee was in honor of Sister M. I. Hummel because the word Hummel, when translated to English, means bumble bee. Nothing could be further from the truth. The V and Bee was the trademark of another company acquired by Goebel and they simply incorporated it into their own trademark. It was only a coincidence.

The foregoing information is possibly in error although its authenticity has never been questioned and the source of the information is impeccable. There is, however, another story now that also has a legitimate claim to authenticity. Records of the earlier days of the company, as we have seen, are sometimes incomplete and, albeit infrequently, occasionally in error. The other (official) story is as follows: About 1950, four years after Sister Maria Innocentia (Hummel) died, the company decided to honor her by incorporating her name in some way in their trademark. Hummel means bee in German. This bee in German. The bee was placed flying in a V, the V was for the German word for "distributing company", "verkaufsgesellschaft".

The elimination of the V and Bee from the company trademark for all their products was disappointing, but under the circumstances of the time, Goebel made a necessary and sensible change. The company has said that the V and Bee will never again be used. With the new trademark exclusive to Hummel items, we can now hope that Goebel will reconsider with the next change.

Other Marks Found Associated with the Trademarks

Throughout the history of the trademark there appear several colors and different wordings to accompany the mark. The colors found to date are:

BLACK	BROWN
BLUE (exclusively since 1972)	PURPLE
GREEN	RED

There have been combinations of the colors uncovered.

The following list contains the various wordings one may encounter on the pieces. There are probably more to be discovered, but these represent those found by the author to date.

GERMANY	(C) by W. Goebel
WEST GERMANY	(c) W. Goebel
WESTERN GERMANY	M. I. HUMMEL
W. GERMANY	Copr. W. Goebel
MADE IN U.S. ZONE	(R)
U.S. ZONE, GERMANY	(c) by W. Goebel, Oeslau 1957
U.S. ZONE	*II Gbl. 1948
OCCUPIED GERMANY	

*Stamped in purple. Found on 85/0, Serenade, 4¾". No trademark apparent.

31

The various U.S. ZONE markings are sometimes found within a frame as illustrated below:

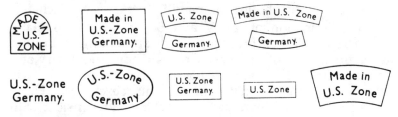

The "U.S. ZONE" markings usually were stamped on after the painting and glazing, and are easily lost over the years through wear or cleaning. The mark was applied in the years 1946 through 1948.

As you can see, over the years the factory has seen fit to change and vary the trademarks many times. This serves sometimes to confuse and complicate the identification of the figures. The changes, although confusing, do enable the collector to determine the age of the pieces with some degree of accuracy. It is quite possible that there will be yet another trademark design change in the near future.

First Issue and Final Issue

Starting in 1990 Goebel began marking any newly issued piece with the words "FIRST ISSUE" during the first year only, of its initial production. Also, in 1991, they began to place a stamp saying "FINAL ISSUE" on those being retired, during the last year of production. Both these marks will be found on the underside of its base where the trademark is also normally found. The words are also accompanied by the year date of the event. They are reproduced for you here. The first to bear the Final Issue backstamp is both sizes of Hum 203, Signs of Spring. It will also have a commemorative retirement medallion hung around the figure.

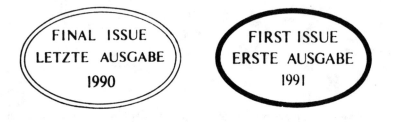

EXPLANATION OF MOLD NUMBER
AND SIZE DESIGNATOR SYSTEM

Mold Numbers

All Hummel molds are assigned a model or mold number upon its induction (when mold is first made) and appears incised into the piece when taken from the mold and finished. It generally appears on the underside of the base, but for practical reasons may appear elsewhere on the item.

Until recent years it was thought that the highest mold number used in production of the pieces was somewhere in the mid-400's. The extensive research conducted by writers, collectors, dealers and Goebel over the years has revealed much new information. Some of the findings render many of the earlier assumptions and theories erroneous. It is now believed that there are roughly 650 unique designs in existence. A great many of these have not yet been put into production and are designated Possible Future Editions (PFE) by Goebel. A precious few of these have somehow found their way into collectors hands, but this occurence is exceedingly rare. More often than not, those sample pieces bear an earlier trademark than that placed on the piece when eventually put into production.

Size Designators

The size designation system is complicated but with study you can understand it. The system has changed over the years and, as is almost always the case, there are exceptions to the rule. The exceptions will be covered as the system is explained.

Beginning with the first piece in 1934-35 and continuing to about 1952, the first size of a particular piece produced was considered by the factory to be the "standard" size. If plans were to produce a smaller or larger version, the factory would place an 'O' or a decimal point after the model or mold number. Frequently, but not always, the 'O' would be separated from the mold number by the placing of a slash mark (/) between them. There are many cases where the 'O' or decimal point do not appear. Apparently this signifies that at that time there were no plans to produce other sizes of the same piece. In the case of Hum #1, "Puppy Love", there exists only one "standard" size and no size designator has ever been found on the figure. It is reasonable to assume, however, that subsequent changes in production plans would result in other sizes being produced. Therefore the absence of the 'O' or decimal point is not a reliable indicator that there exists only one "standard" size of the particular piece. *In fact, there are some instances where later versions of a piece have been found bearing the "slash O", decimal point, and even a "slash I", which are smaller than the "standard" for that piece.

The factory used Roman numerals or Arabic numbers in conjunction with the mold numbers to indicate larger or smaller sizes than the "standard".

The best way for the collector to understand the system is by example. The figure "Village Boy" Hum #51, has been produced in 4 different sizes.

---

*After the mold for Hum 218, "Birthday Serenade", the use of the "slash O" size designator was eliminated.

EXAMPLE: 51/0

The number 51 tells us that this is the figurine "Village Boy" and the "slash O" indicates that it is the first size produced, therefore the "standard" size. In this case the size of the piece is roughly 6". The presence of the "slash O" (or of decimal point) is also an indication that the figure was produced sometime prior to 1952.

As discussed earlier, not all the figures produced prior to 1952 were designated with the "slash O" or decimal point, but, if present is a great help in beginning to date a figure. The one exception, in present knowledge, is to the discontinuance of the use of the "slash O" designator is Hum #353, "Spring Dance". It was produced with the 353/0 mold and size designator about 1963, taken out of current production later and recently reinstated.

By checking the reference for mold #51, you will note there exist three more sizes, Hum 51/2/0, Hum 51/3/0 and Hum 51/I. Roman numerals are normally used to denote sizes larger than the "standard" and Arabic numbers indicate sizes smaller than the "standard". When utilized in the normal manner, the Arabic number is always found to the left of the 'O' designator. There are two exceptions to this norm, one specific, the other general. The specific, known exception is "Heavenly Angel", Hum mold number 21/0/1/2. This is the only known instance of the use of a fractional size designator. The last two numbers are read as one-half (½). The general exception is the occasional use of an Arabic number in the same manner as the Roman numeral. The Roman numeral size indicator is never used with the 'O' designator present, and the Arabic number is never normally used without the 'O' designator; therefore, if you were to find a mold number *51/2, you would know to read it *51/II and that it represents a piece larger than the "standard."

Continuing with our example, we will take Hum 52/I.
EXAMPLE: 51/I

As before the number 51 identifies the piece for us. The addition of the "slash I" tells us that this is a larger figure than the standard. In this case it is about one inch larger.
EXAMPLE: 51/2/0 and 51/3/0

Once again we know the identity of the piece is #51, "Village Boy." In both cases there is an Arabic number, the mold number

---

*This mold number does not exist. Used here as an illustrative example only.

and the "slash O", therefore we can assume both are smaller than the "standard." The 51/2/0 is smaller than 5" and the 51/3/0 is even smaller still.

Since the 'O' and decimal point size designators are no longer in use and, keeping in mind the cited exceptions, we can usually assume that a figure with the model number and no accompanying Arabic or Roman numerals is the "standard" size for that model. If the model number is accompanied by Roman numerals, the figure is a larger size, ascending to larger sizes the higher the numeral.

There seems to be no set "standard" size or set increase in size for each of the Arabic or Roman numeral size designators used in the collection. The designators are individually specific to each model and bear no relation to the designators on other models.

ADDITIONAL DESIGNATORS

There are a number of pieces in the collection: table lamps, candy boxes, book ends, ash trays, fonts, plaques, music boxes, candle holders, plates and sets of figures, some of which have additional or different designators. The following is a list of them and explanations of how each is marked:

TABLE LAMPS – are numbered in the traditional manner. Some later price lists show the number preceded by an M. Example: M/285.

CANDY BOXES (CANDY BOWLS) – are covered cylindrical deep bowls, the cover being topped with one of the Hummel figures. They are numbered with the appropriate model number for the figure and preceded with the Roman numeral III. Example: III/57 is a candy box topped with Hum 57, "Chick Girl."

BOOK ENDS – are both large figures with provisions for weighting with sand, and smaller figures placed on wooden bookend bases. The only sand-weighted book ends are the "Book Worms". The designation for a book end is accomplished by placing A and B after the assigned Hum model number for the book ends.

Example: Hum 61/A and Hum 61/B is a set of book ends utilizing Hum 58 and Hum 47, "Playmates" and Chick Girl." These are the current designations. In some cases, if the figurines are removed from the bookend bases, they are indistinguishable from a regular figurine.

ASH TRAYS – are numbered in the traditional manner.

FONTS – are numbered in the traditional manner. Exception: There is a font, Hum #91, "Angel At Prayer", in two versions. One faces left, the other right. They are numbered 91/A and 91/B respectively.

PLAQUES – are numbered in the traditional manner.

MUSIC BOXES – are round wooden boxes in which there is a music box movement, topped with a traditional Hummel model which rotates as the music plays. The number for the music box is the Hummel number for the piece on the box followed by the letter 'M'. If the figure is removed from the top, it will not have the 'M' but will be marked in the traditional manner.

CANDLE HOLDERS – are numbered in the traditional manner. They sometimes have Roman numerals to the left of the model designator. These indicate candle size. I: .6 cm. II: 1.0 cm.

PLATES – are numbered in the traditional manner. To date, none has been produced with the size designator, only model number.

SETS OF FIGURES – are numbered with one model number sequence and followed by the designation /A, /B, /C . . . /Z, to indicate each figure is part of one set.

Example: The Nativity Set 214 contains 15 Hummel figures, numbers 214/A, 214/B, 214/C, and so on. In the case of Nativity Sets there are some letters which are not used. The letters I and Q are not utilized because of the possibility of confusing them with the Roman numeral I or Arabic 1 and 0.

SOME ADDITIONAL NOTES ON SPECIAL MARKINGS

Sets

Any time there have been two or more pieces in the collection which were meant to be matched as a pair or set, the alphabetical listings A through Z appropriately are applied to the Hummel model numbers in some way. Exception: Sometimes called "The Little Band" are the three figures Hum 389, Hum 390, and Hum 391. They do not bear the A, B, C designating them as a set. The piece actually entitled "The Little Band" is Hum 392, an incorporation of these three figures on one base together. References to the "Little Band" and the "Eight Piece Orchestra" are occasionally found in price lists which include Hummel Numbers 2/0, 1/I, 89/I, 89/II, 129, 389, 390, 391. A charming group, but not officially a set.

Finishes

In price lists, some of the Madonnas and Infants of Krumbad, you may encounter numbers *after* the size designators. These numbers indicate whether the figure is painted in colors or finished in a white overglaze. The numbers are 11 (meaning painted in color) and 89 (meaning white overglaze). The letter 'W' appearing after the size designator also means white overglaze. These numbers and letters are in the *price lists only* and *do not appear on the piece itself.*

Additional odd marks found on the figures are internal production control codes and artists' marks. They are presently felt to be of no value in identification or establishing age of figures.

Any other oddities in marking will be discussed under the individual listings.

MISCELLANEOUS NOTES
OF INTEREST TO COLLECTORS
The Making Of Hummel Figurines and Plates

The question most asked by those uninitiated to the Hummel world is "Why do they cost so much?" It is not an unreasonable question and the answer can be simply that they are hand-made. That, however, really doesn't do justice to the true story. The making of Hummel pieces is immensely complex; truly a hand operation from start to finish. The process requires no less than *seven hundred* steps! Those few of you who have been lucky enough to visit Goebel's northern Bavaria facility know how complicated the operation is. Others of you who have seen the Goebel film and/or visited the facsimile factory on its 1985 U.S. tour have a pretty good idea.

To call the facility a factory is misleading, for the word factory causes the majority of us to conjure up an image of machinery and automated assembly lines. It is not that at all. It is an enormous artists' and artisans' studio and workshop complete with friendly relaxed surroundings including good music, hanging baskets and potted plants. In short, a pleasant place to create and work. It is packed with highly trained and skilled artists and craftsmen. Each of them must undergo a full three year apprenticeship before actually taking part in the fashioning of the figurines and other items that are made available to the collector. This apprenticeship is required no matter whether the worker is a mold-maker or painter. Each specialist in the process must understand the duties of the others.

There is insufficient space to elaborate on all seven hundred steps in making the pieces so I have grouped them into six basic areas: Sculpting the Master Model, Mother or Master Mold Making, Molding the Pieces, Bisque Firing, Glaze Firing, Painting and Decor Firing.

1. SCULPTING THE MASTER MODEL

It is estimated that there are 1200-1500 M. I. Hummel artworks from which Goebel may pick to render into a three-dimensional piece. Once a piece of art is chosen a master sculptor fashions a model in a water base Bavarian black clay. This is a long process during which the artist must not just reproduce the art but interpret it. He must visualize for instance, what the back of the piece must look like and sculpt it as he thinks M.I. Hummel would have rendered it. Once the wax model is deemed acceptable it is taken to the Siessen Convent where it is presented for approval or disapproval. If the preliminary model is approved it is then taken back to Goebel for the next step.

Master wax model of Goose Girl

39

2. MASTER OR MOTHER MOLD MAKING

A figurine cannot be made from a single mold because of its complexity. Therefore after very careful study of the wax model it is strategically cut into several pieces. Some figurines

Master wax model of Goose Girl cut into seven parts preparatory to molding.

require being cut up into as many as thirty pieces for molding. For example, Ride Into Christmas had to be cut into twelve separate pieces and Goose Girl into seven. Using the Goose Girl seven pieces we continue. Each of the seven are placed on a round or oval base and secured with more clay. The base is then surrounded by a piece of flexible plastic that extends above the piece to be molded. Liquid plaster of paris is then poured into it. The dry plaster of paris is removed resulting in an impression of the part. This process must be repeated for the other side. After each of the seven parts are molded the result is fourteen separate mold halves. From these are made the Mother (sometimes called Master) molds. These are made from an acrylic resin. The mother molds are cream

Body of Goose Girl embedded in wax on oval base. Preparatory to surrounding with flexible plastic for containing the plaster of paris after pouring.

Result of the pouring of plaster of paris. The wax body has not yet been removed. Note the key slots. The one on the right is still in process of being carved out.

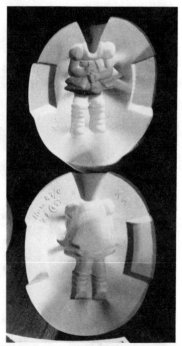

The Master or Mother Mold.

The two halves of a plaster of paris working mold. Note the keys left and right. These insure accuracy of fitting the two halves together for pouring the piece.

colored and very durable. It is from the mother molds that the working molds are made. The plaster of paris working molds can be used only about twenty times at which time a new set must be made from the mother molds.

Before full production of a new figures is commenced, a few samples are made. The figure must again be carried to the Siessen Convent for approval or, as the case may be, rejection or recommendations for changes. Once final approval is given the piece is ready for production. That could be immediate or years later.

3. MOLDING AND ASSEMBLY OF THE PIECES

All the pieces in the collection are made of fine earthenware consisting of a mixture of feldspar, kaolin and quartz. It is the finest earthenware available. Both porcelain and earthenware come under the definition of ceramic. Add just a bit more kaolin and the earthenware would become porcelain. Goebel chooses to use earthenware because of its inherent softness. That softness is considered best for Hummel items.

The liquid mixture of the three ingredients plus water is called slip. The slip is poured into the working molds and left for a period of time. The porous character of the plaster of paris acts like a sponge and draws moisture out of the slip. After a carefully monitored time the remaining slip is poured out of the mold leaving a hollow shell of the desired thickness. The parts are removed from the molds and while

The seven pieces of Goose Girl after removal from the molds and prior to assembly.

The assembled, refined piece prior to bisque firing.

still damp, they are assembled using slip as a sort of glue. The assembled piece is then refined, removing all seams and imperfections and detailing the more subtle areas. The piece is then set aside to dry for about a week.

4. THE BISQUE FIRING

Bisque is fired, unglazed ceramic. The dry assembled pieces are gathered together and fired in a kiln for eighteen hours at 2100 degrees Fahrenheit. This results in a white, unglazed bisque figurine.

Appearance of the Goose Girl after bisque firing.

5. THE GLAZE FIRING

The bisque fired pieces are then dipped into a tinted glaze mixture. The glaze is tinted to assure that the whole piece is covered with the mixture. The tint is usually green and any uncovered area will show up white. The dipped pieces are then fired at 1872 degrees Fahrenheit. When removed from the kiln after cooling, they are a shiny white.

(See next page)

The tinted piece prior to glaze firing. .

6. PAINTING AND DECOR FIRING

The Goebel company maintains a highly sophisticated color laboratory where ceramic paint chemists have developed and produced 2000 different color formula variations under strict quality controls. The paints are metallic oxide with an oil base. The colors used on Hummel pieces are specifically formulated to match M.I. Hummel's original colors and upon firing, to blend into the glaze resulting in the soft matte finish on the figures.

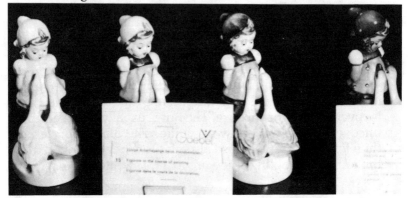

These four pieces illustrate a few of the many stages of painting before and during decor firing(s).

44

The colors are mixed in small amounts and given to the painters only as needed. Some of the colors react to each other upon firing, so oftentimes the item must be painted with one or a few colors and fired before others can be applied. This results in multiple decor firings before the pieces are finished. In some cases up to ten separate firings are required before they are finished and ready for distribution.

As you can see now, the making of the pieces is a long, involved and painstaking operation. As noted earlier there are 700 separate operations, the workers are highly trained and experienced, and there are 25 different quality control inspection points. In spite of this each piece is unique because it is a hand operation. No matter how a piece is assembled or painted, no matter how experienced a worker is, he is still a human being, inherently incapable of creating identical copies. That is part of the magic. Each piece is a joy, each unique, each a hand-made work of art.

Mold Induction Dates

The year date incised on the base of many M.I. Hummel pieces is the source of much confusion to some collectors. The year date is the Mold Induction Date (MID). The MID is the date the original mold for that particular piece was made and not the date the piece was made. It bears no relationship whatsoever with the date of molding the item, only the mold. As a matter of fact there are many molds that are years old and still being used to make figures today. The MID doesn't always appear on the older pieces but all those currently being made will have it.

M.I. HUMMEL DOLLS

The first Hummel dolls were made in 1950. They were made at the time outside of the Goebel factory by arrangement with another company by the Goebel firm. The first dolls had rubber heads and soft stuffed bodies, stood 16½ inches tall, and were delivered to the Goebel factory to be dressed in hand-made clothing. Very shortly thereafter the composition of the body was changed (1951) to rubber also. There were only six dolls produced at first and in 1952 Goebel took over the entire production of the dolls in-house and added a smaller 10 inch tall size.

Over the years it became apparent that the rubber type used in the dolls was unstable and the compound would sometimes break down. This breakdown is exhibited by overall deterioration of the head and body, areas sinking in or collapsing, cracking or a combination of any or all. By 1963 or 1964 the company changed the composition to rubber and vinyl according to their advertising at the time. They are now all made of a soft, durable material which is a type of polyvinylchloride (PVC).

There were nine different dolls of this type produced up until 1983 in a 10 inch size. At that point Goebel introduced a completely new line. These will be discussed on following pages.

THE FIRST SIX DOLLS

NAME	SIMILAR TO	NAME	SIMILAR TO
Bertl	Unknown	Liesl	Unknown
Gretl	Sister	Max	Unknown
Hansel	Unknown	Seppl	Boy with Toothache

Variously over the years the company has called the dolls by different names and have also made an 8 inch high version of some. A 1976 catalog advertised the 8 inch dolls as:

NAME	SIMILAR TO
Vroni	Meditation
Rudi	Home From Market
Seppl	Boy with Toothache
Mariandi	None
Jackl	Happy Traveler (somewhat)
Rosi	Little Sweeper (somewhat)

The 1976 catalog also lists and illustrates a 10 inch tall baby doll in two different costumes (boy and girl) although it is not made completely clear whether or not they are Hummel dolls.

The nine 10 inch dolls that were in production up until the introduction of the new line in 1983 were as follows:

NAME	SIMILAR TO
Felix	Chimney Sweep
Ganseliesl	Goose Girl
Gretl	Sister
Hansl	Brother
Peterle	School Boy
Radibub	For Father
Rosi	School Girl
Striekliesl	A Stitch In Time (somewhat)
Wanderbub	Merry Wanderer

All the bodies of the girls and of the boys were the same (two styles only). It is the costumes and accessories that made them different.

Identification of the above Hummel dolls is made relatively easy by the presence of an incised M.I. Hummel signature and Goebel trademark found on the back of the neck of each;

and one or more articles of clothing also bear the M.I. Hummel signature. In addition, if not lost, a tag (usually triangular) will be found attached to each that bears the Goebel trademark and the doll's name. Costumes, patterns, styles and colors may differ considerably.

There is not presently a large, established secondary market for the dolls. Therefore a reasonable value for the older models is not possible to establish yet. Because of the tendency for some of the older ones to deteriorate, condition would be of paramount importance, obviously. Some sources have placed values in excess of $100.00 on them but this is not a substantiated trade figure, only an estimate.

Current Production Dolls

In 1983 the Goebel company announced a completely new line of M.I. Hummel dolls. The heads, hands and feet of the new dolls are made of the same or similar ceramic-type material as are the figurines. The bodies are still of a soft, stuffed material.

The new dolls are readily identifiable from the material of the heads, hands and feet but there are additional, unmistakable identifying characteristics. They are 15 inches in height, each having the M.I. Hummel signature and the date of production year. The bodies will also carry a label containing the production date along with identifying remarks. The vinyl dolls are still being made, but they are for European distribution only.

The first four to be released were as follows:

Postman
On Holiday
Boy from Birthday Serenade
Girl from Birthday Serenade

They were released at a suggested retail price of $175.00 each and production was limited to the year 1984.

The dolls for the year 1985 and limited in production to that year were as follows:

Lost Sheep
Easter Greetings
Signs of Spring
Carnival

All eight are at $210.00 each suggested retail price as of March 1987.

Two of the Four Hummel Dolls for 1984

Left:
"Girl from Birthday Serenade"
Right:
"Postman"

CARING FOR AND DISPLAYING HUMMEL FIGURINES

It is best to keep your collection in a well lighted, dust-free display case of some sort. This allows minimum risk of breakage and keeps the pieces dust-free and clean.

Some of the older pieces may have discolored somewhat over the years due to environmental and atmospheric pollution. In the early years the pigments used in the paints were not as durable and lasting as those used in the present day and are more subject to the caustic elements of air pollution. This type of deterioration is not reversible. However, should you obtain a piece which is merely dirty or dusty, you may safely wash it in warm water with a mild soap. Many knowledgeable dealers and collectors use strong detergents to clean the figure without harm, but I would be reluctant to use detergents as they sometimes contain chemicals which may be harmful to the finish.

What To Do When It's Broken

The following is a short list of specialists in repairing porcelains. It is by no means complete, for there are dozens of firms around the country doing competent, professional repair work. This list is arranged alphabetically and does not necessarily constitute a recommendation. Many of them however, have demonstrated expertise in repairs and restoration. Over the years I have heard from or spoken to dealers and collectors who have not been satisfied with the work or service of some of them but on the other hand I have heard praise from others regarding the same restorers. In fairness to all of them I can no longer be responsible for recommendations and therefore offer only the list.

MR. ALLAN B. MITTELMARK
366 Clinton Ave.
Cedarhurst, NY 11516

HARRY A. EBERHARDT & SONS, INC.
Bill Eberhardt
2010 Walnut Street
Philadelphia, Pennsylvania 19103

ELY HOUSE
118 Patterson Avenue
Shrewsbury, New Jersey 07701

GEPPETTO IMPORTS & RESTORATION, INC.
31143 Via Colinas No. 506
Westlake Village, California 91362

RICHARD GERHARDT
66 Jayson Avenue
Great Neck, New York 11021

SIERRA STUDIOS
37W222 Rt. 64 Ste., 103
St. Charles, IL 60175

A Word About Insurance

With the ever increasing value of pieces from the Hummel collection comes ever increasing loss if some or all are destroyed or damaged. Just about everyone carries some amount of homeowners or household insurance against loss due to fire or natural disaster, but so few actually have enough.

Pictured here is an example of what intense heat and smoke can do to a Hummel figurine. As a result of underinsurance, the sad situation represented by these few pieces resulted in the insurance settlement for the loss being about $200.00 when, in fact, the collection was worth in excess of $1000.00 at the time. An

$800.00 plus loss! Not to mention the heartbreak experienced by the loss. Some consolation would have been derived from their ability to at least have the insurance money to replace their pieces in kind.

Do investigate insurance on your collection.

THE THREE LINE MARK PIECES

The Three Line Mark is illustrated and discussed on page 27. The list of original Hummel pieces here is of those designs first released in the United States in 1971-72 and can generally be found bearing only the Three Line Mark, the Stylized Bee Mark, the Last Bee Mark or Missing Bee. There have been a few from this list uncovered which bear earlier trademarks but these are very rare occurrences. **Don't be confused that these are the only pieces with the Three Line Mark for there are many others.** The list following is **only** those Three Line Mark pieces that were **new releases in 1971-72.**

MOLD NUMBER	NAME	
#304	THE ARTIST	
#308	LITTLE TAILOR	
#314	CONFIDENTIALLY	(cont.)

#327	THE RUN-A-WAY
#331	CROSSROADS
#334	HOMEWARD BOUND
#337	CINDERELLA
#340	LETTER TO SANTA CLAUS
#342	MISCHIEF MAKER
#344	FEATHERED FRIENDS
#345	A FAIR MEASURE
#347	ADVENTURE BOUND, THE SEVEN SWABIANS
#355	AUTUMN HARVEST
#356	GAY ADVENTURE
#363	BIG HOUSECLEANING
#369	FOLLOW THE LEADER
#374	LOST STOCKING
#377	BASHFUL!
#378	EASTER GREETINGS
#381	FLOWER VENDER
#382	VISITING AN INVALID
#384	EASTER PLAYMATES
#385	CHICKEN-LICKEN
#386	ON SECRET PATH
#396	RIDE INTO CHRISTMAS

Reinstated Pieces

In 1978 the W. Goebel firm announced its intention to place back into current production status, some designs previously thought to be permanently out of production by collectors and dealers. The following is a list of those pieces that have been or will be placed back in the line. The availability of any of these varies from dealer to dealer.

MOLD NUMBER	NAME
#83	ANGEL SERENADE
#153/I	AUF WIEDERSEHN
#176/I	BIRTHDAY SERENADE
#3/III	BOOK WORM
#143/I	BOOTS
#139	FLITTING BUTTERFLY (Plaque)
#183	FOREST SHRINE
#52/I	GOING TO GRANDMA'S
#176/I	HAPPY BIRTHDAY
#150/O	HAPPY DAYS

#150/I	HAPPY DAYS
#113	*HEAVENLY SONG
#124/I	HELLO (Chef Hello)
#27/III	JOYOUS NEWS
#2/III	LITTLE FIDDLER
#24/III	LULLABY
#45/III	MADONNA
#46/III	MADONNA
#151	MADONNA (Blue Cloaked)
#151	MADONNA (White Overglaze)
#13/II	MEDITATION
#13/V	MEDITATION
#7/III	MERRY WANDERER
#82/II	SCHOOL BOY
#353/O	SPRING DANCE
#168	STANDING BOY (Plaque)
#165	SWAYING LULLABY (Plaque)
#196/I	TELLING HER SECRET
#49/I	TO MARKET
#180	TUNEFUL GOOD NIGHT (Plaque)
#50/O	VOLUNTEERS
#50/I	VOLUNTEERS
#154/O	WAITER
#360A, 360B, 360C	WALL VASES (Set of 3)
#163	WHITSUNTIDE
#84/V	WORSHIP

*The Goebel company has announced that this piece has been removed from the Open Edition status and placed in Closed Edition status because of its similarity to Hum 54, Silent Night which continued in production.

FIVE YEAR SUSPENSION

In late 1989 Goebel announced that it was suspending production of a number of M.I. Hummel pieces for a period of five years. They provided no explanation so you must draw your own conclusion. In any case the following is a list of those suspended items:

MOLD NUMBER	NAME
2/II	Little Fiddler
2/III	Little Fiddler
3/II	Bookworm
3/III	Bookworm
7/II	Merry Wanderer
7/III	Merry Wanderer
13/V	Meditation
46/I	Madonna w/Halo (color & white)
78	Infant of Krumbad (all sizes)
84/V	Worship
151/I	Madonna & Child (color & white)

CANDLEHOLDERS

24/I	Lullaby
25	Angelic Sleep
37	Herald Angels
241B	Angel Lights w/Plate
388	Little Band
388M	Little Band Music Box

BOOKENDS

250/A&B	Little Goat Herder
	Feeding Time
252/A&B	Apple Tree Boy
	Apple Tree Girl

PLAQUES

48/0	Madonna
92	Merry Wanderer
93	Little Fiddler
125	Vacation Time
126	Retreat to Safety
140	Mail is Here
165	Swaying Lullaby
168	Standing Boy
180	Tuneful Goodnight

Five Year Suspension

CANDY BOXES

III/53	Joyful
III/57	Chick Girl
III/58	Playmates
III/110	Let's Sing

OTHER

260	Nativity Set
All Ashtrays	
All Vases	
All Table Lamps	

RARE, UNUSUAL AND UNIQUE HUMMEL AND HUMMEL RELATED PIECES

The International Figures

One of the most interesting and exciting aspects of collecting Hummel figurines and other related pieces is the omnipresent chance to turn up a relatively uncommon to a significantly rare piece. This fortuitous circumstance has happened many times. It has often occurred as a result of painstaking research and detective work, but more often it is pure chance.

One such example is the story of the "Hungarians". A knowledgeable and serious collector of Hummel articles, Mr. Robert L. Miller, regularly advertises that he will buy original Hummel pieces in various collector periodicals around the world. He received a postcard from Europe one day describing some "Hummels" an individual had for sale. After he obtained photographs of a few figurines which appeared to be Hummel designs, some were obviously the familiar figurines but some were apparently in Hungarian costume. In relating his story to the author Mr. Miller said he felt at first that they were probably not real Hummel pieces but were attractive and he thought they might make a nice Christmas present for his wife. He sent a check and after some thought he called the factory to inquire as to their possible authenticity. He was informed that they knew of no such figures. By the time the pieces arrived he had begun to think that they might be genuine. Upon opening and examining he saw that each bore the familiar "M.I. Hummel" signature! He again called the factory and was told again they knew nothing of them but would investigate. A short time later he received a letter from the W. Goebel firm stating that the eight figurines were indeed produced by the factory as prototypes for a dealer in Hungary before the war and that they believe them to be the only eight ever produced! As most of us are aware now, many more have turned up since Mr. Miller's discovery. In fact there have been something like twenty-six or more different designs to be found. In the beginning, they were so unique that the price they commanded was as much as $20,000.00 at one time! The old law of supply and demand came very much into play as more were found and today the price hovers around $7500.00, but can go below or above that because of duplicate examples found and some, at present, are unique, one of a kind examples. These superb figurines are no longer referred to as Hungarians because several have now been found with costumes from countries other than Hungary. Among them are: Bulgaria, Czechoslovakia, Serbia, Sweden, Slovakia. There may be others to be found yet. The term presently used to describe these pieces collectively is the "International Figures". Please see color section for illustrations of several of these figurines.

These are the first eight "International Figures" discovered by Robert Miller. They are still part of his collection. Photographed on display and used with his permission.

So far there have been at least 26 unique models found; and counting variations and those figures that are different, but bear the same mold number, there are at least 36. When considering numbers missing in the sequence of those found so far, a conservative estimate of those left unfound would be 25-35, but there is a distinct, however remote, possibility that upwards of 100 may yet be out there.

The following is a list of the different designs that have so far been found.

806 Bulgarian	Similar to SERENADE
807 Bulgarian	Entirely different from other known Hummel designs. Could be a redesign of FEEDING TIME.
808 Bulgarian	Similar to SERENADE
809 Bulgarian	Similar to FEEDING TIME
810 Bulgarian	Entirely different from other known Hummel designs.
810 Bulgarian	Similar to SERENADE
811 Bulgarian	Entirely different from other known Hummel designs.
812 Serbian	Entirely different from other known Hummel designs.
813 Serbian	Entirely different from other known Hummel designs.
824 Swedish	Similar to MERRY WANDERER

825 Swedish	Similar to MEDITATION
831 Slovak	Similar to SERENADE
832 Slovak	Similar to MEDITATION
833 Slovak	Similar to SERENADE, but with different instrument.
841 Czech.	Similar to LOST SHEEP
842 Czech.	Similar to GOOSE GIRL.
851 Hungarian	Similar to LITTLE HIKER
852 Hungarian	Entirely different from other known Hummel designs.
853 Hungarian	Similar to NOT FOR YOU
853 Hungarian	Entirely different from other known Hummel designs.
854 Hungarian	Similar to the girl on the right in HAPPY BIRTHDAY.
904 Serbian	Similar to LITTLE FIDDLER
913 Serbian	Similar to MEDITATION.
947 Serbian	Similar to GOOSE GIRL
968 Serbian	Similar to LOST SHEEP

Known only to a few is a tentative plan to issue a new set of thirty of the original International designs in a larger size. The International Figures found so far, all have a basic size of 5''. The proposed new set will be molded in a basic size of 7''. Exactly when or if this proposed set becomes a reality is not yet known. Advanced collectors and dealers are speculating that this issue might have a negative effect on one of the most exciting aspects of collecting Hummel items, i.e. the value of those Internationals now known and those yet to be uncovered. In the final analysis, it will be the collector that makes that determination. The fact remains, regardless of whether or not this new series becomes a reality, is that the 5'' Internationals are unique. They were never produced and released in large quantities, but rather a very limited number of sample pieces therefore very rare. They will remain just as rare and sought after. I am always excited and will remain so every time a collector writes me that they have discovered one.

The M.I. Hummel Miniatures

There is another division of Goebel, based in California, Goebel Miniatures. They are the sold producers of the painted bronze miniature renditions of M.I. Hummel figurines.

There is an interesting story behind the formation of Goebel Miniatures. Back a few years before the division existed, a talented artist named Robert Olszewski produced several miniature replicas of Hummel figurines, innocently unaware of the need to obtain permission to do so. It is unlikely that the company would have allowed it and that's what makes the story interesting. Prior to Geobel finding out about his work and stopping him, he produced miniatures of each of the following five figurines:

Barnyard Hero
Stormy Weather
Kiss Me
Ring Around the Rosie
Ride into Christmas

He had also fashioned a very small number of solid gold bracelets with each one of the above miniatures attached. Those bracelets and the unauthorized have since become highly sought and if sold can command extraordinary high prices.

Out of this incident came Goebel's recognition of Olszewski's talent and the fact that there was a market for the miniature figurines. It resulted in his association with Goebel and the creation of Goebel Miniatures with Olszewski as its head. Over the years the acceptance of the miniatures of Hummel figurines and other artist's work rendered in miniature has been excellent. The line, known as KinderWay has also been enhanced by Goebel production of little Barvarian buildings and settings to display the figurines on. The following is a list of the Hummel miniatures to be produced so far:

1983-84
Valentine Gift pendant (club exclusive)

1986
What Now? (club exclusive)

1989
Postman
Visiting and Invalid
Apple Tree Boy

1990
Baker
Waiter
Cinderella

1991
Accordion Boy
Busy Student
We Congratulate
Serenade
Dealer Display Plaque
Morning Concert (Club exclusive)

1992
School Boy
Wayside Harmony
Goose Girl

THE CLUB PIECES

The M.I. Hummel Club, sponsored by the company, was founded in 1976* and as part of the benefits of membership the company began producing pieces that would be available only through membership in the organization. Each year, following renewal of membership, the member receives a redemption card allowing the purchase of that year's annual exclusive offering. The pieces are available only through officially sanctioned dealers representing the club.

Where practical, in the past, each of these exclusive pieces bear the following inscription:

"EXCLUSIVE SPECIAL EDITION
No. (1, 2, 3, etc.) FOR MEMBERS
OF THE GOEBEL COLLECTORS'
CLUB"

Concurrent with the transition of the Goebel Collector's Club to the M.I. Hummel Club came a change in the club exclusives backstamp. The stamp now incorporates a black and yellow bumble bee in a lined half-circle and the words "M.I. HUMMEL CLUB" beneath the half-circle. See the listing for Hum $79 for an illustration of the backstamp.

*1976 was the year the Goebel Collectors' Club was founded. It became the M.I. Hummel Club in 1989.

With only one exception so far, each piece has been an M.I. Hummel design. This exception was the third redemption piece. It is a bust of Sister M.I. Hummel (HU-3) designed by Goebel master sculptor Gerhard Skrobek and illustrated here.

A most unusual club piece was offered in addition to the figurine for 1983-84 club exclusive. This was a miniature of the first exclusive club piece, "Valentine Gift". It was made in the form of a tiny ¾ inch figurine mounted in a 14K gold plated cage hanging from a chain and worn as a necklace. It is easily removed from the cage for display as a free-standing figurine.

Valentine Gift

What Now?

1986 saw the introduction of a second M.I. Hummel miniature, "What Now?" as an exclusive piece available to members. Photo on previous page.

For the club year 1991-92 Goebel Miniatures created another miniature figurine exclusive for the club. This one is a freestanding figurine, Morning Concert at 7/8". It is supplied with an earthenware Bavarian Bandstand setting and a protective glass display dome and base. The release price was $175.00.

Goebel announced in 1984 that from that point on there would be a cut-off date for use of the redemption certificates after which the pieces would no longer be available and the molds destroyed. Following here is a list of each of the exclusive club pieces and their respective cut-off dates.

Release Date	Name	Mold No.	Cut-off Date
1977-78	Valentine Gift	387	5/31/84
1978-79	Smiling Through (Plaque)	690	5/31/84
1979-80	M.I. Hummel Bust	HU-3	5/31/84
1980-81	Valentine Joy	399	5/31/84
1981-82	Daisies Don't Tell	380	5/31/85
1982-83	It's Cold	421	5/31/85
1983-84	What Now?	422	5/31/85
1984-84	Valentine Gift (Miniature)	––	12/31/84
1984-85	Coffee Break	409	5/31/86
1985-86	Smiling Through	408	5/31/87
1986-87	What Now? (Miniature)	––	5/31/88
1986-87	Birthday Candle	440	5/31/88
**1986-87	Valentine Gift (6" plate)	738	5/31/88
1987-88	Morning Concert	447	5/31/89
**1987-88	Valentine Joy (6" plate)	399	5/31/89
1988-89	The Surprise	431	5/31/89
**1988-89	Daisies Don't Tell (6" plate)	736	5/31/90
1988-89	Daisies Don't Tell	380	5/31/89
1989-90	*I Brought You a Gift	479	5/31/90
**1989-90	It's Cold 6" plate	735	5/31/90
1989-90	Hello World	429	5/31/90

*This is a special edition piece given to all old members who renew and new members who join in the year beginning June 1, 1989.

**A four plate series called the Celebration Plate Series.

Release Date	Name	Mold No.	Cut-off Date
1990-91	I Wonder	486	5/31/91
1991-92	Gift From a Friend	485	5/31/92
1991-92	Two Hands, One Treat	493	5/31/93

There are three new pieces available to club members at or after their 5th, 10th and 15th anniversary of membership.

Five Year - Flower Girl	548
Ten Year - The Little Pair	449
Fifteen Year - Honey Lover	412

Please refer to the collection listing beginning on page 73 for further details and current values of the various exclusive club pieces.

M.I. HUMMEL ORNAMENTS

There have been many Christmas ornaments produced bearing M.I. Hummel artwork, but only four under the auspices of the Goebel company to date.

There is one, called "Blessed Event", bearing a rendering of the figurine of the same name. The other three (as of 1984) are in the Annual Christmas Ornament Series. The first was released for 1983 and is "Ride into Christmas" and the second in the continuing series is "Letter to Santa Claus." Each bears a rendering of the figurine of the same name. All three ornaments have the signature of M.I. Hummel as used by Goebel. The fourth (not pictured) is the Merry Christmas plaque design.

| Ride Into Christmas | Letter to Santa Claus | *Blessed Event |

Busts of M.I. Hummel

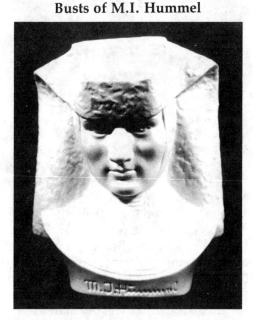

*On-going production – not limited to one year.

(cont.)

The bust of Sister M.I. Hummel (HU-3) mentioned as one of the Goebel Collectors' Club exclusives on page 56 is actually the third bust of her to be produced. While none of the three are Hummel original designs, they are of special interest to collectors. Each does carry the M.I. Hummel incised signature. The club exclusive edition is rendered in full color, but the two previous releases were in bisque (white) only.

The first bust (HU-1) is very large at 13'' and was originally intended to be only a display piece for dealer promotion. A few of them have found their way into private collections.

The second bust (HU-2) another bisque piece but smaller at 5½'' was released to dealers for retail sale in 1967 but was soon after placed in a suspended production status. It became briefly available again in the 1970's but once again taken out of production.

Factory Workers' Plate

This plate was produced for distribution to the Goebel factory workers involved in plate production, in commemoration of the tenth (1980) annual plate. Because it was produced for this purpose it obviously would have been made in an extremely low edition as it was never intended for general distribution and retail sales. The edition is reported to be 60-100. It is not rendered in bas relief as are all the other Goebel plates but was made by utilizing the decal method. The design depicts the ten plates in miniature in a counter clockwise circle with the 1971 plate in the 12 o'clock position. The inscription in the center reads:

1971
10 JAHRE
TELLERGRUPPE
1980

The collector value of these plates is between $2200.00 and $2500.00. A few reside in private collections.

Of some interest is an unauthorized version of this plate. It seems that someone produced a few of the plates in full color. When Goebel found out about this, they quickly put a stop to it. Some collectors place a value of about $300.00 on these, but most are uninterested because they were not produced by or under the auspices of W. Goebel Porzellanfabrik.

GOEBEL EMPLOYEE SERVICE PLAQUE

This very unique piece is quite similar to the Hum 187 display plaque but does not have the usual "Original Hummel Figures" inscription. On the occasion of the employee's 25th, 40th and 50th anniversary with the company each is presented with one of these plaques personalized with the employee's name and the date of the event. A very small number of these pieces have surfaced in private collections. They are valued at $1200-1500.00.

WOODEN DISPLAY PLAQUE

There have been at least seven of these plaques found in recent years. They are each magnum sized (34'' x 23'', 20 lbs.), carved from wood and beautifully painted duplicating the Hum 187 Display Plaque in a jumbo size.

The only identifying mark that could be found on the plaque was a curious "A" within a circle with the crossbar in the "A" appearing to be a bolt of lightning.

For several years the origin of this plaque remained elusive giving rise to much speculation regarding the circle A mark. The "A" gave rise to the theory that the plaques were produced in the famous ANRI wood carving workshops in Italy for the character of the carving and painting seemed to be the same as their style and quality.

Some of the circle A marks were placed upside down on the back of the plaques and not rendered very clearly. This anomaly made the mark resemble the Goebel Vee and Bee trademark giving rise to yet another theory that it might have been a Goebel product.

Both of these theories have since been discredited as the origin of the plaques has finally been traced. It seems that a furniture company quite close to the Goebel factory in Oeslau, Germany was the manutacturer. When queried about them, company spokesmen said they did indeed produce them, but have not done so for 30 or so years. It seems there was some sort of changeover in the type of production facility resulting in the company no longer employing the wood carvers necessary to produce them. No doubt the Goebel company would take a dim view of this endeavor in any case.

There is no record of how many of these were made, but they are in short supply. They have been found both in Europe and the United States. The last one I know of was found in the U.S. Virgin Islands.

The Full Flying Bee

In the mid 1940's Goebel made a complete change in their trademark. The new trademark is now known as the ''Full Bee'' (TMK-2). The promotional display piece shown here was made to show the new trademark. Secondary market value is around $1500-2000.00

PATCHES, PLAQUES AND PINS

Many collectors like to add related Hummel items to their collections. There have been various items made by Goebel with their knowledge and permission to commemorate particular events in the world of M.I. Hummel collecting. There may be one or two more than listed here, privately made with little or no knowledge on the company's part.

Pictured above is an example of a display plaque few collectors are aware of. It is a modified Hum 187 Display Plaque that was made available for a short time to members of local chapters of the Goebel Collectors' Club. It was personalized with the name of the member and local chapter name.

There are more Archive Tour plaques than are listed here. It proved difficult to track them all down in time for publication.

There are twelve to fourteen additional unauthorized pins floating around, in addition to those listed following.

Patches

Year	Design	Event
1977	Merry Wanderer	Hummel Festival Eaton, Ohio
1978	Merry Wanderer	Hummel Festival Eaton, Ohio
1978	Silent Night with Black Child, Hum 31	Hummel Festival Eaton, Ohio
1979	Mountaineer	Hummel Festival Eaton, Ohio
1979	Singing Lesson (plate)	Collectors' Exposition Rosemont, Illinois
1980	Meditation	Hummel Festival Eaton, Ohio
1981	Little Fiddler	Hummel Festival Eaton, Ohio
1982	Goose Girl	Hummel Festival Eaton, Ohio

Year	Design	Event
--	Text only	"Goebel Collectors' Club LOCAL CHAPTER MEMBER
1983	Confidentially	M.I. Hummel Fiesta Sierra Vista, Arizona
1986	Friends	Hummel Festival Eaton, Ohio

Plaques

Year	Design	Event
--	Merry Wanderer	Free to each visitor to the Goebel factory
1977 to May 31, 1989 Merry Wanderer		Free to each new member of the Goebel Collectors' Club. States membership
1979	Merry Wanderer	Hummel Festival Eaton, Ohio
1980	Meditation	Hummel Festival Eaton, Ohio
1981	Little Fiddler	Hummel Festival Eaton, Ohio
1982	Goose Girl	Hummel Festival Eaton, Ohio
1983	Merry Wanderer	Archive Tour Spenser-Zaring, Ltd., Carefree, Arizona
1983	Merry Wanderer	Archive Tour Carol's Gift Shop Artesia, California
1983	Merry Wanderer	Archive Tour Henri's Belmont, California
1983	Merry Wanderer	South Bend Plate Collectors Convention, Goebel Facsimile Factory Display, South Bend, Indiana
1983	Confidentially	M.I. Hummel Fiesta Misty's Gift Gallery Sierra Vista, Arizona

Year	Design	Event
	Pins	
--	Merry Wanderer	5 year membership pin for members the Whittier, CA chapter
1983	Confidentially	M.I. Hummel Fiesta Misty's Gift Gallery Sierra Vista, Arizona
	Miscellaneous	
1986	Commemorative plaque (DeGrazia figure)	Goebel Fest Las Vegas, Nevada
1986	Mug (Chapel Time)	Goebel Fest Las Vegas, Nevada

The Crystal Pieces

In the fall of 1991 Goebel announced that twelve new Hummel designs were rendered in lead crystal and added to the Goebel Crystal Collection. The figurines have a matte finish and range in height from 2-7/8'' to 3-5/8''. The designs are as follows:

Apple Tree Girl
Visiting an Invalid
The Botanist
Meditation
Postman
Merry Wanderer
Soloist
Little Sweeper
Village Boy
Sister
For Mother

Most Serious collectors are aware of a glass rendering of Goose Girl that was made and sold with candy inside. The candy was held in by a cardboard insert at the bottom of the figure. This glass piece was not made by Goebel. It predates the crystal pieces by at least two decades.

THE 'MEL' PIECES

At least seven of a possible twenty-four or more of these interesting pieces are known to exist today. Some are more common than others, but on a relative basis for they are all scarce. Generally speaking, the rule of identification is that each of the pieces have the three letter prefix "MEL" incised along with the mold number. It is now known that these were produced as prototypes and marked with the last three letters of Hummel to identify them as such. Only two of these so far have been found with the M.I. Hummel incised signature and they are unique. The remaining pieces do not have the signature so cannot be considered original Hummel pieces in the strictest sense. Their claim to authenticity otherwise is obvious.

So far those positively identified as MEL pieces are:

Mel 1   Girl with Nosegay
Mel 2   Girl with Fir Tree
Mel 3   Boy with Horse
Mel 6   Child in Bed Candy Dish
Mel 7   Tiny Child Angel (sitting on lid of candy dish)
Mel 9   International figure (Bulgarian)
Mel 24*   International figure (Swedish)

Of all these the first three are so far the most commonly found. It is a matter of interest that these three (Mel 1 through Mel 3) have subsequently been released as HUM 115, 116 and 117. The other Mel piece with the signature is only assumed to be so through an old Goebel catalog listing for it does not have the Mel prefix in the mold number. It is unique with only one known to exist in a private collection.

There is some information in existence that suggests there may be more of these pieces to be found. There are the obvious missing numbers between nine and twenty-four and factory

*This particular Mel piece bears the incised M.I. Hummel signature. Only one known to be in a private collection.

records of the modeling of Mel 4 and Mel 5, both candy dishes, one with a boy on top and the other with a girl indicate their existence.

GOOSE GIRL BOWL

This mysterious piece was uncovered in Germany about 1989. It has an incised Crown Marked. It is a 4-3/4'' Goose Girl with an attached bowl. Upon close examination, it appears that they were joined before firing, lending legitimacy to the presumption that it was fashioned at the factory. The bowl is a Double Crown piece with an incised mold number ''1''.

PRAYER BEFORE BATTLE
Hum 20

This very unusual version of Prayer before Battle exhibits extreme color variations from the norm. The hobby horse is gray, black and white instead of the normal tan, the wagon is dark green with red wheels, socks and the same green and the clothes are dark green and brown. The most unusual variation is the shiny gold gilded horn.

SIGNS OF SPRING
Hum 203

A very rare and unusual version of Signs of Spring. Note the several significant differences such as the fourth fence post and extra flowers. The base is an unusual split style. It has a stamped Full Bee as you can see, and although not readily discernible in the photo here, the mold number appears to have been incised by hand after the un-fired piece was removed from the mold. This rare piece will command $15-$20,000 in the collector market.

73

The Faience or "Doll Face" Pieces

In 1986 a U.S. Army officer stationed in Germany discovered a most unusual Little Fiddler with the M.I. Hummel incised signature and the Crown trademark in a German flea market. It was painted different, brighter colors than the normal ones and even more unusual was the china white face, hands and base and the very shiny glaze. Subsequent investigation not only authenticated the piece as genuine, but uncovered some new and interesting information with regard to the early history of the development of M.I. Hummel figurines. It seems that early on, while experimenting with different mediums for the pieces, glazed porcelain was used. As far as is known, Goebel did not go into mass production of the porcelain pieces for it was found that the fine earthenware with a matte finish was more amenable to the true reproduction of the soft pastel colors used by M.I. Hummel in her artwork. What we do know is that they were produced in sufficient numbers for many to end up in private collections. Models and colors vary widely, but the majority reflect the normal colors. The one the officer found had a bright blue coat, red kerchief instead of the normal blue and a brown hat instead of black. Some collectors refer to these as the "Doll Face Pieces". The accompanying photos illustrate the differences between the normal and the Doll Face pieces of the same era. If found, these are valued at about 20% higher than their Crown marked counterparts.

The two unusual Crown Marks shown here are often found incised on the underside of the base of the Doll Face pieces. The reason for the odd devices over the mark is as yet unexplained.

Hum 4, Little Fiddler. The Doll Face piece is on the left. Note the different head posture, white hands, face and base and the lack of a kerchief. Both are 5⅛" high and bear the Crown Mark.

Hum 9, Begging His Share. The Doll Face piece is on the left. This one nicely illustrates the high glaze typically found on them. Both measure 5⅝", have donut bases and bear both the incised and stamped Crown Marks.

Miniature Annual Plates 1971-76 mini-plates in a oval wooden frame. Edition limited to 15,000.

MINIATURE ANNUAL PLATES

Made by Goebel and marketed by Ars Edition. This is a series of six miniature plates (1'') that are replicas of the first six plates in the Annual Plate Series, 1971 through 1976. The total production is 15,000 sets worldwide. The complete set, released in 1986 was offered at $150.00 including a wooden oval display frame designed for the set.

WOODEN MUSIC BOXES

Ride into Christmas Music Box

Announced in late 1986, this is the first officially authorized hand-carved wooden M.I. Hummel design. In a cooperative effort with Goebel the Anri Workshops in Italy has rendered Ride into Christmas in relief on top of a music box that plays Winter Wonderland. This is the first in a series of four and is limited to 10,000 worldwide. Each music box will be accompanied by a sequentially numbered ceramic medallion made by Goebel. The release price was $389.95. The 1988 music box motif is Chick Girl and was released at $400.00. The 1989 version is In Tune and the release price was $425.00. The 1990 motif is Umbrella Girl and the price was $450.00

THE ENGLISH PIECES

There have been several interesting pieces found that are intriguing in that some mystery surrounds their origin. They have become known collectively as The English Pieces because of what is so far known about them. At present they are not accepted by most collectors as authentic but there is some indication, however slight, that they may be. Certainly there has never been any hard evidence uncovered if it exists at all.

By looking at the accompanying photographs of two of them here you can see they are quite obviously Hummel-like. What sets them apart from fakes or copies is the fact that many of them so far found have the incised M.I. Hummel signature on their bases and beneath the bases the markings as drawn below.

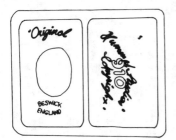 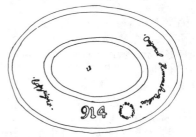

Each of the two in the pictures and drawings not only bear the signature but also the inscription "Original Hummel Studios". They each also have the word "Copyright" inscribed. The back stamp of "Beswick-England" indicates they were made by an old and respected English Porcelain manufacturer that was later bought out by Royal Doulton. The Goebel company has not acknowledged the authenticity of these figurines and they are after all, the final authority unless someone else can come up with irrefutable evidence one way or the other. Until then it must be left to you, the collector, to make your own judgment. There have been twelve different designs identified with Beswick mold numbers 903 through 914. Two of these have yet to be found. See list following:

Beswick Mold No.	Beswick Mold No.
903 Trumpet Boy	909 Unknown Design
904 Bookworm	910 Meditation
905 Goose Girl	911 Max and Moritz
906 Strolling Along	912 Farm Boy
907 Puppy Love	913 Globe Trotter
908 Stormy Weather	914 Shepherd's Boy

The majority of those found so far are signed "M.I. Hummel" and bear Beswick markings. There are, however, some that bear one or the other or no markings at all. A value of around $950.00 is placed on those that are not signed. The signed pieces will bring $1200.00 to $1500.00 on the retail secondary market.

The underside of the base of the figurine showing the German language Jubilee backstamp. It reads: "50 JAHRE M.I. HUMMEL-FIGUREN 1935-1985".

The limited edition, gold base Little Fiddler, Hum 2/I.

Limited Edition Little Fiddler

Little known in the U.S. is the limited production of a 7-1/2", Hum 2/I, Little Fiddler with a gilded gold base. According to company promotional literature only fifty of these were made and they were part of a Goebel contest give-a-way in Germany. This is probably one of the most severely limited production figures that Goebel has ever produced. The collector value is about $2500.

RECOMMENDED BOOKS FOR COLLECTORS

AUTHENTIC M. I. HUMMEL FIGURINES
Copyright by W. Goebel, Rodental, W. Germany. Available through Goebel United States, P.O. Box 10, Route 31, Pennington, NJ 08534-0010.

This is the illustrated catalog published by the factory.

FORMATION OF AN ARTIST, THE EARLY WORKS OF BERTA HUMMEL
James S. Plaut. Copyright 1980, Schmid Brothers, Inc., Randolph, Massachusetts.

This paperbound book is actually a catalog of the 1980-82 tour of an exhibition of paintings, drawings, photographs and a tapestry from the collection of the Hummel family.

GOEBEL MINIATURES OF ROBERT OLZEWSKI by Dick Hunt. 595 Jackson Ave., Satellite Beach, FL.
Hunt's Collectibles.
GUIDE FOR COLLECTORS
Copyright by W. Goebel, Rodental W. Germany. Available through Goebel United States, P. O. Box 10, Route 31, Pennington, NJ 08534-0010.

This is a beautiful full color catalog illustrating the current Goebel Hummel collection. A good color reference.

HUMMEL
By Robert L. Miller. Copyright 1979, Portfolio Press Corporation, Huntington, New York 11743.

This is a supplment to the original *Hummel, the Complete Collector's Guide and Illustrated Reference* by Ehrmann and Miller.

HUMMEL ART
By John Hotchkiss. Copyright 1982. Wallace-Homestead Book Co., 1912 Grand Avenue, Des Moines, Iowa 50305.

This is a full color handbook that essentially updates the first and second editions.

THE HUMMEL BOOK
17th Edition; by Berta Hummel and Margarete Seeman. Copyright 1972 by W. Goebel, Rodental, W. Germany

Available from several dealers around the country; this charming little book is full of illustrations by Sister M.I. Hummel and poetry by Margarete Seeman. A must for anyone interested in collecting Hummel figurines. It is available in both English and German.

HUMMEL FACTS
By Pat Arbenz, Misty's Gift Gallery, 228 Fry Blvd., Sierra Vista, Arizona 85635.

This is a reprint collection of all Mr. Arbenz' columns for Plate Collector Magazine. It is inexpensive and indispensable to the collector.

HUMMEL, THE COMPLETE COLLECTOR'S GUIDE AND ILLUSTRATED REFERENCE
By Erich Ehrmann and special contributor, Robert L. Miller, 1976. Portfolio Press Corporation, Huntington, NY 11743.

Mr. Ehrmann, publisher of Collectors Editions Magazine, and Mr. Miller, acknowledged expert and owner of one of the world's largest Hummel collections, have collaborated to present this large work. As a reference it is invaluable to collectors.

M.I. HUMMEL ALBUM
A Goebel publication. See you dealer.

M.I. HUMMEL: THE GOLDEN ANNIVERSARY ALBUM
By Eric W. Ehrmann, Robert L. Miller and Walter Pfeiffer. Copyright 1984, Portfolio Press Corporation, Huntington, NY 11743
A beautiful book full of color photos and much good information for collectors.

PRICE GUIDE TO M.I. HUMMEL FIGURINES, PLATES, MORE ... 5th Edition
By Robert L. Miller. Copyright 1991, Portfolio Press Corporation, Huntington, NY 11743
A well organized and handy reference by this noted collector.

SKETCH ME BERTA HUMMEL
By Sister M. Gonsalva Wiegand, O.S.F. Published in reprint by Robert L. Miller and available at most dealers or from Mr. Miller at P.O. Box 210, Eaton, Ohio 45320.

SOME USEFUL PERIODICALS
the following is a list of periodicals you may find useful in collecting Hummel figurines.

ANTIQUES JOURNAL
P. O. Box 1046
Dubuque, Iowa 52001   (monthly)
Has occasional articles about Hummel collecting and ads for buying and selling Hummels.

THE ANTIQUE TRADER WEEKLY
P.O. Box 1050
Dubuque, Iowa 52001   (weekly)
Occasional Hummel articles and extensive ads for buying and selling Hummels.

COLLECTOR EDITIONS (incorporating ACQUIRE)
170 Fifth Avenue
New York, NY 10010   (quarterly)
Has occasional Hummel column.

COLLECTORS JOURNAL
Box 601
Vinton, Iowa 52349   (weekly)
    Has ads for Hummel buying and selling.

COLLECTORS MART
15100 W. Kellogg
Wichita, Kansas 67235   (bi-monthly)

COLLECTORS NEWS
606 8th Street
Grundy Center, Iowa 50638   (monthly)
    Has ads for Hummel buying and selling occasional Hummel articles.

COLLECTORS' SHOWCASE
P.O. Box 6929
San Diego, California 92106   (bi-monthly)

THE TRI-STATE TRADER
P.O. Box 90
Knightstown, Indiana 46148   (weekly)
    Has ads for Hummel buying and selling.

CLUBS AND ORGANIZATIONS

    There are many dealers who sponsor "collectors clubs". Most are valuable to collectors. This is a good marketing tech--nique which doubles as a means of educating the collector as to what the artists and manufacturers are presently doing. The following two of these are highly recommended:
    M.I. HUMMEL CLUB (formerly Goebel Collectors' Club)
Goebel Plaza
P.O. Box 11
Pennington, NJ 08534

    This club is under the direct sponsorship of Goebel Art, Inc., the manufacturers of the Hummel figurines and related pieces. The club issues a beautiful and informative quarterly newsletter which no collector shoud be without.

    THE HUMMEL COLLECTORS CLUB
P.O. Box 257
Yardley, Pennsylvania 19067
Taken over around 1974-75 by Dorothy Dous, she and her husband have developed the club into a very valuable and worthwhile organization for collectors of Hummel figurines. Mrs. Dous (Dotty) writes an interesting quarterly newsletter

which is lengthy, easy to read, and crammed with information. The cost of membership includes a subscription to the newsletter.

SECTION III

MASTER INDEX
ALPHABETICAL ENGLISH NAME LISTING
OF THE COLLECTION
WITH CORRESPONDING MOLD NUMBER

A few of the names of pieces have been changed by the factory over the years and this has confused collectors from time to time. Some are even known by two names, due to the changes and different translations from the original German name. As many of these as possible have been included in this listing to facilitate location of those figures.

You may look up the name of the figure, ascertain its appropriate mold number and locate it in the Master Listing of the collection. It begins on page 97 and is arranged in ascending numerical order.

NAME	HUMMEL MOLD NUMBER
The Accompanist	453
Accordion Boy	185
Adoration	23
Adoration with Bird (Bird Lovers)	105
Advent Group - Candle Holders	115, 116 & 117
Advent Group with Candle	31
Adventure Bound, The Seven Swabians	347
An Apple A Day	403
An Emergency	436
Angel At Prayer-Font	facing left 91/a
	facing right 91/B
Angel Cloud-Font	206
Angel Duet	261
Angel Duet-Candle Holder	193
Angel Duet-Font	164
Angel Lights-Candle Holder	241
Angel Serenade with Lamb	83
Angel Trio (Christmas Angels)	
Angel with Lute	238/A
Angel with Accordion	238/B
Angel with Trumpet	238/C
The Angel Trio-Candle Holders	
Joyous News-Angel with Lute	38

NAME	HUMMEL MOLD NUMBER
Annual Plate 1986, Playmates	279
Annual Plate 1987, Feeding Time	283
Annual Plate 1988, Little Goat Herder	284
Annual Plate 1989, Farm Boy	285
Annual Plate 1990, Shepherd's Boy	286
Annual Plate 1991, Just Resting	287
Annual Plate 1992, Wayside Harmony	288
Apple Tree Boy (Fall)	142
Apple Tree Boy	252/A
and	
Apple Tree Girl-Bookends	252-B
Apple Tree Boy-Lamp	230
Apple Tree Girl (Spring)	141
Apple Tree Girl-Table Lamp	229
Arithmetic Lesson	303
Art Critic	318
The Artist	304
At the Fence	324
Auf Wiedersehen	153
Autumn Harvest	355
Ba-Bee Rings	30 A&B
Baker	128
Band Leader	129
Band Leader (plate)	742
Banjo Betty (Joyful)	53
Barnyard Hero	195
Bashful	377
Bath Time	412
Being Punished (plaque)	326
Begging His Share	9
Behave!	339
Be Patient	197
Big Housecleaning	363
Bird Duet	169
Bird Lovers (Adoration with Bird)	105
Bird Watcher	300
Birthday Candle	440
Birthday Present	341
Birthday Serenade	218
Birthday Serenade-Table Lamp	231
Birthday Serenade-Table Lamp	234
Birthday Wish	338
Blessed Event	333

NAME	HUMMEL MOLD NUMBER
Blessed Mother	372
Blue Cloaked Madonna (Madonna)	151
Bookworm	3
Bookworm	8
Bookworms-Bookends	14 A&B
Boots	143
The Botanist	351
Boy With Accordion (Part of Little Band)	390
Boy With Bird-Ash Tray	166
Boy With Toothache	217
Brother (Our Hero)	95
A Budding Maestro	477
The Builder	305
Busy Student	367
Call to Worship (clock)	441
Candlelight	192
Carnival	328
Celestial Musician	188
Chapel Time (clock)	442
Chef Hello (Hello)	124
Chick Girl	57
Chick Girl-Candy Box	111/57
Chicken-Licken	385
Chicken-Licken (mini-plate)	748
Child-In-Bed-Plaque	137
Child Jesus-Font	26
Child with Flowers-Font	36
Children Standing	
Girl With Flowers	239/A
Girl With Doll	239/B
Boy With Toy Horse	239/C
Children's Prayer	448
Chimney Sweep (Smokey)	12
Christmas Angels (Angel Trio)	238/A,B&C
Christmas Bells here and ornaments	
Christmas Song	343
Christ Child	18
Cinderella	337
Close Harmony	336
Coffee Break	409
Companions	370
Concentration	302
Confidentially	314

NAME	HUMMEL MOLD NUMBER
Congratulations	17
Coquettes	179
Country Song (clock)	443
Cradle Song (Lullaby)-Candle Holder	24
Crossroads	331
Culprits	56A
Culprits-Table Lamp	44/A
Christmas Bell 1988, Ride into Christmas	775
Christmas Bell 1990, Letter to Santa Claus	776
Christmas Bell 1991, Here Ye, Here Ye	777
Christmas Bell 1992, Harmony in Four Parts	778
Christmas Ornament 1990, Peace on Earth	484
Christmas Ornament 1991, Angelic Guide	571
Christmas Ornament 1992, Light Up the Night	622
Daddy's Girls	371
Daisies Don't Tell	380
Daisies Don't Tell (6'' plate)	736
Delicious	435
Delivery Angel	301
Devotion-Font	147
Display Plaque (Tally)	460
Do I Dare?	411
Doctor	127
Doll Bath	319
Doll Mother	67
Doll Mother	76/A
and	
Prayer Before Battle-Book Ends*	76/B
Don't Be Shy	379
Dove (font)	393
Drummer (Little Drummer)	240
Duet	130
Easter Greetings	378
Easter Playmates	384
Errand Girl (The Little Shopper)	96
Eventide	99
Evening Prayer	495
A Fair Measure	345
Farewell (Goodbye)	65
Farewell-Table Lamp*	103
Farm Boy (Three Pals)	66

NAME	HUMMEL MOLD NUMBER
Farm Boy	60/A
and	
Goose Girl-Bookends	60/B
Fall (Apple Tree Boy)	142
Father's Joy (For Father)	87
Favorite Pet	361
Feathered Friends	344
Feeding Time	199
Festival Harmony (Angel with Flute)	173
Festival Harmony (Angel with Mandolin)	172
Flitting Butterfly-Plaque	139
The Florist	349
Flower Girl	**548**
Flower Madonna	10
Flower Vendor	381
Flowers for Mother (plate)	500
Flute Song	407
Flying Angel	366
Flying High	452
Follow The Leader	369
Forest Shrine	183
For Father (Father's Joy)	87
For Mother	257
Forty Winks	401
Friend or Foe	434
Friends	136
For Father (7'' plate)	
Friends Forever,	plate series
Meditation	292
For Father	293
Sweet Greetings	294
Surprise	295
Gay Adventure (Joyful Adventure)	356
A Gentle Glow	439
A Gift From a Friend	**485**
Girl With Frog (Little Velma)	219
Girl With Horn (Part of Little Band)	391
Girl With Sheet Music (Part of Little Band)	389
Globe Trotter	79
Going To Grandma's	52
Goodbye (Farewell)	65

*Not known to exist in any collector's hands.

NAME	HUMMEL MOLD NUMBER
Good Friends	182
Good Friends	251/A
and	
She Loves Me, She Loves Me Not (Bookends)	251/B
Good Friends-Table Lamp	228
Good Hunting	307
Good Luck	419
Good Night	214C
Good Shepherd	42
Good Shepherd-Font	35
Goose Girl	47
Grandma's Girl	561
Grandpa's Boy	562
Guardian, The	455
Guardian Angel-Font	29
Guardian Angel-Font	248
Guiding Angel	357
Happiness	86
Happiness, Puppy Love & Serenade	
(triple figure on a wooden base)*	122
Happy Birthday	176
Happy Bugler (Tuneful Goodnight) Plaque	180
Happy Days (Happy Little Troubadours)	150
Happy Days-Table Lamp	232
Happy Days-Table Lamp	235
Happy Little Troubadours (Happy Days)	150
Happy New Year (Whitsuntide)	163
Happy Pastime	69
Happy Pastime-Ash Tray	62
Happy Pastime-Candy Box	111/69
Happy Traveler	109
Harmony in Four Parts	471
Hear Ye, Hear Ye	15
Heavenly Angel	21
Heavenly Angel-Font	207
Heavenly Lullaby	262
Heavenly Protection	88
Heavenly Song*	113
Helly (Chef, Hello)	124
Hello World	429
Helping Mother	325
Herald Angels-Candle Holder	37

*Not known to exist in any collector's hands.

NAME	HUMMEL MOLD NUMBER
High Tenor (Soloist)	135
The Holy Child	70
Holy Family-Font	246
Home From Market	198
Homeward Bound	**334**
Honey Lover	312
Horse Trainer	423
Hosanna	480
I Brought You a Gift	479
I Forgot	362
I Wonder	486
I Won't Hurt You	428
I'll Protect Him	438
I'm Here	478
In D-Major	430
In The Meadow	459
In Tune	414
Infant of Krumbad	78
Is It Raining?	420
It's Cold	421
It's Cold (6" Plate)	735
Joyful (Betty Banjo)	53
Joyful Adventure (Gay Adventure)	356
Joyful and Let's Sing (double figure on a wooden base)**	120
Joyful-Ash Tray	33
Joyful-Candy Box	111/53
Joyous News	27
Jubilee	416
Just Resting	112
Just Resting-Table Lamp	225
Kindergartner	**467**
Knit One, Purl One	432
Kiss Me	311
Knitting Lesson	256
Land in Sight	**530**
Latest News	184
Let's Sing	110
Let's Sing-Ash Tray	114
Let's Sing-Candy Box	111/110
Let's Tell the World	487

*Removed by Goebel from "Open Edition" status in mid-1981.
**Not known to exist in any collector's hands.

NAME	HUMMEL MOLD NUMBER
Letter To Santa Claus	340
Little Band	see Hummel Nos. 389, 390, 391
Little Band	392
Little Band-Candle Holder	388
Little Band-Candle Holder/Music Box	388/M
Little Band-Music Box	392/M
Little Bookkeeper	306
Little Cellist	89
Little Drummer (Drummer)	240
Little Fiddler (Violinist)	2
Little Fiddler (Violinist)	4
Little Fiddler-Plaque	93
Little Fiddler-Plaque	107
Little Gabriel	32
Little Gardener	74
Little Goat Herder	200
Little Goat Herder	250/A
and	
Feeding Time-Bookends	250/B
Little Guardian	145
Little Helper	73
Little Hiker	16
Little Nurse	376
The Little Pair	**449**
Little Pharmacist	322
Little Scholar	80
Little Shopper (Errand Girl)	96
Little Sweeper	171
Little Tailor	308
Little Thrifty	118
Little Velma (Girl with Frog)	219
Littlest Angel	365
Lost Sheep	68
Love From Above (Ornament)	481
Lost Stocking	374
Lucky Boy	335
Lullaby (Cradle Song)-Candle Holder	24
Lute Song	368
Madonna-Plaque	48
Madonna ("Blue Cloaked Madonna")	151
Madonna Plaque (with metal frame)	222
Madonna and Child-Font	243

NAME	HUMMEL MOLD NUMBER
Madonna praying (no halo)	46
Madonna with Halo	45
Mail Coach-Plaque	140
Mail Coach (The Mail Is Here)	226
Make A Wish	**475**
March Winds	43
Max and Moritz	123
Meditation	13
Meditation (7″ plate)	**292**
Merry Wanderer	7
Merry Wanderer	11
Merry Wanderer-Plaque	92
Merry Wanderer-Plaque	106
Merry Wanderer-Plaque	263
Mischief Maker	342
Morning Concert	**447**
Morning Stroll	375
Mother's Aid	325
Mother's Day Plate (Flowers for Mother)	500
Mother's Darling	175
Mother's Helper	133
Mountaineer	315
A Nap	**534**
Nativity Set	214/A,B,C,D,E,F,G,H,J,K,M,N,O
Nativity Set (large)	260/A,B,C,D,E,F,G,H,J,L,M,N,O,P,R
Naughty Boy (Being Punished)	326
Not For You	317
Off To School	329
One for You, One for Me	482
On Holiday	350
On Our Way	**472**
On Secret Path	386
Our Hero (Brother)	95
Out Of Danger	56B
Out of Danger-Table Lamp	**44/B**
The Poet	397
The Photographer	178
Playmates	58
Playmates-Candy Box	111/58
Playmates	61/A
and	
Chick Girl-Bookends	61/B

NAME	HUMMEL MOLD NUMBER
Pay Attention	426
Pleasant Journey	406
Pleasant Moment	425
Postman	119
Prayer Before Battle	20
The Professor	320
Puppy Love	1
Quartet-Plaque	134
Relaxation	316
Retreat To Safety	201
Retreat To Safety-Plaque	126
Ride Into Christmas	396
Ring Around The Rosie	348
The Run-Away	327
Sad Song	404
Scamp	553
School Boy (School Days)	82
School Boys	170
School Days (School Boy)	82
School Girl	81
School Girls	177
Seated Angel (with bird)-Font	167
Sensitive Hunter	6
Serenade	85
She Loves Me, She Loves Me Not	174
She Loves Me, She Loves Me Not-Table Lamp	227
Shepherd Boy	395
Shepherd's Boy	64
Shining Light	358
Shrine-Table Lamp	100
Signs of Spring	203
Silent Night-Candle Holder	54
Sing Along	433
Sing With Me	405
Singing Lesson-Ash Tray	34
Singing Lesson	63
Singing Lesson-Candy Box	111/63
Sister	98
Skier	59
Sleep Tight	424
Smiling Through	408
Smiling Through-Plaque	690

NAME	HUMMEL MOLD NUMBER
Smokey (Chimney Sweep)	12
The Smart Little Sister	346
Soldier Boy	332
Soloist (High Tenor)	135
Song of Praise	454
Sounds of the Mandolin	438
Sound the Trumpet	457
Spring (Apple Tree Boy)	141
Spring Bouquet	398
Spring Cheer	72
Spring Dance	353
Standing Boy-Plaque	168
Star Gazer	132
St. George	55
A Stitch In Time	255
A Stitch in Time (mini-plate)	747
Store Plaque (English)	187
Store Plaque (English) (Schmid Brothers plaque)	210
Store Plaque (English)	211
Store Plaque (French)	208
Store Plaque (German)	205
Store Plaque (Spanish)	213
Store Plaque (Swedish)	209
Store Plaque (English, new in 1986)	460
Stormy Weather (Under One Roof)	71
Storybook Time	458
Street Singer	131
Strolling Along	5
Sunny Morning	313
Supreme Protection	364
Surprise	94
Surprise (7'' plate)	295
The Surprise	431
Swaying Lullaby	165
Sweet Greetings	352
Sweet Greetings (7'' plate)	294
Sweet Music	186
Tally (display plaque)	460
Telling Her Secret	196

NAME	HUMMEL MOLD NUMBER
Thoughtful (I Forgot)	415
Three Pals (Farm Boy)	66
Timid Little Sister	394
To Market	49
To Market-Table Lamp	101
To Market-Table Lamp	223
Truant	410
True Friendship	402
Trumpet Boy	97
Tuba Player	437
Tuneful Angel	359
Tuneful Goodnight (Happy Bugler)-Plaque	180
Two Hands, One Treat	**493**
Umbrella Boy	152/A
Umbrella Girl	152/B
Under One Roof (Stormy Weather)	72
Vacation Time-Plaque	125
Valentine Gift	387
Valentine Gift (6″ Plate)	738
Valentine Joy	399
Valentine Joy (6″ Plate)	737
Village Boy	51
Violinist (Little Fiddler)	2
Visiting An Invalid	382
Volunteers	50
Volunteers-Table Lamp	102
Waiter	154
Wall Vases (3)	
Boy and Girl	360/A
Boy	360/B
Girl	360/C
Wash Day	321
Watchful Angel (Angelic Care)	194
Wayside Devotion	28
Wayside Devotion	90/A
and	
Adoration-Bookends	90/B
Wayside Devotion-Table Lamp	104
Wayside Harmony	111
Wayside Harmony and Just Reading	121
(double figure on a wooden base)*	
Wayside Harmony-Table Lamp	224

*Existence unsubstantiated outside factory archives.

NAME	HUMMEL MOLD NUMBER
Weary Wanderer	204
We Congratulate	214E
We Congratulate (with base)	220
We Wish You the Best	600
Well Done!	400
What Now?	422
What's New?	418
Where Are You?	427
Where Did You Get That?	417
Which Hand?	258
Whistler's Duet	413
White Angel-Font	75
Whitsuntide (Happy New Year)	163
Winter Song	476
With Loving Greetings	309
Worship	84
Worship-Font	164

**Pieces listed chronologically by Mold Number
beginning on next page.
Alphabetical Cross Referencing starting on page 83.**

THE HUMMEL COLLECTION LISTING

The following list of pieces in the Hummel collection is arranged by the appropriate Hummel mold number in ascending order. To fully understand all of the notations you must read and study the first 96 pages of this book very carefully.

You will find the price listings almost complete, but it is impossible to conscientiously assign a value to each and every model that exists today. (Please refer to the introduction and to page 15 for a discussion of value determination.) I have tried to count the possible number of pieces according to size and the number in the listing is approximately 1500. This number does not take into consideration all of the size variations due to mold size variation, color variation and model design differences, so as you can see the number would be incredibly large. Where it was impossible to obtain any pricing information on a particular figure size or variation, the appropriate space is left blank or the listing is omitted altogether. In the latter case, it was not possible to ascertain and document all existing models. From time to time it is possible to establish the existence of a piece but without sure information as to size or trademark. In these cases the corresponding space is left blank.

As evidence by this ninth edition, the book is periodically updated and improved as information is gained and these values and other information will be incorporated in subsequent editions.

As stated earlier, the sizes are approximate but as accurate as was possible to establish. Almost all lists are contradictory, but in most cases within reasonable agreement. The sizes listed are those most frequently encountered in those listings and notated as the Basic Size. (See definition in glossary.) Most of the time this is the smallest size for each figure. Frequently, however, there would be one smaller size listed, but the preponderance of other listings would indicate a ¼'' or ½'' larger size. In these cases the larger size was assumed the more representative.

For purposes of simplification the various trademarks have been abbreviated in the list. Most are obvious but, should you encounter any trouble interpreting them, refer to the list of abbreviations below or to the Glossary.

Dbl. Crown – Double Crown Trademark (TMK 1)
CM – Crown Trademark (TMK 1)
FB – Full Bee Trademark (TMK 2)   (cont.)

Sty. Bee – Stylized Bee Trademark (TMK 3)
3-line – Three Line Trademark (TMK 4)
LB – Last Bee Trademark or Goebel Bee (TMK 5)
MB - Missing Bee Trademark (TMK 6)
HM - Current Mark or Hummel Trademark (TMK 7)

PUPPY LOVE
Hum 1

This figure is similar to Hum 2 and Hum 4 except that this piece has the addition of a small dog at the boy's feet. The one in the photograph here is the more commonly found mold design. They are found in all marks from the Crown to the current trademarks. There is an early Crown mark mold variation where the boy's head is tilted to his right and he wears no tie. These are valued at a bit more than the Crown mark value listed below. Out of production; retired in 1988.

Hum No.	BASIC SIZE	TRADE MARK	CURRENT VALUE
1	5''	CM	360-465.00
1	5''	FB	300-350.00
1	5''	Sty.Bee	200-250.00
1	5''	3-line mark	100-125.00
1	5''	LB	

LITTLE FIDDLER
Hum 2

Originally known as the "Violinist" this figure appears in five basic sizes. There are only five listed below, however, because the sixth and next smallest size bears another model number (Hum 4).

All sizes here are in current production. The two larger sizes of this piece have been temporarily withdrawn from production. The smallest (3½") of the five sizes of the Hum 4 was introduced into the line in 1984 and will remain as an open edition. It is the first of a series of new small figures of similar size to be offered over the next few years. It was issued at $39.00 and now retails for about $60-80.00.

Hum No.	BASIC SIZE	TRADE MARK	CURRENT VALUE
2/4/0	3½"	MB	60-80.00
2/0	6"	CM	400-500.00
2/0	6"	FB	190-250.00
2/0	6"	Sty. Bee	
2/0	6"	3-line mark	140-175.00
2/0	6"	LB	
2/I	7½"	CM	700.00
2/I	7½"	FB	400-500.00
2/I	7½"	Sty.Bee	
2/I	7½"	3-line mark	250-300.00
2/I	7½"	LB	

Hum No.	BASIC SIZE	TRADE MARK	CURRENT VALUE
2/II	11''	CM	1700-1900.00
2/II	11''	FB	1150-1500.00
2/II	11''	Sty. Bee	
2/II	11''	3-line mark	750- 1000.00
2/II	11''	LB	
2/III	12¼''	CM	2000-2500.00
2/III	12¼''	FB	1650-2000.00
2/III	12¼''	Sty. Bee	900-1200.00
2/III	12¼''	LB	

BOOKWORM
Hum 3

This figure appears more than once in the collection. A girl reading a book. It is also found in a smaller size as Hum 8 and in the Hum 14A and B, bookends with a companion figure of a boy reading. The largest Hum 3/III, has been out of current production for some time but recently reinstated. This larger size with older trademarks is avidly sought by collectors. The numbers 3/II and 3/III are occasionally found with the Arabic number size designator (3/2 and 3/3 respectively). See Hum 8 for photo. The two larger sizes have been temporarily withdrawn from current production.

Hum No.	BASIC SIZE	TRADE MARK	CURRENT VALUE
3/I	5½''	CM	600-800.00
3/I	5½''	FB	275-300.00
3/I	5½''	Sty.Bee	250-275.00
3/I	5½''	3-line mark	200-250.00
3/I	5½''	LB	
3/II	8''	CM	1800-2300.00
3/II	8''	FB	1200-1600.00
3/II	8''	Sty.Bee	850-1000.00
3/II	8''	LB	810.00
3/III	9½''	CM	2500-3000.00
3/III	9½''	FB	1600-2100.00
3/III	9½''	Sty.Bee	950-1200.00
3/III	9½''	LB	900.00

LITTLER FIDDLER
Hum 4

This is the same as Hum 2 and only one basic size exists with the Hum 4 mold number (see page 99).

Hum No.	BASIC SIZE	TRADE MARK	CURRENT VALUE
4	4¾''	CM	300-425.00
4	4¾''	FB	135-180.00
4	4¾''	Sty.Bee ⎫	
4	4¾''	3-line mark ⎬	115-125.00
4	4¾''	LB ⎭	

STROLLING ALONG
Hum 5

STROLLING ALONG HUM 5. Mold variations. Note position of umbrellas.

Appears in only one basic size, 4¾''. This figure similar to Hum 7, MERRY WANDERER. The most notable variation found in Hum 5 is that the latest figures to be produced have the boy looking straight ahead while the older ones have him looking to the side. Strolling Along was removed from production at the end of 1989.

Hum No.	BASIC SIZE	TRADE MARK	CURRENT VALUE
5	4¾''	CM	450-700.00
5	4¾''	FB	300-350.00
5	4¾''	Sty.Bee	250.00
5	4¾''	3-line mark	95-120.00
5	4¾''	LB	

SENSITIVE HUNTER
Hum 6

The most notable variation is the "H" shape of the suspenders used with the lederhosen. This variation is associated with all of the Crown marked figures and most of those with the Full Bee and will generally bring about 30% more than the value for the "X" pieces. The later models have an "X" shape configuration. At least one Crown mark piece has been found having the "X" shape suspenders. The color of the rabbit was usually orange until 1981 when the company changed it to brown for all newly produced pieces. Effective December 31, 1984 Goebel has announced that the new production piece in the 7½'' size (Hum 6/II) was placed on a temporary withdrawn from production status.

Hum No.	BASIC SIZE	TRADE MARK	CURRENT VALUE
6/2/0	4''	MB	90-95.00
6	4¾''	CM	500.00 +
6/0	4¾''	CM	330-450.00
6/0	4¾''	FB	135-180.00
6/0	4¾''	Sty.Bee	
6/0	4¾''	3-line mark	100-125.00
6/0	4¾''	LB	
6/I	5½''	CM	470-570.00
6/I	5½''	FB	185-230.00
6/I	5½''	Sty.Bee	165-175.00
6/I	5½''	LB	155-160.00
6/II	7½''	CM	1100-1500.00
6/II	7½''	FB	875-1050.00
6/II	7½''	Sty.Bee	225.00
6/II	7½''	LB	195.00

MERRY WANDERER
Hum 7

MERRY WANDERER   Hum 7/I. Shows the rare two-level or double base.

Also appears as Hum 11. This figure is probably found in more sizes and size variations than any other single figure in the collection. There are at least twelve different sizes known to exist. It appears numerous times in various forms and is used extensively by the W. Goebel firm in promotion and advertising. There is even a huge concrete replica of the figure on the factory grounds in Germany and a figure, 8 feet high, on the grounds of the Goebel Collectors Club in New York. It is found as a part of every single dealer (store) and display plaque until the 1986 release of a new dealer plaque (see Hum 460). The many size variations are due to base variations, possibly mold growth and mold changes. The rarest of the sizes is Hum 7/III size approximately 11'' to 12''. The rarest of the base variations is the two-level base. This variation appears on mold number 7/I in Crown, Full Bee and Stylized Bee marks. The number 7/II is also found as 7/2.

Hum No.	BASIC SIZE	TRADE MARK	CURRENT VALUE
7/0	6¼''	CM	450-650.00
7/0	6¼''	FB	180-225.00
7/0	6¼''	Sty.Bee	
7/0	6¼''	3-line	125-170.00
7/0	6¼''	LB	
7/I	7''	CM	1200-1500.00
7/I	7''	FB	900-1000.00
7/I Double Step Base	7''	Sty.Bee	
7/I	7''	3-line	240-300.00
7/I	7''	LB	
7/II	9½''	CM	1600-2000.00
7/II	9½''	FB	1200-1500.00
7/II	9½''	Sty.Bee	
7/II	9½''	3-line	850-1000.00
7/II	9½''	LB	
7/III	*11¼''	CM	2500-3000.00
7/III	*11¼''	FB	1800-2100.00
7/III	*11¼''	Sty.Bee	
7/III	*11¼''	3-line	950-1100.00
7/III	*11¼''	LB	
7/X	30''	LB	**16,900.00

*The 11¼'' size has been temporarily withdrawn from production.

**1990 suggested retail. There are a few of these ''Jumbo'' figures in collectors' hands. They are generally used as promotional figures in showrooms and shops. They rarely bring full retail price. The Aug. 1990 price list from Geobel states ''Production Suspended''.

BOOKWORM
Hum 8

See Hum 3 and 14A and B. This figure is the same but smaller. The BOOKWORM bearing the Hum 8 number is found in only one basic size, approximately 4''.

Hum No.	BASIC SIZE	TRADE MARK	CURRENT VALUE
8	4''	CM	400-520.00
8	4''	FB	175-210.00
8	4''	Sty.Bee	150-165.00
8	4''	3-line	150-165.00
8	4''	LB	140-150.00

BEGGING HIS SHARE
Hum 9

BEGGING HIS SHARE   HUM 9. Left: Stylized Bee mark, no
candle hole. Right: Full Bee mark with candle hole.

Appears in only one basic size, approximately 5½''. The
most notable variation is that some have a hole in the cake pro-
viding for a candle. The Full Bee piece always has this hole and
the Stylized Bee piece is found with and without the hole.

Hum No.	BASIC SIZE	TRADE MARK	CURRENT VALUE
9	5½''	CM	600.00
9 (hole)	5½''	FB	500.00
9 (w/o hole)	5½''	FB	395.00
9 (hole)	5½''	Sty.Bee	200-240.00
9 (w/o hole)	5½''	Sty.Bee ⎫	140-200.00
9	5½''	LB ⎭	

The 9 mold number designator is sometimes found as ''9''.

FLOWER MADONNA
Hum 10

There are several color and mold variations known. The figure appears in color and in white overglaze in both sizes. There have been reports of the figure occurring in tan, beige or brown, and in a royal blue. Has also been found in terra cotta in 10/III (13'') and in 10/I size (9½'') with the Crown mark. The "donut" or open halo and regular or closed halo is found in both sizes. The Full Bee trademarked figures are the pieces in which both type halos are found. The Full Bee pieces with open halo bring about 20% more than those with closed halos. This variation has no significant influence on the white overglaze pieces. There isn't sufficient trade data to establish a collector value for any of the 10/I or 10/III sizes when they appear in any of the rare colors reported. The Flower Madonna has been temporarily suspended from current production with no date given for reinstatement.

Hum No.	BASIC SIZE	TRADE MARK	CURRENT VALUE
10/I (white)	9½''	CM	350-420.00
10/I (white)	9½''	FB	125-175.00
10/I (white)	9½''	Sty.Bee	90-125.00
10/I (white)	8¼''	LB	90-100.00
10/I (color)	9½''	CM	350-450.00
10/I (color)	9½''	FB	225-325.00
10/I (color)	8¼''	Sty.Bee	175-220.00
10/I (color)	8¼''	LB	175-200.00

Hum No.	BASIC SIZE	TRADE MARK	CURRENT VALUE
10/III (white)	13''	CM	250-450.00
10/III (white) - open halo	13''	FB	200-300.00
10/III (white) - closed halo	13''	FB	150-300.00
10/III (white)	13''	Sty.Bee	150-250.00
10/III (white)	11½''	LB	175-190.00
10/III (color)	13''	CM	500-800.00
10/III (color) - open halo	13''	FB	450-700.00
10/III (color, closed halo)	13''	FB	400-650.00
10/III (color)	13''	Sty.Bee	350-400.00
10/III (color)	11½''	LB	315-345.00

MERRY WANDERER
Hum 11

MERRY WANDERER   HUM 11/2/0. This photo shows the 5, 6 and 7 button variations.

Same design as Hum 7. This Hum 11 is found in only two basic sizes. There are 6 button and 7 button variations to be found on the 11/2/0 size. The 5 button version is the most common.

Hum No.	BASIC SIZE	TRADE MARK	CURRENT VALUE
11/2/0	4¼''	CM	275-330.00
11/2/0	4¼''	*FB	120-180.00
11/2/0	4¼''	Sty.Bee	75-115.00
11/2/0	4¼''	3-line	75-115.00
11/2/0	4¼''	LB	75-115.00

*The 6 and 7 button variation of this one will bring $195-225.00.

Hum No.	BASIC SIZE	TRADE MARK	CURRENT VALUE
11/0	4¾''	CM	400-460.00
11/0	4¾''	FB	175-220.00
11/0	4¾''	Sty.Bee ⎫	
11/0	4¾''	3-line ⎬	100-150.00
11/0	4¾''	LB ⎭	

CHIMNEY SWEEP
Hum 12

Chimney Sweep, Hum 12/0, Stylized Bee.

This figure has been called "Smokey" in the past. Sizes found in various lists are 4'', 5½'', 6¼'' and 6⅜''. There are only three basic sizes, others are variations.

Hum No.	BASIC SIZE	TRADE MARK	CURRENT VALUE
12/2/0	4''	FB	75-100.00
12/2/0	4''	Sty.Bee ⎫	
12/2/0	4''	3-line ⎬	54-70.00
12/2/0	4''	LB ⎭	
12	5½''	CM	400-500.00
12	5½''	FB	200-300.00
12/I	5½''	CM	360-450.00
12/I	5½''	FB	200-250.00
12/I	5½''	Sty.Bee ⎫	
12/I	5½''	3-line ⎬	100-125.00
12/I	5½''	LB ⎭	
12/II	7¼''	FB	*

*Insufficient available data to establish value. Existence unsubstantiated.

MEDITATION
Hum 13

There are several variations associated with this piece. The 13/II is found with the basket half full of flowers, the 13/2/0 has no flowers, and the 13/V size is completely filled with flowers. The Crown marked 13/II is the rarest and when sold commands a premium price. The 13/II and 13/V are listed as reinstated, but the new 13/II* has no flowers in the basket.

Hum No.	BASIC SIZE	TRADE MARK	CURRENT VALUE
13/2/0	4¼"	FB	125-200.00
13/2/0	4¼"	Sty.Bee	125.00
13/2/0	4¼"	3-line	90.00
13/2/0	4¼"	LB	85.00
13/0	5¼"	CM	400-500.00
13/0	6"	FB	220-250.00
13/0	5¼"	Sty.Bee	210.00
13/0	5"	3-line	150-200.00
13/0	5"	LB	

*Effective December 31, 1984 the 13/II was temporarily withdrawn from current production with no date given for reinstatement.

Hum No.	BASIC SIZE	TRADE MARK	CURRENT VALUE
13/II (13/2) (w/flowers)	7''	CM	3000-4500.00
13/II (13/2) (w/flowers)	7''	FB	2500-4000.00
13/II (13/2) (w/flowers)	7''	Sty.Bee	2250.00
13/II (13/2) (w/flowers)	7''	3-line	2000.00
13/II (13/2)	7''	LB	275.00
13/V	13¾''	FB	4000-5000.00
13/V	13¾''	Sty.Bee	1800-2500.00
13/V	13¾''	3-line	1200-1500.00
13/V	13¾''	LB	900-1000.00

BOOKWORMS
(BOOKENDS)
Hum 14A and B

Bookworm – Bookend, Hum 14A, 5¼'', Full Bee.

Bookworm – Bookend, Hum 14B, 5¾'', Full Bee.

These are two figures, a boy and a girl (see Hum 3 and Hum 8). As far as is known to date, there is no other occurrence of the Boy Bookworm anywhere else in the collection. It occurs only in conjunction with the Book Ends (Hum 14 A and B) in only one size. There are no wooden bases as is the case with the other book ends in the collection. There are holes provided where the figures are weighted with sand, etc., and usually sealed with a factory sticker, gold in color. These are listed as "Temporarily Withdrawn" on current Goebel lists.

Hum No.	BASIC SIZE	TRADE MARK	CURRENT VALUE
14/A&B	5½''	CM	1000-1200.00
14/A & B	5½''	FB	375-550.00
14/A & B	5½''	Sty.Bee	320-355.00
14/A & B	5½''	3-line	250-320.00
14/A & B	5½''	LB	

HEAR YE HEAR YE
Hum 15

Hum No.	BASIC SIZE	TRADE MARK	CURRENT VALUE
15/II/0	4''	MB	95-120.00
15/0	5''	CM	375-500.00
15/0	5''	FB	190-240.00
15/0	5''	Sty.Bee	120-150.00
15/0	5''	3-line	
15/0	5''	LB	
15/I	6''	CM	450-600.00
15/I	6''	FB	220-215.00
15/I	6''	Sty.Bee	150-200.00
15/I	6''	3-line	
15/I	6''	LB	

Hum No.	BASIC SIZE	TRADE MARK	CURRENT VALUE
15/II	7½''	CM	800-1100.00
15/II	7½''	FB	440-600.00
15/II	7½''	Sty.Bee	
15/II	7½''	3-line	245-350.00
15/II	7½''	LB	

LITTLE HIKER
Hum 16

Sizes encountered in lists were 4¼'', 5¾'' and 6''.

Hum No.	BASIC SIZE	TRADE MARK	CURRENT VALUE
16/2/0	4¼''	CM	225-325.00
16/2/0	4¼''	FB	115-195.00
16/2/0	4¼''	Sty.Bee	
16/2/0	4¼''	3-line	70-85.00
16/2/0	4¼''	LB	
16/I	5½''	CM	385-450.00
16/I	5½''	FB	200-325.00

Hum No.	BASIC SIZE	TRADE MARK	CURRENT VALUE
16/I	5½''	Sty.Bee	
16/I	5½''	3-line	125-150.00
16/I	5½''	LB	

CONGRATULATIONS
Hum 17

CONGRATULATIONS   HUM 17/0. Left: Last Bee trademark, 1971 MID. Right: Older trademark. Note no socks.

Size variations from 5½'' to 6'' were encountered in various lists. A later model of the figure is slightly taller, hair appears a little longer in a different style, flowers are larger and, most significantly, the later version has socks while the earlier ones have no socks. The earlier no-socks variation is the most desirable to collectors and the Crown marked 17/2 (8¼'') size commands a premium price if sold.

Hum No.	BASIC SIZE	TRADE MARK	CURRENT VALUE
17/0 (no socks)	6''	CM	325-375.00

Hum No.	BASIC SIZE	TRADE MARK	CURRENT VALUE
17/0 (no socks)	6''	FB	220-290.00
17/0 (no socks)	6''	Sty.Bee	130-150.00
17/0 (no socks)	6''	3-line	110-150.00
17/0 (socks)	6''	3-line	90-110.00
17/0 (socks)	6''	LB	
17/2 or 17/II	8¼''	CM	5000-7500.00
17/2 or 17/II	8¼''	FB	4000-5000.00
17/2 or 17/II	8¼''	Sty.Bee	3000-4000.00

CHRIST CHILD
Hum 18

This figure is very similar to the Christ Child figure used in the Nativity Sets, Hum 214 and 260. It is known to have been produced in a solid white overglaze. The white piece is rare. Christ Child has been temporarily withdrawn from production.

Hum No.	BASIC SIZE	TRADE MARK	CURRENT VALUE
18	2''x6''	CM	250-300.00
18	2''x6''	FB	100-125.00
18	2''x6''	Sty.Bee	95.00
18	2''x6''	3.line	90.00
18	2''x6''	LB	80-90.00

PRAYER BEFORE BATTLE
(Large Tray)
Hum 19
Closed Number

Until 1986, when one of these surfaced in the United States, it was thought this was a Closed Number and the piece never produced. Even though one was found (temporarily) it may well be the only one ever made. The reason I noted "temporarily found" follows: It seems that a lady brought the piece to the Goebel Collectors' Club in Tarrytown, NY for identification. The paint finish was badly damaged as a result of her putting it in a dishwasher to clean it, Goebel Master Sculptor Gerhard Skrobek coincidentally was there. He speculated that the reason the paint was damaged was because it was probably a sample piece, painted but never fired so that the paint had not bonded to the figurine. Subsequent investigation of Goebel records revealed that the design was rejected by the Siessen Convent therefore never placed in production. Furthermore there is no example in the company archives. How it got out of the factory and to the U.S. remains a mystery. It seems the lady left, taking her piece with her, and no one present could remember her name or where she was from. Too unique to place a value on.

PRAYER BEFORE BATTLE
Hum 20

Until recent years it has been thought that only minor, insignificant variations existed. At least one major variation has been uncovered, with regard to color. The figure is illustrated and discussed in more detail on page —. Has been listed variously as 4'' and 4-1/2'' in the past and is currently listed at 4-1/4'' in the Goebel recommended price list. If found and placed on sale it very likely would fetch at least $5000.00

Hum No.	BASIC SIZE	TRADE MARK	CURRENT VALUE
20	4¼''	CM	420-500.00
20	4¼''	FB	160-250.00
20	4¼''	Sty.Bee ⎫	
20	4¼''	3-line ⎬	100-145.00
20	4¼''	LB ⎭	

(See illustration next page)

PRAYER BEFORE BATTLE

Crown	CM	TMK-1	1934-1950
Full Bee	FB	TMK-2	1940-1959
Stylized Bee	Sty Bee	TMK-3	1958-1972
Three Line Mark	3-Line	TMK-4	1964-1972
Last Bee Mark	LB	TMK-5	1970-1980
Missing Bee Mark	MB	TMK-6	1979-1991
Hummel Mark (Current)	HM	TMK-7	1991-Present

HEAVENLY ANGEL
Hum 21

Sizes found references in various lists are 4¼'', 4½'', 6'', 6¾'' and 8¾''. Has been made in white overglaze. The white piece is very rare.

Hum No.	BASIC SIZE	TRADE MARK	CURRENT VALUE
21/0	4¼''	CM	250-300.00
21/0	4¼''	FB	115-160.00
21/0	4¼''	Sty.Bee	
21/0	4¼''	3-line	75-100.00
21/0	4¼''	LB	
*21/0/½	6''	CM	400-500.00
*21/0/½	6''	FB	195-250.00
*21/0/½	6''	Sty.Bee	
*21/0/½	6''	3-line	125-175.00
*21/0/½	6''	LB	
21/I	6¾''	CM	440-530.00
21/I	6¾''	FB	230-295.00

Hum No.	BASIC SIZE	TRADE MARK	CURRENT VALUE
21/I	6¾''	Sty.Bee	
21/I	6¾''	3-line	130-190.00
21/I	6¾''	LB	
21/II	8¾''	CM	920-1100.00
21/II	8¾''	FB	450-550.00
21/II	8¾''	Sty.Bee	
21/II	8¾''	3-line	250-400.00
21/II	8¾''	LB	

ANGEL WITH BIRDS – Font
Hum 22

Sometimes known as Seated or Sitting Angel with birds. This font has variations in bowl design and appears in two basic sizes. The mold number 22 has been known to appear with the decimal point size designator. The 22/I size is a closed edition.

Hum No.	BASIC SIZE	TRADE MARK	CURRENT VALUE
22/0	2¾''x3½''	CM	85-100.00
22/0	2¾''x3½''	FB	40-50.00
22/0	2¾''x3½''	Sty.Bee	
22/0	2¾''x3½''	3-line	25-40.00
22/0	2¾''x3½''	LB	
22/I	3¼''x4''	CM	400-500.00
22/I	3¼''x4''	FB	350-400.00
22/I	3¼''x4''	Sty. Bee	300-350.00

ADORATION
Hum 23

HUM 23/I
ADORATION
White overglaze

Although listed in the current factory price lists, this figure is considered rare (especially the larger sizes). ADORATION was also produced in solid white overglaze in the 23/I size. See Hum 100 and 105.

Hum No.	BASIC SIZE	TRADE MARK	CURRENT VALUE
23/I	6¼''	CM	600-750.00
23/I	6¼''	FB	325-450.00
23/I	6¼''	Sty. Bee	
23/I	6¼''	3-line	225-300.00
23/I	6¼''	LB	
23/III	9''	CM	900-1300.00
23/III	9''	FB	400-550.00

Hum No.	BASIC SIZE	TRADE MARK	CURRENT VALUE
23/III	9''	Sty.Bee ⎫	
23/III	9''	3-line ⎬	350-450.00
23/III	9''	LB ⎭	

LULLABY
Candleholder
Hum 24

LULLABY (Candleholder) HUM 24   LULLABY HUM 262

This piece is quite similar to Hum 262, except that this one is a candleholder.

The larger (Hum 24/III) was out of production for some time, but has recently been reissued. The 24/III bearing older marks commands premium prices. The 24/III is sometimes found as 24/3. This, the larger size, has been removed temporarily from current production with no given reinstatement date.

Hum No.	BASIC SIZE	TRADE MARK	CURRENT VALUE
24/I	3¼''x5''	CM	385-460.00
24/I	3¼''x5''	FB	150-205.00
24/I	3¼''x5''	Sty.Bee ⎫	
24/I	3¼''x5''	3-line ⎬	110-140.00
24/I	3¼''x5''	LB ⎭	
24/III	6''x8''	CM	1400-1700.00
24/III	6''x8''	FB	500-700.00
24/III	6''x8''	Sty.Bee ⎫	
24/III	6''x8''	LB ⎬	310-400.00

ANGELIC SLEEP
Candleholder
Hum 25

Has been produced in color and white overglaze. The white figure is quite rare.

Hum No.	BASIC SIZE	TRADE MARK	CURRENT VALUE
25	3½''x5''	CM	400-475.00
25	3½''x5''	FB	160-225.00
25	3½''x5''	Sty.Bee	
25	3½''x5''	3-line	125-140.00
25	3½''x5''	LB	

CHILD JESUS
Font
Hum 26

Although the color of the dress on the figure is ordinarily orange, there is an extremely rare variation where the color is blue.

Appears in two basic sizes, though the larger size does not appear in current factory lists.

Hum No.	BASIC SIZE	TRADE MARK	CURRENT VALUE
26/0	1½"x5"	CM	85-100.00
26/0	1½"x5"	FB	40-50.00
26/0	1½"x5"	Sty.Bee	
26/0	1½"x5"	3-line	25-35.00
26/0	1½"x5"	LB	
26/I	2½"x6"	—	350-500.00

JOYOUS NEWS
Hum 27

This piece is considered to be fairly scarce in the first three trademarks. As far as is presently known, there are somewhere between 25 and 50 in collectors' hands. The 27/III is sometimes found as 27/3. It was out of production for several years, but has been back in production for some time now. Older marked figures command a premium price. There is smaller size (27/I) but it is extremely rare. This 2¾'' version is a candleholder. There are only four presently known to exist.

Hum No.	BASIC SIZE	TRADE MARK	CURRENT VALUE
27/III	4¼''x4¾''	CM	1500-1800.00
27/III	4¼''x4¾''	FB	750-1000.00
27/III	4¼''x4¾''	Sty.Bee	500-750.00
27/III	4¼''x4¾''	3-line	300-500.00
27/III (27/3)	4¼''x4¾''	LB	160-185.00

WAYSIDE DEVOTION
Hum 28

The 28/II has been found with the Arabic size designator 28/2, and in white overglaze. The larger (28/II) size is occasionally found without the "II" designator but a "28" only.

Hum No.	BASIC SIZE	TRADE MARK	CURRENT VALUE
28/II	7½''	CM	825-990.00
28/II	7½''	FB	400-485.00
28/II	7½''	Sty.Bee	
28/II	7½''	3-line	250-350.00
28/II	7½''	LB	
28/III	8½''	CM	1000-1300.00
28/III	8½''	FB	500-620.00
28/III	8½''	Sty.Bee	
28/III	8½''	3.line	350-450.00
28/III	8½''	LB	

GUARDIAN ANGEL
Font
Hum 29

This figure is not in current production and highly sought by collectors. A similar piece (Hum 248) exists and is considered to be a redesign of Hum 29. It is, therefore, unlikely to ever be reissued. It has been known to have been found with the decimal point designator.

Hum No.	BASIC SIZE	TRADE MARK	CURRENT VALUE
29	2½''x5⅝''	CM	1200.00
29	2½''x5⅝''	FB	1000.00
29	2½''x5⅝''	Sty.Bee	800.00
29/0	2½''x5⅝''	CM	1100.00
29/0	2½''x5⅝''	FB	900.00
29/0	2½''x5⅝''	Sty.Bee	900.00

BA-BEE RINGS
Plaques
Hum 30 A and 30 B

These are fashioned for hanging. They consist of right and left facing babies' heads in a ring. All sizes except the 30/I are in current production. One pair with red painted rings is known to exist.

Hum No.	BASIC SIZE	TRADE MARK	CURRENT VALUE
30/A&B	5''diam.	CM	300-450.00
30/OA&B	5''diam.	FB	250-300.00
30/OA&B	5''diam.	Sty.Bee	
30/OA&B	5''diam.	3-line	120-150.00
30/OA&B	5''diam.	LB	
30/IA&B	6''diam.	CM	2500-3000.00

ADVENT GROUP
With Candleholder
Hum 31

This is a multifigure piece quite similar to Hum 54 "Silent Night". Extremely rare. This piece was produced around 1935 with a black child angel appearing on the left side. It is otherwise almost identical to SILENT NIGHT and is frequently referred to as "Silent Night with Black Child". It is believed that it was removed from production due to Hitler's extreme racial prejudice. There are none of these known to be for sale, but if found and placed on the market it would probably bring $12,000-15,000.00.

There have been a few Hum 31's discovered in recent years in which there is no black child. The value for this all-white-children Hum 31 is about $10,000-12,000.00.

LITTLE GABRIEL
Hum 32

Little Gabriel has recently been redesigned. The older pieces have the arms that are attached to each other up to the hands. The new design has the arms separated.

Hum No.	BASIC SIZE	TRADE MARK	CURRENT VALUE
32/O	5″	CM	275-325.00
32/O	5″	FB	140-165.00
32/O	5″	Sty.Bee	80-115.00
32/O	5″	3-line	
32/O	5″	LB	
32/I	6″	CM	4000.00
32/I	6″	FB	2500-3000.00
32/I	6″	Sty. Bee	2000-2500.00

JOYFUL
Ashtray
Hum 33

An ashtray utilizing a figure very similar to Hum 53 and with the addition of a small bird on the edge of the tray next to the figure. This piece has been temporarily removed from current production effective December 31, 1984 with no date for reinstatement given.

Hum No.	BASIC SIZE	TRADE MARK	CURRENT VALUE
33	3½''x6''	CM	325-390.00
33	3½''x6''	FB	120-160.00
33	3½''x6''	Sty.Bee	85-100.00
33	3½''x6''	3-line	70-85.00
33	3½''x6''	LB	

SINGING LESSON
Ashtray
Hum 34

An ashtray utilizing a figure very similar to Hum 63, with a small bird perched on the edge of the tray instead of the boy's shoes.

Hum No.	BASIC SIZE	TRADE MARK	CURRENT VALUE
34	3½''x6¼''	CM	400-480.00
34	3½''x6¼''	FB	140-200.00
34	3½''x6¼''	Sty.Bee	
34	3½''x6¼''	3-line	110-140.00
34	3½''x6¼''	LB	

THE GOOD SHEPHERD
Font
Hum 35

Hum No.	BASIC SIZE	TRADE MARK	CURRENT VALUE
35/0	2¼''x4¾''	CM	100-150.00
35/0	2¼''x4¾''	FB	55.00
35/0	2¼''x4¾''	Sty.Bee	
35/0	2¼''x4¾''	3-line	24-30.00
35/0	2¼''x4¾''	LB	
35/I	2¾''x5¾''	CM	300-350.00
35/I	2¾''x5¾''	FB	200.00
35/I	2¾''x5¾''	Sty.Bee	100-150.00

CHILD WITH FLOWERS
Font
Hum 36

Hum No.	BASIC SIZE	TRADE MARK	CURRENT VALUE
36/0	2¾″x4″	CM	100-150.00
36/0	2¾″x4″	FB	50.00
36/0	2¾″x4″	Sty.Bee	
36/0	2¾″x4″	3-line	25-35.00
36/0	2¾″x4″	LB	
36/I	3½″x4½″	CM	300-350.00
36/I	3½″x4½″	FB	150-250.00
36/I	3½″x4½″	Sty.Bee	100-150.00
36/I	3½″x4½″	LB	50-100.00

HERALD ANGELS
Candleholder
Hum 37

This is a group of figures very similar to Hum 38, 39 and 40, placed together on a common round base and provided with a candle receptacle in the center. There are two versions, one with a low and one with a higher candle holder. The higher holder is found on the older pieces (photo above). This candleholder has been temporarily withdrawn from current production.

Hum No.	BASIC SIZE	TRADE MARK	CURRENT VALUE
37	2¼''x4''	CM	420-500.00
37	2¼''x4''	FB	165-225.00
37	2¼''x4''	Sty.Bee	
37	2¼''x4''	3-line	120-150.00
37	2¼''x4''	LB	

THE ANGEL TRIO
Candleholders
Hum 38, Hum 39, Hum 40

These three figures are presented as a set of three and are usually sold as a set. They each come in three versions according to size and candle size.

Hum 38 **Joyous News** – Angel with lute
Hum 39 **Joyous News** – Angel with accordion
Hum 40 **Joyous News** – Angel with horn

I/38/0, I/39/0, I/40/0	2″	0.6 cm candle diameter
III/38/0, III/39/0, III/40/0	2″	1.0 cm candle diameter
III/38/I, III/39/I, III/40/I	2¾″	1.0 cm candle diameter

Crown Mark (as a set).................... 325-395.00
Full Bee (as a set)......................... 120-175.00
Stylized Bee (as a set)....................⎫
3-line Mark (as a set) ....⎬100-115.00
Last Bee (as a set)........................⎭

SINGING LESSON
(without base)
Closed Number   Hum 41

Has been listed as a closed number but the existence of this piece has now been substantiated. Details are not known but the piece is said to be similar to Hum 63 "Singing Lesson" without the base.

GOOD SHEPHERD
Hum 42

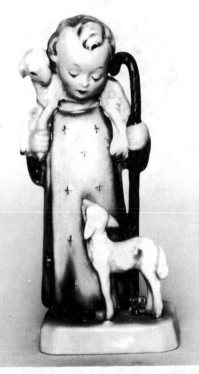

The 42 mold number has been found with the decimal point designator. There are two very rare variations; a blue gown rather than the normal brownish color and a white gown with blue stars. No longer produced in the 7½" size.

Hum No.	BASIC SIZE	TRADE MARK	CURRENT VALUE
42.	6¼"	CM	350-425.00
42/0	6¼"	CM	270-325.00
42/0	6¼"	FB	220-270.00
42/0	6¼"	Sty.Bee	}
42/0	6¼"	3-line	} 125-200.00
42/0	6¼"	LB	}
42/1	7½"	CM	4000-6000.00
42/1	7½"	FB	3000-3800.00

MARCH WINDS
Hum 43

There appear to be two slightly different designs. In the earlier pieces the boy looks more toward the rear than in the newer ones.

Hum No.	BASIC SIZE	TRADE MARK	CURRENT VALUE
43	5″	CM	300-350.00
43	5″	FB	150-180.00
43	5″	Sty.Bee	
43	5″	3-line	85-100.00
43	5″	LB	

CULPRITS
Table Lamp
Hum 44/A

The figure utilized as this lamp base is very similar to Hum 56/A. In current production.

Hum No.	BASIC SIZE	TRADE MARK	CURRENT VALUE
44/A	9½''	CM	450-600.00
44/A	9½''	FB	350-400.00
44/A	9½''	Sty.Bee	275-320.00
44/A	9½''	3-line	225-260.00
44/A	9½''	LB	225-260.00

OUT OF DANGER
Table Lamp
Hum 44/B

Out of Danger table lamp Hum 44/B, Full Bee, black Germany with (c) W. Goebel.

The figure utilized as this lamp base is very similar to Hum 56/B. In current production.

Hum No.	BASIC SIZE	TRADE MARK	CURRENT VALUE
44/B	9½''	CM	450-600.00
44/B	9½''	FB	350-400.00
44/B	9½''	Sty.Bee	275-320.00
44/B	9½''	3-line	225-260.00
44/B	9½''	LB	225-260.00

MADONNA WITH HALO
Hum 45

Left figure is Hum 46. The other three are each Hum 45.

At least nine variations have been found. The chief differences are in the size and in color and glaze treatment. Sizes found in various lists: 10½'', 11⅞'', 12'', 13¼'', 16¾''. The figure is found in color and in white overglaze. There are many color variations known. Those known are beige, rose, light blue and ivory. In 1982 the 45/III was temporarily withdrawn from production in regular color and white overglaze. The 45/0 size in regular color and white overglaze has been temporarily withdrawn from production as of December 31, 1984. No reinstatement date is given for either. Has been found in terra cotta.

Hum No.	BASIC SIZE	TRADE MARK	CURRENT VALUE
45/0	10½''	CM	200-250.00
45/0	10½''	FB	75-105.00

Hum No.	BASIC SIZE	TRADE MARK	CURRENT VALUE
45/0	10½''	Sty.Bee	
45/0	10½''	3-line	45-65.00
45/0	10½''	LB	
45/I	12''	CM	225-300.00
45/I	12''	FB	90-130.00
45/I	12''	Sty.Bee	
45/I	12''	3-line	70-85.00
45/I	12''	LB	
45/III	16¼''	CM	500-600.00
45/III	16¼''	FB	180-260.00
45/III	16¼''	Sty.Bee	
45/III	16¼''	3-line	115-145.00
45/III	16¼''	LB	

MADONNA WITHOUT HALO
Hum 46

At least nine variations have been found. The chief differences are in the size and in color and glaze treatment. Sizes found in various lists: 10½'', 11⅞'', 12'', 13¼'', 16¾''. The figure is found in color and in white overglaze. There are many color variations known. Those known are beige, rose, light blue and ivory. In 1982 the 46/III was temporarily withdrawn from production in regular color and white overglaze.

There have been at least two versions of this piece found, that are of a reddish terra cotta finish. They are both signed with the incised M.I. Hummel signature and inexplicably marked with the mold number "18" incised on the bottom.

The Goebel company lists the 46/0 size in both regular color and white overglaze as temporarily withdraw from current production status effective December 31, 1984. There is no reinstatement date given for either the 46/III or 46/0.

Hum No.	BASIC SIZE	TRADE MARK	CURRENT VALUE
46/0	10¼''	CM	200-250.00
46/0	10¼''	FB	75-105.00
46/0	10¼''	Sty.Bee	
46/0	10¼''	3-line	45-65.00
46/0	10¼''	LB	
46/I	11¼''	CM	225-300.00
46/I	11¼''	FB	90-130.00

Hum No.	BASIC SIZE	TRADE MARK	CURRENT VALUE
46/I	11¼''	Sty.Bee ⎫	
46/I	11¼''	3-line ⎬	70-85.00
46/I	11¼''	LB ⎭	
46/III	16''	CM	500-600.00
46/III	16''	FB	180-260.00
46/III	16''	Sty.Bee ⎫	
46/III	16''	3-line ⎬	115-145.00
46/III	16''	LB ⎭	

GOOSE GIRL
Hum 47

A very popular piece in the collection and occurs in three basic sizes. The 47/II size has been found with the Arabic number designator (47/2). Goose Girl has been found in terra cotta.

Hum No.	BASIC SIZE	TRADE MARK	CURRENT VALUE
47/3/0	4''	CM	310-350.00
47/3/0	4''	FB	160-195.00
47/3/0	4''	Sty.Bee ⎫	
47/3/0	4''	3-line ⎬	110-140.00
47/3/0	4''	LB ⎭	
47/0	4¾''	CM	450-540.00

Hum No.	BASIC SIZE	TRADE MARK	CURRENT VALUE
47/0	4¾''	FB	200-265.00
47/0	4¾''	Sty.Bee	
47/0	4¾''	3-line	140-185.00
47/0	4¾''	LB	
47/II	7½''	CM	1000-1200.00
47/II	7½''	FB	415-470.00
47/II	7½''	Sty.Bee	
47/II	7½''	3-line	290-380.00
47/II	7½''	LB	

MADONNA
Plaque
Hum 48

MADONNA PLAQUE   HUM48
Shows painted and white overglaze pieces.

A relatively rare piece. Has been known to appear in a white overglaze in the 48/0 and the 48/II in a bisque finish. The 48/II can sometimes be found as 48/2. There are two variations of the 48/II in the Crown Mark. The 48/II size in current use trademark has been temporarily withdrawn from production. The effective date was December 31, 1984 with no reinstatement date given.

(cont.)

Hum No.	BASIC SIZE	TRADE MARK	CURRENT VALUE
48/0	3"x4"	CM	250-300.00
48/0	3"x4"	FB	100-115.00
48/0	3"x4"	Sty.Bee	
48/0	3"x4"	3-line	75-90.00
48/0	3"x4"	LB	
48/II	4¾"x6"	CM	400-520.00
48/II	4¾"x6"	FB	185-250.00
48/II	4¾"x6"	Sty.Bee	105-135.00
48/II	4¾"x6"	LB	
48/V	8¼"x10½"	CM	2200.00
48/V	8¼"x10½"	FB	1500-2000.00
48/V	8¼"x10½"	Sty.Bee	1000-1500.00

TO MARKET
Hum 49

The 49/I size was out of current production for at least 20 years and then reinstated in the early 1980's. Once again it is out of current production. Goebel placed it on a temporarily withdrawn from production status on December 31, 1984. The 49 mold number has occasionally been found with the decimal point size designator. There have been 49/0's to surface having no bottle in the basket. The 49/3/O size is routinely produced with no bottle in the basket.

Hum No.	BASIC SIZE	TRADE MARK	CURRENT VALUE
49/3/0	4″	CM	310-390.00
49/3/0	4″	FB	195.00
49/3/0	4″	Sty.Bee	
49/3/0	4″	3-line	110-145.00
49/3/0	4″	LB	
49/0	5½″	CM	450-650.00
49/0	5½″	FB	240-305.00
49/0	5½″	Sty.Bee	
49/0	5½″	3-line	175-220.00
49/0	5½″	LB	
49.	6¼″	CM	1100-1300.00
49/I	6¼″	CM	800-1100.00
49/I	6¼″	FB	500-750.00
49/I	6¼″	Sty.Bee	
49/I	6¼″	3-line	265-330.00
49.	6¼″	LB	300-400.00
49/I	6¼″	LB	265-275.00

VOLUNTEERS   Hum 50

(cont.)

The 50/0 and 50/I sizes were out of production for some years and difficult to find with the older trademarks. Both were reinstated in 1979 with the new pieces having the Last Bee (TMK-5). The 50/I has once again been withdrawn from current production with no published reinstatement date.

The small, Hum 50/2/0 Volunteers was released with a special backstamp commemorating the allied victory in Operation Desert Storm. Reportedly limited to 10,000 pieces worldwide, it was to be sold only through military post and base exchanges. There has not been sufficient time to determine if this piece will rise in value or remain stable in the collector market.

Hum No.	BASIC SIZE	TRADE MARK	CURRENT VALUE
50/2/0	5''	CM	525-600.00
50/2/0	5''	FB	205-285.00
50/2/0	5''	Sty.Bee	
50/2/0	5''	3-line	155-185.00
50/2/0	5''	LB	
50/0	5½''	CM	675-800.00
50/0	5½''	FB	275-360.00
50/0	5½''	Sty.Bee	
50/0	5½''	LB	195-230.00
50/I	6½''	CM	900-1450.00
50/I	6½''	FB	420-600.00
50/I	6½''	Sty.Bee	
50/I	6½''	LB	265-345.00

VILLAGE BOY   Hum 51

Placed in production around 1934-35, this figure is still being produced. The 51/I was taken out of production sometime in the 1960's and the early figures are considered rare. Out of production for some twenty years, the 51/I was placed back in production for a short time and has once again been temporarily withdrawn effective December 31, 1984 with no known date for reinstatement. Sizes encountered in various lists: 3¼'', 4½'', 5'', 5¼'', 6'', 6¾'', 6⅞'', 7¼''.

Hum No.	BASIC SIZE	TRADE MARK	CURRENT VALUE
51/3/0	4''	CM	225-265.00
51/3/0	4''	FB	110-135.00
51/3/0	4''	Sty.Bee	
51/3/0	4''	3-line	75-85.00
51/3/0	4''	LB	
51/2/0	5''	CM	270-320.00
51/2/0	5''	FB	125-160.00
51/2/0	5''	Sty.Bee	
51/2/0	5''	3-line	90-100.00
51/2/0	5''	LB	
51/0	6''	CM	440-550.00

Hum No.	BASIC SIZE	TRADE MARK	CURRENT VALUE
51/0	6''	FB	240-305.00
51/0	6''	Sty.Bee	
51/0	6''	3-line	175-220.00
51/0	6''	LB	
51/I	7¼''	CM	800-1100.00
51/I	7¼''	FB	500-750.00
51/I	7¼''	Sty.Bee	265-330.00
51/I	7¼''	LB	

GOING TO GRANDMA'S
Hum 52

Hum 52/0 with square base (older model).   Hum 52/I.

The most significant variation associated with this piece is the rectangular base found on some of the figures in the 52/0 size. The cone is sometimes found without candies in the large sizes and with candies in the small size. A more accurate description is a rough or smooth appearing top on the cone. The 52/I size was out of production for many years and reinstated with a redesigned base (oval). It has been temporarily withdrawn from production once again, effective December 31, 1984.

Hum No.	BASIC SIZE	TRADE MARK	CURRENT VALUE
52/0	4¾''	CM	500-600.00
52/0	4¾''	FB	250-315.00
52/0	4¾''	Sty.Bee	
52/0	4¾''	3-line	160-180.00
52/0	4¾''	LB	
52/I	6''	CM	800-1000.00
52/I	6''	FB	500-625.00
52/I	6''	Sty.Bee	300-330.00
52/I	6''	LB	265-300.00

JOYFUL
Hum 53

Shows major size variations.

This figure has also been known as "Banjo Betty". Sizes encountered in various lists vary from 3½'' to 4¼''. The oversize pieces consistently bring premium prices. Has been found in the decimal point size designator. There are major color variations in this piece. The older more rare piece with an orange dress is the most significant color variation.

Hum No.	BASIC SIZE	TRADE MARK	CURRENT VALUE
53	4″	CM	300-400.00
53	4″	FB	125-150.00
53	4″	Sty.Bee	
53	4″	3-line	75-95.00
53	4″	LB	

JOYFUL
Candy Box
Hum III/53

Hum No.	BASIC SIZE	TRADE MARK	CURRENT VALUE
III/53	6¼″	CM	450-530.00
III/53	6¼″	FB	300-350.00
III/53	6¼″	Sty.Bee	150-295.00
III/53	6¼″	3-line	
III/53	6¼″	LB	120-150.00

SILENT NIGHT
Candle Holder
Hum 54

This piece is almost identical to Hum 31, except that the child angel standing on the left in most 31's is *black*. In 54 the child is white. There were two distinctly different sizes encountered in various lists, 3½'' x 5'' and 4¾'' x 5½''.

The author has seen at least two distinct molds. The older Crown marked piece shown here has a girl as the middle figure, newer ones appear to have a boy in the middle. In the fifth edition it was reported that there was reason to believe the existence of this piece with a black child on the left. This has now been substantiated. It is highly speculative to place a value on this rare variation but it would likely fall somewhere between a retail value of $10,000 and $12,000 depending upon the trademark. Photo of this piece on following page.

Hum No.	BASIC SIZE	TRADE MARK	CURRENT VALUE
54	4¾''x5½''	CM	500-600.00
54	4¾''x5½''	FB	250.00
54	4¾''x5½''	Sty.Bee	
54	4¾''x5½''	3-line	175-225.00
54	4¾''x5½''	LB	

Silent Night
Candle Holder
Hum 54

ST. GEORGE
Hum 55

Last Bee trademark.

This figure is substantially different in style from most others in the collection and is difficult to locate most of the time, even though it is listed as in current production. Sizes encountered in various lists: 6¼", 6⅝", 6¾". Some of the early (crown mark) pieces will have a bright red painted saddle. This is the rarest variation and brings $1500-2000.00 when sold. Has been reported to appear in white overglaze.

Hum No.	BASIC SIZE	TRADE MARK	CURRENT VALUE
55	6¾"	CM	800-1000.00
55	6¾"	FB	250-360.00
55	6¾"	Sty.Bee	
55	6¾"	3-line	200-250.00
55	6¾"	LB	

CULPRITS
Hum 56/A

Early model Culprits (eyes open).

Similar figure used in lamp base Hum 44 A. Has been found without the 'A' designator. Later models have eyes appearing closed.

Hum No.	BASIC SIZE	TRADE MARK	CURRENT VALUE
56/A	6¼''	CM	525-625.00
56/A	6¼''	FB	260-315.00
56/A	6¼''	Sty.Bee	}
56/A	6¼''	3-line	} 170-220.00
56/A	6¼''	LB	}

OUT OF DANGER
Hum 56/B

Shows eyes open and eyes closed variation.
Similar figure used as lamp base in Hum 44B. Variations:
late model figures have eyes closed.

Hum No.	BASIC SIZE	TRADE MARK	CURRENT VALUE
56/B	6¼''	FB	260-290.00
56/B	6¼''	Sty.Bee	
56/B	6¼''	3-line	170-245.00
56/B	6¼''	LB	

CHICK GIRL
Hum 57

There are many mold types and sizes. The chief mold variations show different numbers of chicks on the base. For instance, the 57/0 has two chicks and the larger, 57/I, has three. Has been found with mold number and no size designator in the 4¼'' size (57).

Hum No.	BASIC SIZE	TRADE MARK	CURRENT VALUE
57/2/0	3''	MB (current)	125-140.00
57/0	3½''	CM	360-425.00
57/0	3½''	FB	160-210.00
57/0	3½''	Sty.Bee	
57/0	3½''	3-line	115-145.00
57/0	3½''	LB	
57/I	4¼''	CM	500-600.00
57/I	4¼''	FB	240-315.00
57/I	4¼''	Sty.Bee	
57/I	4¼''	3-line	175-220.00
57/I	4¼''	LB	

CHICK GIRL
Candy Box
Hum III/57

Overall size of this figure and box is 5¼″ or 6¼″, depending upon source of information. Differences probably due to a design change in the type of bowl and lid used. Newer lids also show green grass painted around the figures, older models do not.

Hum No.	BASIC SIZE	TRADE MARK	CURRENT VALUE
III/57	5¼″	CM	450-530.00
III/57	5¼″	FB	300-350.00
III/57	5¼″	Sty.Bee	150-295.00
III/57	5¼″	3-line	120-145.00
III/57	5¼″	LB	

PLAYMATES
Hum 58

Similar figures used on book end Hum 61 A and candy box on next page.

Hum No.	BASIC SIZE	TRADE MARK	CURRENT VALUE
58/2/0	3½''	MB	100-125.00
58/0	4''	CM	360-425.00
58/0	4''	FB	160-210.00
58/0	4''	Sty.Bee	
58/0	4''	3-line	100-145.00
58/0	4''	LB	
58/I	4½''	CM	500-600.00
58/I	4½''	FB	245-325.00
58/I	4½''	Sty.Bee	
58/I	4½''	3-line	175-225.00
58/I	4½''	LB	

PLAYMATES
Candy Box
Hum III/58

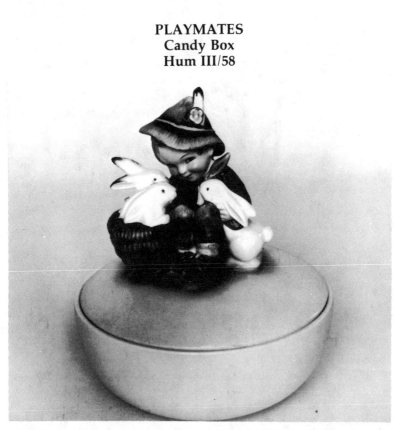

Overall size of this figure and box is 5¼'' or 6¼'', depending upon source of information. Difference probably due to a
design change in the type of lid used.

Hum No.	BASIC SIZE	TRADE MARK	CURRENT VALUE
III/58	5¼''	CM	450-530.00
III/58	5¼''	FB	300-350.00
III/58	5¼''	Sty.Bee	150-295.00
III/58	5¼''	3-line	120-145.00
III/58	5¼''	LB	

SKIER
Hum 59

Newer models have metal ski poles and older have wooden poles. For a short time this figure was made with plastic poles. The poles are replaceable and are not considered significant in the valuation of the piece in the case of wooden and metal poles. There is, however, some difficulty with the plastic ski poles found on most of the Stylized Bee (TMK-3) pieces. The small round discs at the bottom of the poles are molded integral with the pole. Some collectors and dealers feel that the intact plastic ski poles on the Stylized Bee pieces are a bit more valuable than those with wooden or metal replacements.

Hum No.	BASIC SIZE	TRADE MARK	CURRENT VALUE
59	5¼''	CM	440-530.00
59	5¼''	FB	225-400.00
59	5¼''	Sty.Bee	
59	5¼''	3-line	175-200.00
59	5¼''	LB	

FARM BOY and GOOSE GIRL
Bookends
Hum 60/A Hum 60/B

Overall size of each is 6'', the figures being 4¾'' each. If the pieces are removed from the base, there are no trademarks evident. The trademark is stamped on the wooden base itself.

These bookends have been temporarily withdrawn from current production status effective December 31, 1984 with no date for reinstatement given.

Hum No.	BASIC SIZE	TRADE MARK	CURRENT VALUE
60/A&B	6''	CM	600-1000.00
60/A&B	6''	FB	400-600.00
60/A&B	6''	Sty.Bee ⎫	225-300.00
60/A&B	6''	LB ⎭	

PLAYMATES and CHICK GIRL
Bookends   Hum 61/A Hum 61/B

Overall size of each is 6'', the figures being 4'' each. If the pieces are removed from the base, there are no trademarks evident. The trademark is stamped on the wooden base itself.

These bookends have been temporarily withdrawn from current production status effective December 31, 1984 with no date for reinstatement given.

Hum No.	BASIC SIZE	TRADE MARK	CURRENT VALUE
60/A&B	6''	CM	600-1000.00
60/A&B	6''	FB	400-600.00
60/A&B	6''	Sty.Bee ⎫	225-300.00
60/A&B	6''	LB ⎬	

HAPPY PASTIME
Ashtray
Hum 62

Figure used is similar to Hum 69 except that the bird is positioned on the edge of the tray rather than on the girl's leg.

Hum No.	BASIC SIZE	TRADE MARK	CURRENT VALUE
62	3½″x6¼″	CM	400-480.00
62	3½″x6¼″	FB	140-200.00
62	3½″x6¼″	Sty.Bee	
62	3½″x6¼″	3-line	105-130.00
62	3½″x6¼″	LB	

SINGING LESSON
Hum 63

Hum No.	BASIC SIZE	TRADE MARK	CURRENT VALUE
63	2¾″	CM	275-330.00
63	2¾″	FB	105-140.00
63	2¾″	Sty.Bee	
63	2¾″	3-line	75-95.00
63	2¾″	LB	

SINGING LESSON
Candy Box
Hum III/63

Shows old (right) and new (left) style boxes.

Overall size of this figure and box is 5¼" or 6", depending upon source of information. Difference probably due to a recent design change in the type of lid used.

Hum No.	BASIC SIZE	TRADE MARK	CURRENT VALUE
III/63	5¼"	CM	450-530.00
III/63	5¼"	FB	300-350.00
III/63	5¼"	Sty.Bee	150-295.00
III/63	5¼"	3-line	120-145.00
III/63	5¼"	LB	

SHEPHERD'S BOY
Hum 64

SHEPHERD'S BOY HUM64   LOST SHEEP HUM68

There seems to be many size variations of this figure. References were found to the following sizes in lists: 4½'', 5½'', 6'', and 6⅛''. Some references place 5½'' as the basic size of the figure.

Hum No.	BASIC SIZE	TRADE MARK	CURRENT VALUE
64	5½''	CM	440-530.00
64	5½''	FB	225-250.00
64	5½''	Sty.Bee	140-195.00
64	5½''	3-line	
64	5½''	LB	

FAREWELL
Hum 65

Farewell, Hum 65, 5″, Full Bee mark.

Sizes found in various price lists: 4½″, 4¾″, 5⅛″. Once known as "Good Bye." The mold number 65/I was used for a while, but all pieces produced now utilize the 65 alone. Originally designed for production in two sizes, Farewell in the smaller 65/0 size is quite rare. Apparently very few of them were made. The piece has been found with the decimal point size designator. The 1979 Annual Bell motif.

Hum No.	BASIC SIZE	TRADE MARK	CURRENT VALUE
65	4¾″	CM	550-650.00
65	4¾″	FB	240-325.00
65	4¾″	Sty.Bee ⎫	
65	4¾″	3-line ⎬	165-225.00
65	4¾″	LB ⎭	
65/0	4″	FB	5000-6000.00

FARM BOY
Hum 66

Similar figure used in Bookends Hum 60/A. Older versions have larger shoes than the newer ones. In fact, the whole piece appears fatter over all. Has been known as "THREE PALS" in the past and is occasionally found with the decimal point size designator.

Hum No.	BASIC SIZE	TRADE MARK	CURRENT VALUE
66	5¼''	CM	500-600.00
66	5¼''	FB	240-275.00
66	5¼''	Sty.Bee	
66	5¼''	3-line	140-200.00
66	5¼''	LB	

DOLL MOTHER
Hum 67

Sizes found referenced in various lists are as follows: 3½'', 4¼'', 4¾'', and 5½''.

Hum No.	BASIC SIZE	TRADE MARK	CURRENT VALUE
67	4¾''	CM	500-600.00
67	4¾''	FB	240-275.00
67	4¾''	Sty.Bee	
67	4¾''	3-line	155-170.00
67	4¾''	LB	

LOST SHEEP
Hum 68

Sizes found referenced in lists are as follows: 4¼'', 4½'', 5½'' and 6½''. This figure is found most commonly with green pants. A reference to a figure with orange pants (6½'') was found, but the color variation considered rare is the one with brown pants. There are four or five different color variations involving the coat, pants and shirt of the figure. Oversize pieces bring premium prices.

The 68/0 and 68/2/0 sizes are to be retired at the end of 1992. Each of them made in 1992 will bear the special ''Final Issue'' backstamp indicating this. See the introductory pages for an explanation and illustration of this mark. In addition there will be a medallion accompanying these particular figures.

Hum No.	BASIC SIZE	TRADE MARK	CURRENT VALUE
68/2/0	4½''	FB	140-175.00

Hum No.	BASIC SIZE	TRADE MARK	CURRENT VALUE
68/2/0	4½''	Sty.Bee ⎫	
68/2/0	4½''	3-line ⎬	80-95.00
68/2/0	4½''	LB ⎭	
68/0	5½''	CM	525-600.00
68/0	5½''	FB	200-250.00
68/0	5½''	Sty.Bee ⎫	
68/0	5½''	3-line ⎬	130-140.00
68/0	5½''	LB ⎭	
68.	5½''	CM	580-690.00
68.	5½''	FB	200-275.00
68.	5½''	Sty.Bee	

LOST SHEEP, HUM 68

HAPPY PASTIME
Hum 69

This is the figure used on the 1978 Plate (see Hum 271).

Hum No.	BASIC SIZE	TRADE MARK	CURRENT VALUE
69	3¼''	CM	330-395.00
69	3¼''	FB	150-195.00
69	3¼''	Sty.Bee	
69	3¼''	3-line	105-120.00
69	3¼''	LB	

HAPPY PASTIME
Candy Box
Hum III/69

Older Style Candy Box.

Hum No.	BASIC SIZE	TRADE MARK	CURRENT VALUE
III/69	6''	CM	450-530.00
III/69	6''	FB	300-350.00
III/69	6''	Sty.Bee	100-295.00
III/69	6''	3-line	120-145.00
III/69	6''	LB	

THE HOLY CHILD
Hum 70

Sizes found referenced in lists are as follows: 6¾'' and 7½''. The oversize pieces bring premium prices.

Hum No.	BASIC SIZE	TRADE MARK	CURRENT VALUE
70	6¾''	CM	350-425.00
70	6¾''	FB	175-225.00
70	6¾''	Sty.Bee	110-140.00
70	6¾''	3-line	
70	6¾''	LB	

STORMY WEATHER
Hum 71

This figure has been known as UNDER ONE ROOF. Some earlier models were produced with a split base under. The split base model with the Full Bee mark, upon examination, shows that the split is laterally oriented. The new models also have the split base, but it is oriented longitudinally. There has been a Crown Mark Stormy Weather found that is different from the norm. Among other things the boy figure in the piece has no kerchief. Too unique to price.

Hum No.	BASIC SIZE	TRADE MARK	CURRENT VALUE
71/2/0	5''	MB	175-185.00
71	6¼''	CM	800-900.00
71	6¼''	FB	425-500.00
71	6¼''	Sty.Bee	
71	6¼''	3-line	300-385.00
71	6¼''	LB	

SPRING CHEER
Hum 72

Left to right: Stylized Bee, green dress, flowers in right hand.
Crown mark, yellow dress, no flowers in right hand. Also older
mold, green dress, no flowers in right hand.

Size references found are 5" and 5¼". There are several
variations which may be encountered. The figure is found with
a yellow dress and flowers in the figures's right hand, and same
dress but no flowers in the hand and a green dress, no flowers
in hand in an old mold style. It is also found with a green dress
(later model and more commonly found). The piece with yellow
dress and no flowers is the most rare and commands a premium
price when sold. Spring Cheer is listed as having been temporarily withdrawn from production as of December 31, 1984
with no reinstatement date. These variations will bring $1500.00
or more.

Hum No.	BASIC SIZE	TRADE MARK	CURRENT VALUE
72	5"	CM	275-330.00
72	5"	FB	125-150.00
72	5"	Sty.Bee	110.00
72	5"	3-line	75-90.00
72	5"	LB	

LITTLE HELPER
Hum 73

Size references found were 4'', 4¼'', and 1¼'' oversize.

Hum No.	BASIC SIZE	TRADE MARK	CURRENT VALUE
73	4¼''	CM	275-330.00
73	4¼''	FB	125-150.00
73	4¼''	Sty.Bee	110.00
73	4¼''	3-line	75-100.00
73	4¼''	LB	

Crown	CM	TMK-1	1934-1950
Full Bee	FB	TMK-2	1940-1959
Stylized Bee	Sty Bee	TMK-3	1958-1972
Three Line Mark	3-Line	TMK-4	1964-1972
Last Bee Mark	LB	TMK-5	1970-1980
Missing Bee Mark	MB	TMK-6	1979-1991
Hummel Mark (Current)	HM	TMK-7	1991-Present

LITTLE GARDENER
Hum 74

This figure was found in several lists with the following sizes: 4'', 4¼'', 4½''. Earlier versions are found on an oval base; newer to current pieces are on the round base. The major variation encountered is a dark green dress rather than the present lighter colored dress. Some of the earliest models have a very light green or yellowish dress (see color section).

LITTLE GARDENER   HUM 74
Left to right: Full Bee, yellow dress. Crown, green dress.

Hum No.	BASIC SIZE	TRADE MARK	CURRENT VALUE
74 (green dress)	4¼''	CM	450.00
74	4¼''	CM	275-330.00
74	4¼''	FB	125-150.00
74	4¼''	Sty.Bee	110.00
74	4¼''	3-line }	75-100.00
74	4¼''	LB }	

WHITE ANGEL FONT
Hum 75

Although this piece is known as the ANGELIC PRAYER of WHITE ANGEL FONT it is painted in color. It has been produced in two sizes, 1¾''x3½'' and 3''x4¼'', but only the larger is still produced. It is the older and smaller one which is usually called the WHITE ANGEL FONT.

Hum No.	BASIC SIZE	TRADE MARK	CURRENT VALUE
75	1¾''x3½''	CM	120-150.00
75	1¾''x3½''	FB	40-50.00
75	1¾''x3½''	Sty.Bee	
75	1¾''x3½''	3-line	25-35.00
75	1¾''x3½''	LB	

DOLL MOTHER and PRAYER BEFORE BATTLE
Book Ends
Hum 76/A   Hum 76/B

These book ends are unique. It is possible, but not likely that they might be found. There are no known examples in private hands. Factory archives only.

CROSS and DOVES FONT
Hum 77

In the last edition of this book it was reported that there was only one example of this piece and it was in the factory archives. Three or four more have surfaced since then and reside in private collections. The one in the photo accompanying is an incised Crown mark piece with the M.I. Hummel signature on the back. It has been reported found in white. If sold, this font would likely bring a low five figure amount, in color or white.

INFANT OF KRUMBAD
(Blessed Child)
Hum 78

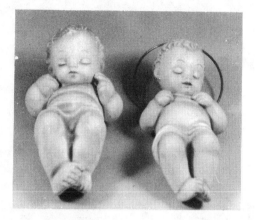

This figure is found in seven sizes and three finishes. The brown-tone bisque models have been in continuous production. The white overglaze finish is reportedly produced for the European market only. The painted pieces were discontinued, but have been put back into production in recent years. Was known as "In the Crib" in the past. Current suggested retail price lists name it "Blessed Child." The tiny 1¾", 78/0 size is a Closed Edition (CE). Production of all sizes was suspended on Jan. 1, 1990.

Hum No.	BASIC SIZE	TRADE MARK	CURRENT VALUE
78/0	1¾"	FB	200-250.00
78/0	1¾"	Sty.Bee	150-200.00
78/I	2½"	CM	105-120.00
78/I	2½"	FB	35-55.00
78/I	2½"	Sty-Bee ⎫	
78/I	2½"	3-line ⎬	30-35.00
78/I	2½"	LB ⎭	
78/II	3½"	CM	130-155.00
78/II	3½"	FB	45-65.00
78/II	3½"	Sty.Bee ⎫	
78/II	3½"	3-line ⎬	35-45.00
78/II	3½"	LB ⎭	
78/III	5¼"	CM	155-180.00
78/III	5¼"	FB	60-80.00
78/III	5¼"	Sty.Bee	45-55.00

Hum No.	BASIC SIZE	TRADE MARK	CURRENT VALUE
78/III	5¼''	3-line ⎫	40-55.00
78/III	5¼''	LB ⎭	
78/V	7¾''	CM	175.00
78/V	7¾''	FB	100.00
78/V	7¾''	Sty.Bee	70.00
78/V	7¾''	3-line	55.00
78/V	7¾''	LB	50.00
78/VI	10''	CM	300.00
78/VI	10''	FB	200.00
78/VI	10''	Sty.Bee	150.00
78/VI	10''	3-line	110.00
78/VI	10''	LB	100.00
78/VIII	13½''	CM	400.00
78/VIII	13½''	FB	300.00
78/VIII	13½''	Sty.Bee	250.00
78/VIII	13½''	3-line	250.00
78/VIII	13½''	LB	200.00

GLOBE TROTTER
Hum 79

Rear view showing the different basket patterns discussed in text. Left is the older mold.

The basket on the boy's back shows a broader, more distinct "checkerboard" type weave pattern on the older models than the new pieces. Some of the older models have a green hat. This figure appears on the 1973 annual plate, Hum 276. Globetrotter was retired in 1991. Those issued in that year all bear a special last year of production "Final Issue" backstamp beneath the base. They each were sold with a special medallion also. See the introductory pages for an explanation and illustration of this mark.

Hum No.	BASIC SIZE	TRADE MARK	CURRENT VALUE
79	5''	CM	450-550.00
79	5''	FB	200-250.00
79	5''	Sty.Bee	
79	5''	3-line	125-200.00
79	5''	LB	

LITTLE SCHOLAR
Hum 80

Hum No.	BASIC SIZE	TRADE MARK	CURRENT VALUE
80	5½''	CM	360-425.00
80	5½''	FB	200-250.00
80	5½''	Sty.Bee	
80	5½''	3-line	125-180.00
80	5½''	LB	

179

SCHOOL GIRL
Hum 81

Left to right: Pink blouse and upper portion of pinafore is dark (purple). Red blouse and pinafore is more or less uniformly colored red.

A variation which should be noted: the girl's basket is found both with and without flowers and it has been reported that sock color varies, although this is not substantiated. The older figures have a black bag and pink blouse, the newer ones have a blue bag and red blouse. Sizes found in various lists are 4¼'', 5'', 5¼'' and 5½''. Has been found with the decimal point size designator.

Hum No.	BASIC SIZE	TRADE MARK	CURRENT VALUE
81/2/0	4¼''	CM	300-400.00
81/2/0	4¼''	FB	140-190.00
81/2/0	4¼''	Sty.Bee	
81/2/0	4¼''	3-line	75-125.00
81/2/0	4¼''	LB	
81/0	5¼''	CM	360-425.00
81/0	5¼''	FB	175-225.00
81/0	5¼''	Sty.Bee	
81/0	5¼''	3-line	125-155.00
81/0	5¼''	LB	

SCHOOL BOY
Hum 82

Sizes found in various lists are 4", 4¾", 5¼", 5½" and 7½". Has been known as SCHOOL DAYS in the past. Is occasionally found having the decimal point size designator.

Hum No.	BASIC SIZE	TRADE MARK	CURRENT VALUE
82/2/0	4"	CM	300-400.00
82/2/0	4"	FB	140-190.00
82/2/0	4"	Sty.Bee ⎫	
82/2/0	4"	3-line ⎬	75-125.00
82/2/0	4"	LB ⎭	
82/0	5½"	CM	360-425.00
82/0	5½"	FB	175-225.00
82/0	5½"	Sty.Bee ⎫	
82/0	5½"	3-line ⎬	125-160.00
82/0	5½"	LB ⎭	
82/II	7½"	CM	750-1000.00
82/II	7½"	FB	500-650.00
82/II	7½"	Sty. Bee ⎫	
82/II	7½"	LB ⎬	300-400.00

ANGEL SERENADE
(with lamb)
Hum 83

Do not confuse this price with Hum 214/D, a part of the NATIVITY SET Hum 214. The figures are dissimilar but have the same name. Sizes vary from 5'' to 6½''. The 6'' to 6½'' sizes are more valuable. There are base variations found. There is a reissue of this piece.

Hum No.	BASIC SIZE	TRADE MARK	CURRENT VALUE
83	5''	CM	500-600.00
83	5''	FB	300-400.00
83	5''	Sty.Bee	250-300.00
83	5''	3-line	150-200.00
83	5''	LB	

Rare Bird Lovers, Hum 105. Double Crown trademark 4¾″. Collection of Kim Marker. and Mrs. Rue Dee Marker.

Congratulations, Hum 17/0. Left: Last Bee trademark, 1971 MID with socks. Right: Full Bee trademark, no socks.

Apple Tree Girl, Hum 141/0, 4″, Full Bee and Apple Tree Boy, Hum 142/3/0, 4″, Stylized Bee. Both figures show old style "Tree Trunk Base".

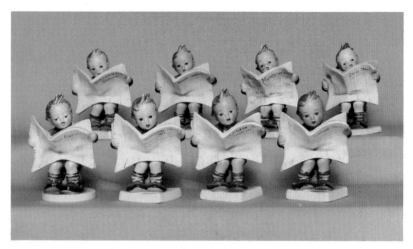

"Latest News", Hum 184. Shows eight different newspaper names.

Meditation. Left: Hum 13/II, Last Bee trademark, 4-1/8″, no flowers in basket. Right: Hum 13/2, Crown trademark, 4¼″, basket full of flowers.

Madonna Hum 45 and Hum 46. Shows color and size variations.

Modonna, Hum 151. The white overglaze, blue cloak and rare brown cloak.
Shows variations of color and size of Flower Madonnas, Hum 10.

Auf Wiedersehen, Hum 153/0. Shows the more commonly found piece on the left and the more rare version wherein the boy wears a Tyrolean cap. Both pieces in this photo are trademarked Full Bee. Collection of Mr. and Mrs. Rue Dee Marker.

Back Row: "For Father", Hum 87. The middle figure shows the major variation orange color radishes.

Front Row: "Brother", Hum 95. Shows the old blue coat variation on right figure. The two figures on the far right are examples of "Mother's Darling", Hum 175 showing the bag color variation.

Back Row: "Lost Sheep", Hum 68. Shows two pants color variations.

Front Row: "Spring Cheer", Hum 72. Left piece has yellow dress, no flowers in right hand (oldest); middle, green dress with no flowers in right hand; far right, green dress and flowers in right hand.

Back Row: "Chef Hello", Hum 124. Left is the gray pants variation and the far right figure shows the green pants variation.

Front Row: "Waiter", Hum 154. The figure on the right is the older one. Note the dark trousers and the label on the wine bottle.

Nine examples of display plaques.
Back Row, left to right: English; Hum 209, Swedish; Hum 208, French; Front
Row, left to right: Hum 205, German; Hum 205, German; the last three show
the Stylized Bee, the Last Bee, and the Missing Bee trademark plaques.

Back Row: "School Girl", Hum 81; "Soldier Boy", Hum 332 showing blue and
red cap medallion variations.
Front Row: "Little Gardener", Hum 74 showing yellow and green dress variations; "Happy Pastime", Hum 69.

The Annual Plates 1976 through 1980.

The special editions released by the Goebel Collector's Club exclusively for members.
Left to right: "Valentine Gift", Hum 387; "Valentine Joy", Hum 399; "Smiling Through" plaque, Hum 690; color bust of M.I. Hummel and the same in bisque (no glaze) finish, and the first plaque issued to members upon joining simply called the membership plaque.

Anniversary Plates: 1975 "Stormy Weather", Hum 280 and 1980, "Spring Dance", Hum 281.

The Annual Plates 1971 through 1975

Top Left: Hum 812. Balkan figure in Serbian costume. Collection of Donald S. Stephens.

Top Right: Hum 913, Balkan figure in Bulgarian costume. Collection of Donald S. Stephens.

Above: Balkan figurine from the collection of Donald S. Stephens. Mold number and origin of costume unknown to the author.

Above: Hum 851. Balkan figure in Hungarian costume. Collection of Donald S. Stephens.

Bottom Left: Hum 968. Balkan figure in Serbian costume. Collection of Donald S. Stephens.

Center: Hum 853. Balkan figurine in Hungarian costume. Incised Crown trademark and measures 4¾''. Private collection.

Bottom Right: Hum 852. Balkan figure in Hungarian costume. Collection of Donald S. Stephens.

Pictured here are seven of the eight "Hungarian" pieces from The collection of Mr. & Mrs. Robert L. Miller. See text for details.

Left: Rare Hum 101 table lamp, "To Market". 8¾" with Double Crown trademark. Center; "Out of Danger" table lamp, Hum 44/B. Newer model. Right: Rare Hum 100 table lamp, "Shrine". 9½" with Double Crown trademark.

Spring Cheer, Hum 72. Left: Incised Crown trademark, 5¼ ", "U.S. Zone, Germany''. Right: Stylized Bee (one-line) trademark, 5".

Bird Duet, Hum 169. Photo shows two lines of music (older) and three lines of music (new mold).

For Father, Hum 87. Left: Crown trademark. Right: Full Bee trademark. Note the rare orange colored vegetables on the right figure. Marker Collection.

Weary Wanderer, Hum 204. Left: Stylized Bee trademark, 1949 MID. Right: Incised Full Bee trademark. Shows scarce blue eye figurine. Collection of Mr. and Mrs. Rue Dee Marker.

The English Pieces. Left: Mold 914, "Johnny Had A Little Lamb". Quite similar to Hum 64, Shepherd's Boy. Right: Mold 910, "A Luckey Letter". Quite similar to Hum 13, Meditation. See page 39 for discussion. Collection of H. L. Jacobs.

Close Harmony, Hum 336. Both have Three Line trademark. Right: figurine is older mold. Shows incised dress pattern and higher socks.

The Run-A-Way, Hum 327. Left: Last Bee trademark. Basket weave is part of the mold. Right: Last Bee trademark figure with painted basket weave.

WORSHIP
Hum 84

Sizes reported in various lists are 5'', 6¾'', and 14½''. Has been found with the decimal point size designator. The 84/V was taken out of production but is being produced again presently. The small (84/0) model has shown up occasionally in white overglaze (rare).

Hum No.	BASIC SIZE	TRADE MARK	CURRENT VALUE
84/0	5''	CM	340-400.00
84/0	5''	FB	150-185.00
84/0	5''	Sty.Bee	
84/0	5''	3-line	110-145.00
84/0	5''	LB	
84/V	13''	CM	1800-2300.00
84/V, 84/5	13''	FB	1350-1650.00
84/V, 84/5	13''	Sty.Bee	
84/V, 84/5	13''	3-line	775-1200.00
84/V, 84/5	13''	LB	

SERENADE
Hum 85

HUM 85/0   (newer design)

The newer design of this figure has the boy's fingers all down on the flute; the older designs show three fingers extended upwards.

Hum No.	BASIC SIZE	TRADE MARK	CURRENT VALUE
85/4/0	3½''	MB	70-85.00
85/0	4¾''	CM	275-330.00
85/0	4¾''	FB	120-155.00
85/0	4¾''	Sty.Bee ⎫	
85/0	4¾''	3-line ⎬	75-115.00
85/0	4¾''	LB ⎭	
85/II	7½''	CM	975-1170.00
85/II	7½''	FB	410-550.00
85/II	7½''	Sty.Bee ⎫	
85/II	7½''	3-line ⎬	300-380.00
85/II	7½''	LB ⎭	

HAPPINESS
Hum 86

Sizes reported in various lists are 4½'', 4¾'', 5'' and 5½''.

Hum No.	BASIC SIZE	TRADE MARK	CURRENT VALUE
86	4¾''	CM	280-325.00
86	4¾''	FB	120-160.00
86	4¾''	Sty.Bee	
86	4¾''	3-line	85-120.00
86	4¾''	LB	

FOR FATHER
Hum 87

Shows all three major variations. There may be a fourth. The variations are in colors found on the radishes. Better distinguished in the color photos.

This figure has also been known as FATHER'S JOY. There has been a recently discovered color variation wherein the radishes are colored orange. These latter pieces are found in Full Bee and Stylized Bee trademarks only and are valued at $3000-4000.00.

Hum No.	BASIC SIZE	TRADE MARK	CURRENT VALUE
87	5½''	CM	410-450.00
87	5½''	FB	200-250.00
87	5½''	Sty.Bee	
87	5½''	3-line	150-185.00
87	5½''	LB	

HEAVENLY PROTECTION
Hum 88

Heavenly Protection, Hum 88, 9⅜'', incised Crown and Full Bee marks (above).It was marked with an 88 only until around the late 1960's. Has been found in white overglaze in Crown and Full Bee marks.

Hum No.	BASIC SIZE	TRADE MARK	CURRENT VALUE
88.	9¼''	CM	1200-1300.00
88.	9¼''	FB	850-950.00
88.	9¼''	Sty.Bee	500-650.00
88/I	6¾''	FB	*
88/I	6¾''	Sty.Bee	450-550.00
88/I	6¾''	3-line	425-450.00
88/I	6¾''	LB	
88/II	9¼''	FB	800-900.00
88/II	9¼''	Sty.Bee	
88/II	9¼''	3-line	500-600.00
88/II	9¼''	LB	

*Insufficient trade data to establish value.

LITTLE CELLIST
Hum 89

This figure appears with eyes open and eyes closed. Eyes open variation occurs on earlier pieces.

Hum No.	BASIC SIZE	TRADE MARK	CURRENT VALUE
89/I	6″	CM	440-515.00
89/I	6″	FB	200-265.00
89/I	6″	Sty.Bee	
89/I	6″	3-line	165-185.00
89/I	6″	LB	
89/II	8″	CM	800-1000.00
89/II	8″	FB	420-570.00
89/II	8″	Sty.Bee	
89/II	8″	3-line	300-400.00
89/II	8″	LB	

EVENTIDE and ADORATION
Book Ends
Hum 90/A   Hum 90/B
Up until late 1984 it was thought that these pieces were never produced except in prototype and never released on the market. The Adoration half of the set has been found. It still may be that they were never released and this particular piece was inadvertantly released. See Hum 23 and Hum 99.

ANGEL AT PRAYER
Font

Hum 91/A Facing Left   **Hum 91/B Facing Right**

The only notable variation is that the older ones have no halo and the newer models do.

Hum No.	BASIC SIZE	TRADE MARK	CURRENT VALUE
91/A&B	2″x4¾″	CM	225.00 (pair)
91/A&B	2″x4¾″	FB	80-105.00 (pair)
91/A&B	2″x4¾″	Sty. Bee	
91/A&B	2″x4¾″	3-line	55-75.00 (pair)
91/A&B	2″x4¾″	LB	

MERRY WANDERER
Plaque
Hum 92

There are different sizes to be found although all bear only the 92 designator.

Hum No.	BASIC SIZE	TRADE MARK	CURRENT VALUE
92	4¾''x5⅛''	CM	300-400.00
92	4¾''x5⅛''	FB	125-170.00
92	4¾''x5⅛''	Sty.Bee	
92	4¾''x5⅛''	3-line	105-125.00
92	4¾''x5⅛''	LB	

LITTLE FIDDLER
Plaque
Hum 93

In current production, this plaque bears the LITTLE FID-DLER motif which appears many times in the collection. Less background detail in older models. Photo shows later version. The older models can bring $2000-3000.00.

Hum No.	BASIC SIZE	TRADE MARK	CURRENT VALUE
93	4¾x5⅛''	CM	300-400.00
93	4¾x5⅛''	FB	120-170.00
93	4¾x5⅛''	Sty.Bee	
93	4¾x5⅛''	3-line	105-120.00
93	4¾x5⅛''	LB	

SURPRISE
Hum 94

Left to right: The square base variation in the 94/I size (older model). The 94/O size, oval base.

Sizes encountered in various lists are 4¼'', 4½'', 5½'' and 5⅜''. Has been found with square and round bases. The square base is the more scarce one. When sold the square base figure commands a premium price.

Hum No.	BASIC SIZE	TRADE MARK	CURRENT VALUE
94/3/0	4¼''	CM	330-380.00
94/3/0	4¼''	FB	145-185.00
94/3/0	4¼''	Sty.Bee ⎫	
94/3/0	4¼''	3-line ⎬	100-125.00
94/3/0	4¼''	LB ⎭	
94/I	5½''	CM	470-550.00
94/I	5½''	FB	250-300.00
94/I	5½''	Sty.Bee ⎫	
94/I	5½''	3-line ⎬	230-250.00
94/I	5½''	LB ⎭	

BROTHER
HUM 95

Left: Newer of the two, dark coat   Right: Older, has blue coat

This figure has been known as OUR HERO. Has occurred with the decimal point size designator. Older mold style comes with a blue coat. (See color section).

Hum No.	BASIC SIZE	TRADE MARK	CURRENT VALUE
95	5½''	CM	350-425.00
95	5½''	FB	180-215.00
95	5½''	Sty.Bee	
95	5½''	3-line	125-175.00
95	5½''	LB	

LITTLE SHOPPER
Hum 96

Hum No.	BASIC SIZE	TRADE MARK	CURRENT VALUE
96	4¾''	CM	325-375.00
96	4¾''	FB	180-215.00
96	4¾''	Sty.Bee	
96	4¾''	3-line	125-170.00
96	4¾''	LB	

TRUMPET BOY
Hum 97

The boy's coat is normally green. Some of the older models, particulary the post-war U.S. Occupation era, have a blue painted coat. Trumpet Boy is not likely to be found with the Crown trademark. The crown mark era piece will have "Design Patent No. 116,464" inscribed beneath instead (see accompanying photo). At present there is no known explanation for this anomaly.

Hum No.	BASIC SIZE	TRADE MARK	CURRENT VALUE
97	4¾''	CM era	500-750.00
97	4¾''	FB	120-160.00
97	4¾''	Sty.Bee	
97	4¾''	3-line	90-110.00
97	4¾''	LB	

SISTER
Hum 98

Hum No.	BASIC SIZE	TRADE MARK	CURRENT VALUE
98/2/0	4¾''	Sty.Bee	180-200.00
98/2/0	4¾''	3-line	150-180.00
98/2/0	4¾''	LB	130-140.00

Hum No.	BASIC SIZE	TRADE MARK	CURRENT VALUE
98/0	5¾''	CM	350-400.00
98/0	5¾''	FB	180-225.00
98/0	5¾''	Sty.Bee	
98/0	5¾''	3-line	125-175.00
98/0	5¾''	LB	

EVENTIDE
Hum 99

There are three mold variations for Eventide. They are found with the sheep on the right as in the accompanying photo. They are also found with the sheep on the left side and the third variation has no sheep at all.

Hum No.	BASIC SIZE	TRADE MARK	CURRENT VALUE
99	4¾''	CM	650-750.00
99	4¾''	FB	320-360.00
99	4¾''	Sty.Bee	
99	4¾''	3-line	225-295.00
99	4¾''	LB	

SHRINE
Table Lamp
Hum 100

Extremely rare 7½'' table lamp. As far as can be determined only three or four exist in collectors' hands presently. The lamps found so far bear the Crown or the Full Bee trademarks and are too unique to price. There are two versions of lamp post. The most commonly found is the tree trunk post. The rarest is the fluted post.

TO MARKET
Table Lamp
Hum 101

To Market Table Lamp, Hum 101, shows the tree trunk lamp stem.

There are two versions of this 7½'' table lamp regarding the lamp stem or post. The majority are found with the tree trunk stem as in the photo here. These are valued at about $600-900.00. The more rare is the plain fluted stem and is valued at around $5000.00 So far there have been only eleven of these known to be in collectors' hands. All eleven have either the Stylized or Full Bee trademarks.

VOLUNTEERS
Table Lamp
Hum 102

There are only a few examples of this piece known to exist in private collections at present. The few found so far all bear the Crown trademark and have a plain white post. They are valued at $3500-5000.00.

FAREWELL
Table Lamp
Hum 103

This is an extremely rare piece of which there are very few known to exist presently. If sold it could bring up to $10,000.

EVENTIDE
Table Lamp
Hum 104

Very few examples of this table lamp known to be in any collector's hands at present. If sold it could bring up to $10,000.

BIRD LOVERS
Hum 105

"Bird Lovers" Hum 105 from the collection of Kim Marker, the original discoverer.

First discovered about 1977 this piece was not previously thought to exist. It bears the mold number 105. This number was a "CLOSED NUMBER", a number supposedly never having been used and never to be used on an original Hummel piece. There have been at least six or seven more found since the initial discovery. As is custom the original finder named the piece "Bird Lovers." It is sometimes known as "Adoration with Bird" because of its similarity to Hum 23, "Adoration." There have been several found. The major variation in them is in the girl's pigtail. A Hum 105 in fine condition is valued at $5,000-7,000. See photo on previous page and in color section.

MERRY WANDERER
Plaque with Wooden Frame
Hum 106

Few examples of this extremely rare piece have been found.

Hum No.	BASIC SIZE	TRADE MARK	CURRENT VALUE
106	4¾''x5⅛''	CM	4000-7500.00

LITTLE FIDDLER
Plaque with Wooden Frame
Hum 107

This plaque has only recently been found. Only two or three presently known to be in any collectors hands.

Hum No.	BASIC SIZE	TRADE MARK	CURRENT VALUE
107	4¾"x5⅛"	CM	4000-7500.00

ANGEL WITH BOY AND GIRL AT FEET (probable)
Plaque in Relief
Hum 108 (Closed Number)

It is unlikely that any of these will ever find their way into collectors' hands. It cannot be certain that it is even an angel with children as described in the name above. There is a 1950's Goebel catalog listing for a plaque as described, but it is not listed as a Hummel design. The deduction is made because of the description similar to the name and the mold number designation of 108 listed in factory records.

HAPPY TRAVELER
Hum 109

Hum No.	BASIC SIZE	TRADE MARK	CURRENT VALUE
109/0	5"	CM	275-325.00
109/0	5"	FB	130-175.00
109/0	5"	Sty.Bee	
109/0	5"	3-line	85-100.00
109/0	5"	LB	
109/II*	8"	CM	1200-1400.00
109/II*	8"	FB	345-490.00
109/II*	8"	Sty.Bee	
109/II*	8"	3-line	260-330.00
109/II*	8"	LB	

*The Goebel company has placed this size of Happy Traveler on "Permanent Retirement" status. It is now a Closed Edition (CE). The 5", 109/0 remains in production.

LET'S SING
Hum 110

Hum No.	BASIC SIZE	TRADE MARK	CURRENT VALUE
110/0	3¼''	CM	250-300.00
110/0	3¼''	FB	115-160.00
110/0	3¼''	Sty.Bee	
110/0	3¼''	3-line	75-100.00
110/0	3¼''	LB	
110/I	3-7/8''	CM	350-420.00
110/I	3-7/8''	FB	155-205.00
110/I	3-7/8''	Sty.Bee	
110/I	3-7/8''	3-line	100-140.00
110/I	3-7/8''	LB	

LET'S SING
Candy Box
Hum III/II0

Overall size of this piece is 5¼'' to 6¼'' depending upon design type of lid. Newer models have a newly designed lid and these are a bit larger.

Let's Sing – Candy Box, Hum III/110, 5⅛'', Last Bee mark.

Hum No.	BASIC SIZE	CURRENT MARK	VALUE
III/110	6''	CM	450-530.00
III/110	6''	FB	300-350.00
III/110	6''	Sty. Bee	
III/110	6''	3-line	150-295.00
III/110	6''	LB	

WAYSIDE HARMONY
Hum 111

This piece has been known to appear with Roman Numeral size designators instead of the Arabic number indictated.

Hum No.	BASIC SIZE	TRADE MARK	CURRENT VALUE
111/3/0	3¾''	CM	260-320.00
111/3/0	3¾''	FB	135-165.00
111/3/0	3¾''	Sty.Bee	
111/3/0	3¾''	3-line	90-110.00
111/3/0	3¾''	LB	

Hum No.	BASIC SIZE	TRADE MARK	CURRENT VALUE
111/1	5''	CM	470-550.00
111/1	5''	FB	240-295.00
111/1	5''	Sty.Bee	
111/1	5''	3-line	150-225.00
111/1	5''	LB	

WAYSIDE HARMONY
Table Lamp
Hum II/111 or II/112

This lamp was made for a short period of time in the 1950's. Perhaps to avoid confusion and/or to conform with the mold numbering system, the lamp was slightly redesigned and assigned a new number, 224 (see page 287). Whatever the reason, there are a few of these II/111 Wayside Harmony lamps around. They occur in the Crown, Full Bee and Stylized Bee trademarks. Quite scarce they are valued at between $1000 and $1500 when found.

JUST RESTING
Hum 112

Some figures have been found with no basket.

Hum No.	BASIC SIZE	TRADE MARK	CURRENT VALUE
112/3/0	3¾''	CM	260-325.00
112/3/0	3¾''	FB	135-165.00
112/3/0	3¾''	Sty. Bee ⎫	
112/3/0	3¾''	3-line ⎬	85-110.00
112/3/0	3¾''	LB ⎭	
112/I	5''	CM	470-550.00
112/I	5''	FB	240-295.00
112/I	5''	Sty.Bee ⎫	
112/I	5''	3-line ⎬	160-225.00
112/I	5''	LB ⎭	

JUST RESTING
Table Lamp
Hum II/112

This lamp was made for a short period of time in the 1950's. Perhaps to avoid confusion and/or conform the mold numbering system the number was changed to 225 with a concurrent slight redesign. Whatever the reason, there are a few of these II/112 Just Resting lamps around. They occur in the Crown, Full Bee and Stylized Bee trademarks. Quite scarce, they are valued at between $1000 and $1500 when found.

HEAVENLY SONG
Candleholder
Hum 113

Heavenly Song,   Hum 113, Full Bee trademark.

This four figure piece is a candleholder. It is quite similar to Hum 54 and was produced in extremely small numbers. There are in fact, only a few known to reside in private collections. The actual number is not known but less than 50 would be a reasonable estimation. They do pop up from time to time and have been found in the Crown, Full Bee, Stylized Bee and Last Bee trademarks. The Goebel company announced in 1981 that they were removing Heavenly Song from production permanently. It is considered extremely rare in any of the trademarks.

Hum No.	BASIC SIZE	TRADE MARK	CURRENT VALUE
113	3½x4¾	CM	5000-6000.00
113	3½x4¾	FB	4000-5000.00
113	3½x4¾	Sty.Bee	3000-4000.00
113	3½x4¾	LB	1000-2000.00

LET'S SING
Ashtray
Hum 114

Both Full Bee. Shows reverse mold variation. Older style on left.

This piece is an ashtray with a figure very like Hum 110 at the edge of the dish. It is found with the figure on either the right or left side of the tray. The older ones have the figure on the right side. There are very few of this variation known. If sold they command premium prices.

Hum No.	BASIC SIZE	TRADE MARK	CURRENT VALUE
114 (rev. mold)	3½''x6¾''	CM	700-900.00
114 (rev. mold)	3½''x6¾''	FB	500-700.00
114	3½''x6¾''	Sty.Bee ⎫	
114	3½''x6¾''	3-line ⎬	90-115.00
114	3½''x6¾''	LB ⎭	

ADVENT GROUP
Candleholders
Hum 115, Hum 116, Hum 117

This is a group of three figures with a Christmas theme, each of the figures provided with a candle receptacle. Hum 115 is a girl holding flowers, Hum 116 is a girl with a Christmas tree, and Hum 117 is a boy with a toy horse. The original models were made with the "MEL" prefix followed by 1, 2 and 3 for 115, 116 and 117 respectively. These were prototypes, but many apparently got into the market (see page 71).

Hum No.	BASIC SIZE	TRADE MARK	CURRENT VALUE
115,116,117	3½''	CM	400-480.00(set)
115,116,117	3½''	FB	140-200.00(set)
115,116,117	3½''	Sty.Bee	
115,116,117	3½''	3-line	110-140.00(set)
115,116,117	3½''	LB	

LITTLE THRIFTY
Hum 118

Left: Full Bee. Note thicker base and lack of pedestal at bottom.
Right: Stylized Bee. Thinner base and has pedestal.

This figure is actually a coin bank and is found with and without a key and lock plug. It is also known to have base variations. They are found on the Crown and Full Bee pieces.

Hum No.	BASIC SIZE	TRADE MARK	CURRENT VALUE
118	5"	CM	650-800.00
118	5"	FB	300-350.00
118	5"	Sty.Bee	130-160.00
118	5"	3-line	
118	5"	LB	100-130.00

POSTMAN
HUM 119

There have been several distinct mold and size variations found despite the one size always listed. The smaller pieces are perhaps a bit more valuable.

Hum No.	BASIC SIZE	TRADE MARK	CURRENT VALUE
119	5¼"	CM	415-490.00
119	5¼"	FB	185-245.00
119	5¼"	Sty.Bee	
119	5¼"	3-line	125-145.00
119	5¼"	LB	

POSTMAN   HUM 119

*JOYFUL and LET'S SING
Double figure on a wooden base
Hum 120

*WAYSIDE HARMONY and JUST RESTING
Double figure on a wooden base
Hum 121

*PUPPY LOVE, and SERENADE WITH DOG
Double figure on a wooden base
Hum 122

*No examples known to exist in collectors' hands.

MAX AND MORITZ
Hum 123

There are some variations with respect to colors used. When found in the Crown mark era, they will command premium prices.

Hum No.	BASIC SIZE	TRADE MARK	CURRENT VALUE
123	5¼''	CM	385-460.00
123	5¼''	FB	210-255.00
123	5¼''	Sty.Bee ⎫	
123	5¼''	3-line ⎬	125-140.00
123	5¼''	LB ⎭	

HELLO
Hum 124

This figure is also known as CHEF HELLO. There are a couple of notable variations to be found. The most important is the different colors of the pants and the vest. The most rare variation is the green pants figure. There has also been found a green pants, pink vest variation. The brown pants, white vest is the common. Pants: green, brown, or black (dark grey); Vest: pink or white. A Crown-marked piece in the 124/I size with gray pants will bring about $750.00.

The 124/I has been found with the decimal point (124.) size designator. The 124. in a Crown mark is valued at about $500.00

and in the Full Bee, $340.00. The 124/I size was listed as temporarily withdrawn from production in 1982 and has not yet been placed back in production.

Left to Right: Hum 124/I, Full Bee, Green Pants; Hum 124/0, Brown Pants; Hum 124/I, Gray Pants.

Hum No.	BASIC SIZE	TRADE MARK	CURRENT VALUE
124/0	6¼''	FB	140-190.00
124/0	6¼''	Sty.Bee	
124/0	6¼''	3-line	105-125.00
124/0	6¼''	LB	
124/I	7''	CM	550-650.00
124/I	7''	FB	195-275.00
124/I	7''	Sty.Bee	
124/I	7''	3-line	140-165.00
124/I	7''	LB	

VACATION TIME
Plaque
Hum 125

There are at least two distinctly different mold designs found. Photo here is of the older style. Newer models are smaller and have only five pickets in the fence.

Hum No.	BASIC SIZE	TRADE MARK	CURRENT VALUE
125	4⅜″x5¼″	CM	500-600.00
125	4⅜″x5¼″	FB	250-325.00
125	4″x4¾″	Sty.Bee ⎫	
125	4″x4¾″	3-line ⎬	135-175.00
125	4″x4¼″	LB ⎭	

RETREAT TO SAFETY
Plaque
Hum 126

Hum No.	BASIC SIZE	TRADE MARK	CURRENT VALUE
126	4¾″x5″	CM	500-600.00
126	4¾″x5″	FB	175-250.00

(See next page)

Hum No.	BASIC SIZE	TRADE MARK	CURRENT VALUE
126	4¾″x4¾″	CM	350-400.00
126	4¾″x4¾″	FB	200-250.00
126	4¾″x4¾″	Sty.Bee	
126	4¾″x4¾″	3-line	135-175.00
126	4¾″x4¾″	LB	

DOCTOR
Hum 127

5⅛″, Full Bee.

In some of the older models of this figure the doll's feet extend slightly over the base. Sizes encountered in various lists were 4¾″ and 5¼″. The larger sizes are generally the older models. (See next page)

Hum No.	BASIC SIZE	TRADE MARK	CURRENT VALUE
127	4¾''	CM	350-425.00
127	4¾''	FB	200-240.00
127	4¾''	Sty.Bee ⎫	
127	4¾''	3-line ⎬	95-120.00
127	4¾''	LB ⎭	

BAKER
Hum 128

Hum No.	BASIC SIZE	TRADE MARK	CURRENT VALUE
128	4¾''	CM	350-425.00
128	4¾''	FB	200-240.00
128	4¾''	Sty.Bee ⎫	
128	4¾''	3-line ⎬	95-120.00
128	4¾''	LB ⎭	

BAND LEADER
Hum 129

Sizes encountered in lists were 5¼'', 5½'', and 5¾''.

Hum No.	BASIC SIZE	TRADE MARK	CURRENT VALUE
129/4/0	3½''	MB	60-80.00
129	5¼''	CM	440-510.00
129	5¼''	FB	185-255.00
129	5¼''	Sty.Bee	
129	5¼''	3-line	140-170.00
129	5¼''	LB	

DUET
Hum 130

Some older Crown trademark pieces have a very small lip on the front of the base; sort of a mini version of the stepped base variation on the Merry Wanderer. These lip base Duets also have incised musical notes on the sheet music and are valued at about $1500.00.

(cont.)

Hum No.	BASIC SIZE	TRADE MARK	CURRENT VALUE
130	5¼''	Cm	500-620.00
130	5¼''	FB	245-325.00
130	5¼''	Sty.Bee	
130	5¼''	3-line	175-200.00
130	5¼''	LB	

STREET SINGER
Hum 131

(cont.)

Hum No.	BASIC SIZE	TRADE MARK	CURRENT VALUE
131	5''	CM	315-370.00
131	5''	FB	170-200.00
131	5''	Sty.Bee ⎫	
131	5''	3-line ⎬	115-150.00
131	5''	LB ⎭	

STAR GAZER
Hum 132

The older figures have a darker blue or purple colored shirt than the newer models (light purple or light blue).

Hum No.	BASIC SIZE	TRADE MARK	CURRENT VALUE
132	4¾''	CM	510-625.00
132	4¾''	FB	200-275.00
132	4¾''	Sty.Bee ⎫	
132	4¾''	3-line ⎬	140-175.00
132	4¾''	LB ⎭	

MOTHER'S HELPER
Hum 133

Hum No.	BASIC SIZE	TRADE MARK	CURRENT VALUE
133	5''	CM	440-500.00
133	5''	FB	175-235.00
133	5''	Sty.Bee	
133	5''	3-line	130-150.00
133	5''	LB	

QUARTET
Plaque
Hum 134

Full Bee trademark

Hum No.	BASIC SIZE	TRADE MARK	CURRENT VALUE
134	6''x6''	CM	700-840.00
134	6''x6''	FB	260-365.00
134	6''x6''	Sty.Bee	
134	6''x6''	3-line	195-250.00
134	6''x6''	LB	

SOLOIST
Hum 135

Size encountered in various lists were 4¾'' and 5''. Has also been known in the past as "HIGH TENOR".

Hum No.	BASIC SIZE	TRADE MARK	CURRENT VALUE
135/4/0	3½''	MB	50-80.00
135	4¾''	CM	260-320.00
135	4¾''	FB	125-165.00
135	4¾''	Sty.Bee	90-110.00
135	4¾''	3-line	
135	4¾''	LB	

FRIENDS
Hum 136

Sizes found in various lists were 5″, 10¾″, and 11½″. There have been at least two examples of this piece found that are made of a terra cotta-like substance; reddish brown in color. These are in the 136/V size. The terra cotta pieces are valued at about $9000-12,000.

Hum No.	BASIC SIZE	TRADE MARK	CURRENT VALUE
136/I	5″	CM	420-490.00
136/I	5″	FB	200-300.00
136/I	5″	Sty.Bee	
136/I	5″	3-line	120-160.00
136/I	5″	LB	
136/V	10¾″	CM	1800-2000.00
136/V	10¾″	FB	1100-1250.00
136/V	10¾″	Sty.Bee	
136/V	10¾″	3-line	900-1100.00
136/V	10¾″	LB	

CHILD-IN-BED
Plaque
Hum 137

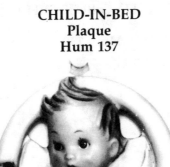

The mold number is found as "137/B" until the Last Bee (TMK-5) when the "B" was dropped. Until recently it was speculated that there might have been a matching piece with the mold number 137/A. A few of these have now surfaced. Apparently they were never produced in any quantity. Hum 137 (no B) is in current production. Appears in the Missing Bee (TMK-6) and Last Bee (TMK-5) trademarks.

Hum No.	BASIC SIZE	TRADE MARK	CURRENT VALUE
137/B	2¾"x2¾" (round)	CM	200.00
137/B	2¾"x2¾" (round)	FB	120.00
137/B	2¾"x2¾" (round)	Sty. Bee	
137/B	2¾"x2¾" (round)	3-line	40-55.00
137	2¾"x2¾" (round)	LB	

BABY IN CRIB - Plaque
Hum 138

Although all records of the factory indicate that this piece was never released for sale to the consumer and only prototypes were produced, at least six are known to reside in private collections. It dates from around 1940. Too unique to place a value on.

FLITTING BUTTERFLY
Plaque
Hum 139

This piece was out of current production for some time. it has been reissued in a new mold design with the same number.

Hum No.	BASIC SIZE	TRADE MARK	CURRENT VALUE
139	2½''x2½''	CM	225-275.00
139	2½''x2½''	FB	150-200.00
139	2½''x2½''	Sty.Bee	
139	2½''x2½''	3-line	40-55.00
139	2½''x2½''	LB	

Trademark	Common Abr.		Years Used
Crown	CM	TMK-1	1934-1950
Full Bee	FB	TMK-2	1940-1959
Stylized Bee	Sty Bee	TMK-3	1958-1972
Three Line Mark	3-Line	TMK-4	1964-1972
Last Bee Mark	LB	TMK-5	1970-1980
Missing Bee Mark	MB	TMK-6	1979-1991
Hummel Mark (Current)	HM	TMK-7	1991-Present

THE MAIL IS HERE
or
MAIL COACH
Plaque
Hum 140

This plaque utilizes the motif from Hum 226. It is known to exist in white overglaze bearing the Crown Mark. The white piece commands premium price when sold.

Hum No.	BASIC SIZE	TRADE MARK	CURRENT VALUE
140	4½''x6¼''	CM	600-750.00
140	4½''x6¼''	FB	235-330.00
140	4½''x6¼''	Sty.Bee ⎫	
140	4½''x6¼''	3-line ⎬	170-235.00
140	4½''x6¼''	LB ⎭	

APPLE TREE GIRL
Hum 141

Full Bee. Shows old style "Tree Trunk Base".

This figure has also been known as "SPRING". Sizes found in various lists are as follows: 4", 4¼", 6", 6¾", 10", 10½", 29". Two references were made in the list to a "rare old base" and a "brown base". This is apparently a reference to the "tree trunk base" variation. When found this variation will bring about ⅓ more than the value in the chart below. The 4" size has no bird perched on the branch as do all the larger sizes, although there has been at least one, a 141/I reported having no bird. Perhaps it was inadvertantly omitted by a factory worker.

Hum No.	BASIC SIZE	TRADE MARK	CURRENT VALUE
141/3/0	4"	CM	250-325.00
141/3/0	4"	FB	135-185.00
141/3/0	4"	Sty.Bee	
141/3/0	4"	3-line	85-100.00
141/3/0	4"	LB	
141/I	6"	CM	500-600.00
141/I	6"	FB	250-330.00

Hum No.	BASIC SIZE	TRADE MARK	CURRENT VALUE
141/I	6''	Sty.Bee	
141/I	6''	3-line	165-195.00
141/I	6''	LB	
141/V	10½''	Sty.Bee	
141/V	10½''	LB	650-800.00
141/X	10½''	LB	*16,900.00

APPLE TREE BOY
Hum 142

Stylized Bee. Shows old style ''Tree Trunk Base''.

This figure has also been known as ''FALL''. Sizes found in various lists are as follows: 3¾'', 4'', 4½'', 6'', 6½'', 10'', 10½'' and 29''. Two references were made in the list to a ''rare old base'' and a ''brown base''. This is apparently a reference to the ''tree trunk base'' variation. When found this variation will bring about ⅓ more than the figure in the value chart below. The 4'' size has no bird perched on the branch as do all the larger sizes.

*There are a few of these ''Jumbo'' figures in collectors' hands. They are generally used as promotional figures in showrooms and shops. Rarely do they bring full retail price. They have been temporarily withdrawn from production.

Hum No.	BASIC SIZE	TRADE MARK	CURRENT VALUE
142/3/0	4''	CM	250-325.00
142/3/0	4''	FB	135-185.00
142/3/0	4''	Sty.Bee	
142/3/0	4''	3-line	85-100.00
142/3/0	4''	LB	
142/I	6''	CM	500-600.00
142/I	6''	FB	250-330.00
142/I	6''	Sty.Bee	
142/I	6''	3-line	165-195.00
142/I	6''	LB	
142/V	10¼''	Sty.Bee	
142/V	10¼''	LB	650-800.00
142/X	29''	LB	*16,900.00

BOOTS
Hum 143

Sizes found referenced in various price lists studied are as follows: 5¼'', 5½'', 5¾'', 6½'', 6¾'' and 7''.

*There are a few of these ''Jumbo'' figures in collectors' hands. They are generally used as promotional pieces in showrooms and shows. Rarely do they bring full retail price. They have been temporarily withdrawn from production.

Hum No.	BASIC SIZE	TRADE MARK	CURRENT VALUE
143/0	5¼"	CM	360-425.00
143/0	5¼"	FB	175-230.00
143/0	5¼"	Sty.Bee	
143/0	5¼"	3-line	125-140.00
143/0	5¼"	LB	
143/1	6¾"	CM	600-750.00
143/1	6¾"	FB	300-390.00
143/1	6¾"	Sty.Bee	
143/1	6¾"	LB	180-230.00

ANGELIC SONG
Hum 144

Sizes found in various lists were 4", 4¼" and 5".

Hum No.	BASIC SIZE	TRADE MARK	CURRENT VALUE
144	4¼"	CM	300-375.00
144	4¼"	FB	140-190.00
144	4¼"	Sty.Bee	
144	4¼"	3-line	100-115.00
144	4¼"	LB	

LITTLE GUARDIAN
Hum 145

Hum No.	BASIC SIZE	TRADE MARK	CURRENT VALUE
145	3¾''	CM	275-330.00
145	3¾''	FB	140-190.00
145	3¾''	Sty.Bee	
145	3¾''	3-line	100-115.00
145	3¾''	LB	

ANGEL DUET
Font
Hum 146

(See next page)

Hum No.	BASIC SIZE	TRADE MARK	CURRENT VALUE
146	2''x4¾''	CM	115-140.00
146	2''x4¾''	FB	50-70.00
146	2''x4¾''	Sty.Bee	
146	2''x4¾''	3-line	30-35.00
146	2''x4¾''	LB	

DEVOTION or ANGEL SHRINE FONT
Hum 147

Hum No.	BASIC SIZE	TRADE MARK	CURRENT VALUE
147	3''x5''	CM	115-135.00
147	3''x5''	FB	50-70.00
147	3''x5''	Sty.Bee	
147	3''x5''	3-line	30-35.00
147	3''x5''	LB	

UNKNOWN
Hum 148
Closed Number Designation

Records indicate that this piece could be a Farm Boy (Hum 66) with no base. No examples have ever been found. You can remove the figure from the bookend Hum 60/A and have the same figure, but the mold number would not be present.

UNKNOWN
Hum 149
Closed Number Designation

Records indicate that this could be a Goose Girl (Hum 47) with no base. No known examples in collectors' hands. You can remove the figure from the bookend Hum 60/B and have the same piece, but the mold number would not be present.

HAPPY DAYS
Hum 150

Sizes reference in price lists were: 4¼'', 5¼'', 6'' and 6¼''. Has been known as "HAPPY LITTLE TROUBADOURS" in the past. Known to appear with the decimal point size designator.

Hum No.	BASIC SIZE	TRADE MARK	CURRENT VALUE
150/2/0	4¼''	FB	170-250.00
150/2/0	4¼''	Sty.Bee ⎫	
150/2/0	4¼''	3-line ⎬	115-145.00
150/2/0	4¼''	LB ⎭	
150/0	5¼''	FB	285-380.00
150/0	5¼''	Sty.Bee ⎫	190-210.00
150/0	5¼''	LB ⎭	
150/I	6''	CM	750-1000.00
150/I	6''	FB	450-625.00
150/I	6''	Sty.Bee ⎫	340-450.00
150/I	6''	LB ⎭	

MADONNA
Hum 151

Sometimes called the "Blue Cloaked Madonna" because of its most common painted finish, this figure was out of current production but has recently been reissued in blue cloak. Sizes found referenced range from 12" to 14" and it has appeared with the Crown, Full Bee and Stylized Bee marks. It has appeared in blue cloak, white overglaze, and in a brown cloak. The brown cloak is the most rare. (See color section.) The white overglaze and blue cloak are both listed as reinstated.

Hum No.	BASIC SIZE	TRADE MARK	CURRENT VALUE
151	12"	CM	See next page
151	12"	FB	
151	12"	Sty.Bee	
151	12"	LB	

Because of their scarcity and lack of mark details on the few pieces found in lists, it was impossible to evaluate prices according to the trademarks; therefore a more general listing follows:

233

	Value Range
Blue Cloaked Madonna	2000-3000.00
White Overglazed Madonna	1500-2500.00
Brown Cloaked Madonna	8,000-10,000.00
New Issue of Madonna (color)	750-800.00
(white)	300-320.00

UMBRELLA BOY
Hum 152/A

Hum No.	BASIC SIZE	TRADE MARK	CURRENT VALUE
152/A/0	5''	FB	540-660.00
152/A/0	5''	Sty.Bee	
152/A/0	5''	3-line	360-450.00
152/A/0	5''	LB	
152/A/II	8''	CM	1500-2500.00
152/A/II	8''	FB	750-1000.00
152/A/II	8''	Sty.Bee	
152/A/II	8''	3-line	650-900.00
152/A/II	8''	LB	

UMBRELLA GIRL
152/B

Hum No.	BASIC SIZE	TRADE MARK	CURRENT VALUE
152/B/0	4¾''	FB	540-660.00
152/B/0	4¾''	Sty.Bee	
152/B/0	4¾''	3-line	360-450.00
152/B/0	4¾''	LB	
152/B/II	8''	CM	1500-2500.00
152/B/II	8''	FB	750-1000.00
152/B/II	8''	Sty.Bee	
152/B/II	8''	3-line	625-900.00
152/B/II	8''	LB	

AUF WIEDERSEHEN
Hum 153

There is an extremely rare version of this double figure piece where the little boy wears a Tryolean cap. This variation is found only in the 153/0 size. In most examples of these pieces he wears no hat but is waving a handkerchief as is the girl. The rare version is valued at about $2200.00. Sizes referenced in various lists follow: 5½'', 5⅞'' and 7''. (See color section.) The 153/I size is listed as reinstated.

Hum No.	BASIC SIZE	TRADE MARK	CURRENT VALUE
153/0	5¼''	CM	450-540.00
153/0	5¼''	FB	225-300.00
153/0	5¼''	Sty.Bee	
153/0	5¼''	3-line	150-175.00
153/0	5¼''	LB	
153/0	7''	CM	750-850.00
153/0	7''	FB	275-375.00
153/0	7''	Sty.Bee	
153/0	7''	LB	180-215.00

WAITER
Hum 154

Left: Older of the two, gray pants. Right: Newer of the two, brown pants, "Rhein Wine" on label. (See color section)

This figure has appeared with several different labels on the wine bottle. All are now produced with a "Rhine Wine" label. Earlier versions have much darker pants than those in current production. The version that has "Whiskey" on the label will bring up to $2500.00.

Hum No.	BASIC SIZE	TRADE MARK	CURRENT VALUE
154/0	6''	CM	500-600.00
154/0	6''	FB	200-280.00
154/0	6''	Sty.Bee	
154/0	6''	3-line	135-170.00
154/0	6''	LB	
154/I	7''	CM	700-800.00
154/I	7''	FB	265-300.00
154/I	7''	Sty.Bee	175-220.00
154/I	7''	LB	

UNKNOWN
Hum 155
Closed Number Designation
Records indicate this to possibly be a Madonna holding child. No known examples.

UNKNOWN
Hum 156
Closed Number Designation
Records indicate this to possibly be a wall plaque of a mother and child. No known examples.

Hum 156 through Hum 162
Closed Number Designations
Until recently these numbers have been listed as unknown. Records indicate these six figures were modeled and considered for production but never released. There are sample models of some of them in the Goebel archives and they are atypical of M.I. Hummel figurines. They do not wear the traditional costumes, but rather appear to be dressed in more modern clothes. Sister Maria Innocentia is known to have asked on at least one occasion, "How shall I draw for the Americans?" It is pure conjecture, but one can only wonder if these pieces were possibly an attempt to produce a few for the American market and not approved. None known outside the archives.

Crown	CM	TMK-1	1934-1950
Full Bee	FB	TMK-2	1940-1959
Stylized Bee	Sty Bee	TMK-3	1958-1972
Three Line Mark	3-Line	TMK-4	1964-1972
Last Bee Mark	LB	TMK-5	1970-1980
Missing Bee Mark	MB	TMK-6	1979-1991
Hummel Mark (Current)	HM	TMK-7	1991-Present

WHITSUNTIDE
Hum 163

Left figure is a new version with no candle in lower figure's hands.

This figure is sometimes known as "Happy New Year". It is one of the early (1934-35) releases and was removed from production about 1960 and reinstated in 1977. The older pieces are very scarce and highly sought by collectors. The angel below appears holding a red or a yellow candle in older versions, without the candle in newer ones.

Hum No.	BASIC SIZE	TRADE MARK	CURRENT VALUE
163	7¼''	CM	900-1200.00
163	7¼''	FB	600-750.00
163	7¼''	Sty.Bee	
163	7¼''	3-line	190-250.00
163	7¼''	LB	

WORSHIP
Font
Hum 164

Hum No.	BASIC SIZE	TRADE MARK	CURRENT VALUE
164	2¾''x4¾''	CM	160-185.00
164	2¾''x4¾''	FB	50-65.00
164	2¾''x4¾''	Sty.Bee ⎫	
164	2¾''x4¾''	3-line ⎬	35-45.00
164	2¾''x4¾''	LB ⎭	

SWAYING LULLABY
Plaque
Hum 165

The older trademarked plaques are considered rare. Has been reinstated.

Hum No.	BASIC SIZE	TRADE MARK	CURRENT VALUE
165	4½''x5¼''	CM	750-1000.00
165	4½''x5¼''	FB	500-700.00
165	4½''x5¼''	Sty.Bee	120-140.00
165	4½''x5¼''	LB	

BOY WITH BIRD
Ashtray
Hum 166

(cont.)

Hum No.	BASIC SIZE	TRADE MARK	CURRENT VALUE
166	3¼″x6¼″	CM	400-475.00
166	3¼″x6¼″	FB	150-200.00
166	3¼″x6¼″	Sty.Bee	
166	3¼″x6¼″	3-line	105-130.00
166	3¼″x6¼″	LB	

ANGEL WITH BIRD
Font
Hum 167

Hum No.	BASIC SIZE	TRADE MARK	CURRENT VALUE
167	3¼″x4¼″	CM	110-140.00
167	3¼″x4¼″	FB	45-60.00
167	3¼″x4¼″	Sty.Bee	
167	3¼″x4¼″	3-line	30-35.00
167	3¼″x4¼″	LB	

STANDING BOY
Plaque
Hum 168

This piece was out of production for many years, but has been placed back in the line.

Hum No.	BASIC SIZE	TRADE MARK	CURRENT VALUE
168	4⅛″x5½″	CM	750-1000.00
168	4⅛″x5½″	FB	500-700.00
168	4⅛″x5½″	Sty.Bee	120-145.00
168	4⅛″x5½″	LB	

BIRD DUET
Hum 169

Hum No.	BASIC SIZE	TRADE MARK	CURRENT VALUE
169	4''	CM	375-450.00
169	4''	FB	135-190.00
169	4''	Sty.Bee	
169	4''	3-line	95-115.00
169	4''	LB	

Crown	CM	TMK-1	1934-1950
Full Bee	FB	TMK-2	1940-1959
Stylized Bee	Sty Bee	TMK-3	1958-1972
Three Line Mark	3-Line	TMK-4	1964-1972
Last Bee Mark	LB	TMK-5	1970-1980
Missing Bee Mark	MB	TMK-6	1979-1991
Hummel Mark (Current)	HM	TMK-7	1991-Present

SCHOOL BOYS
Hum 170

This is a triple figure piece which is still in current production.

Hum No.	BASIC SIZE	TRADE MARK	CURRENT VALUE
170/I	7½''	Sty.Bee ⎫	
170/I	7½''	3-line ⎬	770-900.00
170/I	7½''	LB ⎭	
170/III*	10''	CM	2200-2600.00
170/III*	10''	FB	1500-2200.00
170/III*	10''	Sty.Bee ⎫	
170/III*	10''	3-line ⎬	1250-1500.00
170/III*	10''	LB ⎭	

*The Goebel company announced the permanent retirement of this size of School Boys in 1982. It is now a Closed Edition (CE). The smaller 170/I remains in current production.

LITTLE SWEEPER
Hum 171

Hum No.	BASIC SIZE	TRADE MARK	CURRENT VALUE
171	4½''	CM	275-330.00
171	4½''	FB	125-165.00
171	4½''	Sty.Bee	
171	4½''	3-line	80-95.00
171	4½''	LB	
171/4/0	3''		*80.00

*Suggested retail.

FESTIVAL HARMONY
Angel with Mandolin
Hum 172

The major variations to be found are the Crown and Full Bee trademarked figures. The earliest (CM) and some FB (very rare) have flowers extending from the base well up onto the gown and the bird is perched on top of the flowers rather than on the mandolin as on later models. This variation piece is valued at $3000-3500.00.

The majority of the Full Bee pieces show the flowers just barely extending up over the bottom edge of the gown and the bird is situated on the mandolin as in later designs.

The 172/II size was temporarily withdrawn from current production effective December 31, 1984 with no reinstatement date given.

Hum No.	BASIC SIZE	TRADE MARK	CURRENT VALUE
172/0	8″	3-line ⎫	
172/0	8″	LB ⎭	155-195.00
172/II	10¾″	CM	3000-3500.00
172/II	10¾″	FB	650-900.00
172/II	10¾″	Sty.Bee	400.00
172/II	10¾″	3-line ⎫	
172/II	10¾″	LB ⎭	245-305.00

FESTIVAL HARMONY
Angel with Flute
Hum 173

The major variations to be found are on the Crown and Full Bee trademarked pieces. The Crown and some Full Bee (very rare) pieces have the flowers extending from the base well up onto the gown front. This variation piece is valued at $3000-3500.00.

The Full Bee pieces have the flowers barely extending from the base up over the bottom edge of the gown.

The 173/II size was temporarily withdrawn from current production effective December 31, 1984 with no reinstatement date given.

Hum No.	BASIC SIZE	TRADE MARK	CURRENT VALUE
173/0	8''	3-line ⎫	
173/0	8''	LB ⎬	155-195.00
173/II	11''	CM	3000-3500.00
173/II	11''	FB	650-800.00
173/II	11''	Sty.Bee	400.00

Hum No.	BASIC SIZE	TRADE MARK	CURRENT VALUE
173/II	11''	3-line ⎫	245-305.00
173/II	11''	LB ⎭	

SHE LOVES ME, SHE LOVES ME NOT
Hum 174

Left: Last Bee trademark, eyes closed, large feather. Right: Full Bee trademark, eyes open, small feather.

The figure appears with eyes open and eyes closed. Almost all of the eyes open figures so far have been found only with the Full Bee trademark. There is a third variation found in the Stylized and Full Bee marks that has eyes open, large feather, vertical stripes on socks and additional flowers on the left post.

Hum No.	BASIC SIZE	TRADE MARK	CURRENT VALUE
174	4¼''	CM	450-550.00
174	4¼''	FB	225-275.00
174	4¼''	Sty.Bee	135-175.00
174	4¼''	3-line ⎫	115-135.00
174	4¼''	LB ⎭	

MOTHER'S DARLING
Hum 175

Left: The older piece. Bag in right hand is pinkish and upper part of dress very light. Right: The newer of these two. Bag in right hand is blue and upper part of dress is very dark. (see color section)

The most significant variation found is in the color of the bags. The older versions find the bags color light pink and yellow-green. The newer ones are blue and red.

Hum No.	BASIC SIZE	TRADE MARK	CURRENT VALUE
175	5½''	CM	440-520.00
175	5½''	FB	225-275.00
175	5½''	Sty.Bee	135-210.00
175	5½''	3-line	115-150.00
175	5½''	LB	

HAPPY BIRTHDAY
Hum 176

Incised Crown and
stamped Full Bee trademarks

The 176/0 has been known to be written "176" without using the "slash 0" designator in the Crown and Full Bee marks.

Hum No.	BASIC SIZE	TRADE MARK	CURRENT VALUE
176/0	5½''	FB	200.00
176/0	5½''	Sty.Bee	
176/0	5½''	3-line	130-165.00
176/0	5½''	LB	
176	6½''-7''	CM	700-750.00
176	6½''-7''	FB	350-400.00
176/I	6''	CM	650-700.00
176/I	6''	FB	300-350.00
176/I	6''	Sty.Bee	
176/I	6''	LB	185-240.00

SCHOOL GIRLS
Hum 177

Hum No.	BASIC SIZE	TRADE MARK	CURRENT VALUE
177/I	7½''	Sty.Bee	
177/I	7½''	3-line	770-900.00
177/I	7½''	LB	
177/III*	9½''	CM	2200-2600.00
177/III*	9½''	FB	1500-2200.00
177/III*	9½''	Sty.Bee	
177/III*	9½''	3-line	1250-1500.00
177/III*	9½''	LB	

*The Goebel company announced in 1982 that this size of School Girls was to be placed in permanent retirement. It is now a Closed Edition (CE). The smaller 177/I remains in current production.

THE PHOTOGRAPHER
Hum 178

Hum No.	BASIC SIZE	TRADE MARK	CURRENT VALUE
178	4¾''	CM	525-625.00
178	4¾''	FB	260-330.00
178	4¾''	Sty.Bee	
178	4¾''	3-line	175-185.00
178	4¾''	LB	

COQUETTES
Hum 179

Older versions of this figure have a blue dress and yellow flowers on the back of the fence posts, the girls are a bit chubbier and the hairstyle of the girl with the red kerchief is swept back.

Hum No.	BASIC SIZE	TRADE MARK	CURRENT VALUE
179	5¼''	CM	520-625.00
179	5¼''	FB	260-330.00
179	5¼''	Sty.Bee	
179	5¼''	3-line	175-190.00
179	5¼''	LB	

TUNEFUL GOODNIGHT
Plaque
Hum 180

This plaque is quite rare in the older marks. Sometimes called "Happy Bugler" it is 5" x 4¾" in size and was redesigned toward the end of the Last Bee trademark era. The newer design has the bugle in a more forward position making it very vulnerable to breakage.

Hum No.	BASIC SIZE	TRADE MARK	CURRENT VALUE
180	4"x4¾"	CM	600-750.00
180	4"x4¾"	FB	500-600.00
180	4"x4¾"	Sty.Bee	200-250.00
180	4"x4¾"	3-line	
180	4"x4¾"	LB	130-165.00
180 (new style)	4"x4¾"	LB	

THE MAMAS AND PAPAS
Hum 181
(See page 263)

GOOD FRIENDS
Hum 182

Left: Last Bee trademark - new mold. Right: Older style mold design.

Hum No.	BASIC SIZE	TRADE MARK	CURRENT VALUE
182	4''	CM	410-500.00
182	4''	FB	180-255.00
182	4''	Sty.Bee ⎫	
182	4''	3-line ⎬	125-150.00
182	4''	LB ⎭	

FOREST SHRINE
Hum 183

The figures bearing the older trademarks are very rare. Value range: $1000.00 to $2200.00. Has been recently reissued in a new mold design.

Hum No.	BASIC SIZE	TRADE MARK	CURRENT VALUE
183	7''x9''	CM	1500-2200.00
183	7''x9''	FB	1000-1200.00
183	7''x9''	Sty.Bee	450-550.00
183	7''x9''	LB	375-450.00

(See illustration next page)

Forest Shrine   Full Bee trademark

LATEST NEWS
Hum 184

The photo above is of four older models. First produced in 1946, the older pieces have square bases and wide open eyes. They are found with a variety of newspaper names. In fact there was a period of time when some were produced with any name requested by merchants, i.e. their hometown newspapers. The piece was remodeled in the 1960's and given a round base and lowered eyes so the boy appears more like he is reading his paper. Later models bear the newspaper names: "Das Allerneuste", "Latest News" and "Muchner Press." As of 1985 the only newspaper name used is "Latest News." These three titles are the most common. Some of the more rare titles can range in value from $750 to $2500 for the rarer titles.

Hum No.	BASIC SIZE	TRADE MARK	CURRENT VALUE
184	5¼''	CM	575-675.00
184	5¼''	FB	265-315.00
184	5¼''	Sty.Bee	200-240.00
184	5¼''	3-line	180-195.00
184	5¼''	LB	160-180.00

ACCORDION BOY
Hum 185

Hum No.	BASIC SIZE	TRADE MARK	CURRENT VALUE
185	5¼''	CM	350-420.00
185	5¼''	FB	180-230.00
185	5¼''	Sty.Bee	120-160.00
185	5¼''	3-line	120-160.00
185	5¼''	LB	120-160.00

SWEET MUSIC
Hum 186

Crown mark. Striped slippers.   Newer mold.

The most significant variation of Sweet Music is the striped slippers shown on the left figure in the accompanying photo. It is found on the Crown Mark (TMK-1) figures and will bring $1500-1800 depending upon condition. The plain painted slippers are also found on Crown Mark era figures.

Hum No.	BASIC SIZE	TRADE MARK	CURRENT VALUE
186	5¼″	CM	410-485.00
186	5¼″	FB	180-230.00
186	5¼″	Sty.Bee	
186	5¼″	3-line	125-155.00
186	5¼″	LB	

DISPLAY PLAQUE
(English Language)
Hum 187

Display Plaque, Hum 187/A, Last Bee mark, 1976 MID.

Display Plaque, Hum 187/C, Three Line Mark, 1947 MID. The display plaque showing the Stylized Bee trademark in a Medallion-like area. This is commonly called the Moon Top.

The 187 mold number is the one used on all dealer plaques produced until 1986 when it was taken out of production (see page 391 and Special Display Plaque, pages 47 and 60. The older pieces have the traditional bumblebee perched on top but was redesigned in 1972. The newer design has a raised round area in its place and is imprinted with the Stylized Bee trademark. The plaques in current production do not have this round medallion like area.

Some of the plaques have been found with the mold numbers 187/A and 187/C.

The picture above is of a special edition of the display plaque make available to local chapter members of the Goebel Collectors' Club for a short time. As you can see they were personalized with chapter and member name.

There are a number of the 187 plaques in existence in Europe that were made specifically for individual stores and bearing the store name in addition to the traditional wordings.

Hum No.	BASIC SIZE	TRADE MARK	CURRENT VALUE
187	4''x5½''	CM	650.00
187	4''x5½''	FB	550.00
187	4''x5½''	Sty.Bee	450.00
187 with Bumblebee	4''x5½''	3-line	600.00
187 with Moon Top	4''x5½''	3-line	275-325.00
187*	4''x5½''	LB	75.00
187*		LB	75.00

*A current suggested retail price list from a few years ago indicates the availability of a "Display Plaque Retailer" and a "Display Plaque Collector." The list suggested that each bears the 187 mold number. Neither are offered any more.

CELESTIAL MUSICIAN
Hum 188

Up until 1983 this piece was made in only one size, 7''. The mold number was simply 188. Production of a smaller size was begun. The smaller size is 5½'' and bears the mold number 188/0. At the same time the mold number of the 188 was changed to 188/1 to reflect the difference.

Hum No.	BASIC SIZE	TRADE MARK	CURRENT VALUE
188/0	5''	LB	105-160.00
188	7''	CM	575-695.00
188	7''	FB	255-320.00
188	7''	Sty.Bee	
188	7''	3-line	155-195.00
188	7''	LB	
188/I	7''	MB	180-195.00

OLD PEOPLE
"THE MAMAS AND THE PAPAS"
Hum 181, 189, 190, 191 and 202
Closed Numbers

These are the only known examples of the M.I. Hummel figurines to feature old people as their subject. They are more like characatures than realistic renderings. The first four were discovered in Europe by an American collector. The fifth piece, a table lamp (Hum 202), has subsequently turned up. These discoveries filled in the gaps in the mold number sequence previously unknown and designed as Closed Numbers. The term Goebel applies to pieces never placed in production. At least three complete sets of the five pieces are positively known to exist, a set in the company archives and two others in private collections. There have been other single pieces found and there are reports of three or more sets in the U.S. There is little doubt that some others do exist, either singly or in sets, but the number is likely to be extremely small. They were made in samples only and apparently rejected by the Siessen Convent as atypical of Hummel art. Collector value is about $20,000 for each.

Hum 181   OLD MAN READING NEWSPAPER
Hum 189   OLD WOMAN KNITTING
Hum 190   OLD WOMAN WALKING TO MARKET
Hum 191   OLD MAN WALKING TO MARKET
Hum 202   Hum 181 above as TABLE LAMP

Although it does not bear the incised M.I. Hummel signature, this 6⅝" figure is the same as the Hum 181, Old Man Reading Newspaper. It does bear the notation "RG".

CANDLELIGHT
Candleholder
Hum 192

Shows mold variations discussed in text.

There are two distinct versions of this piece. The chief difference is found in the candle receptacle. In the older version the figure holds a candle which is a molded part of the figure. It extends downward almost to the feet. The upper end has a hole for placing a candle. The newer pieces provide only a candle socket in the hands.

Hum No.	BASIC SIZE	TRADE MARK	CURRENT VALUE
192 long candle	6¼''	CM	700-800.00
192 long candle	6¾''	FB	500-600.00
192 long candle	6¾''	Sty.Bee	350.00
192 regular	6¾''	Sty.Bee ⎫	
192 regular	6¾''	3-line ⎬	100-160.00
192 regular		LB ⎭	

ANGEL DUET
Candleholder
Hum 193

Essentially the same design as Hum 261 except that the 261 is not a candleholder. Has been produced in two variations. The variations are in the rear view of the figure. One shows the angel not holding the song book has an arm around the waist of the other, one shows no arm. The no-arm version is the newer.

Hum No.	BASIC SIZE	TRADE MARK	CURRENT VALUE
193	5″	CM	500.00
193	5″	FB	200-275.00
193	5″	Sty.Bee ⎫	
193	5″	3-line ⎬	135-160.00
193	5″	LB ⎭	

WATCHFUL ANGEL
Hum 194
Sometimes called Angelic Care

Hum No.	BASIC SIZE	TRADE MARK	CURRENT VALUE
194	6½''	CM	675-800.00
194	6½''	FB	300-400.00
194	6½''	Sty.Bee	
194	6½''	3-line	215-250.00
194	6½''	LB	

BARNYARD HERO
Hum 195

Hum No.	BASIC SIZE	TRADE MARK	CURRENT VALUE
195/2/0	4''	FB	160-225.00
195/2/0	4''	Sty.Bee ⎫	
195/2/0	4''	3-line ⎬	115-125.00
195/2/0	4''	LB ⎭	
195/I or 195	5¾''-6''	CM	725-850.00
195/I or 195	5¾''-6''	FB	295-400.00
195/I	5¾''	Sty.Bee ⎫	
195/I	5¾''	3-line ⎬	200-240.00
195/I	5¾''	LB ⎭	

TELLING HER SECRET
Hum 196

A new mold design of 196/I was issued in recent years but has been temporarily withdrawn from current production effective December 31, 1984 with no date of reinstatement.

Hum No.	BASIC SIZE	TRADE MARK	CURRENT VALUE
196/0	5¼''	FB	275-365.00
196/0	5¼''	Sty.Bee ⎫	
196/0	5¼''	3-line ⎬	200-235.00
196/0	5¼''	LB ⎭	

(See illustration next page)

Hum No.	BASIC SIZE	TRADE MARK	CURRENT VALUE
196	6¾''	CM	700-800.00
196/I	6¾''	FB	420-600.00
196/I	6¾''	Sty.Bee	
196/I	6¾''	3-line	275-344.00
196/I	6¾''	LB	

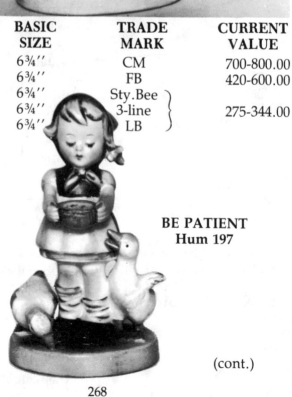

BE PATIENT
Hum 197

(cont.)

Hum No.	BASIC SIZE	TRADE MARK	CURRENT VALUE
197/2/0	4¼''	FB	180-235.00
197/2/0	4¼''	Sty.Bee	
197/2/0	4¼''	3-line	130-145.00
197/2/0	4¼''	LB	
197	6¼''	CM	650-800.00
197/I	6¼''	FB	275-325.00
197/I	6¼''	Sty.Bee	
197/I	6¼''	3-line	175-210.00
197/I	6¼''	LB	

HOME FROM MARKET
Hum 198

Hum No.	BASIC SIZE	TRADE MARK	CURRENT VALUE
198/2/0	4¾''	FB	135-180.00
198/2/0	4¾''	Sty.Bee	
198/2/0	4¾''	3-line	90-100.00
198/2/0	4¾''	LB	
198.	5¾''	CM	500-600.00
198/I	5¾''	FB	300-350.00

Hum No.	BASIC SIZE	TRADE MARK	CURRENT VALUE
198/I	5¾''	Sty.Bee ⎞	
198/I	5¾''	3-line ⎬	135-170.00
198/I	5¾''	LB ⎠	

FEEDING TIME
Hum 199

Each piece bears the 1948 MID. Left: Older, Full Bee piece with blonde hair. Right: Last Bee, darker hair. Note mold variations.

The older pieces have blonde hair and the newer ones dark hair.

Hum No.	BASIC SIZE	TRADE MARK	CURRENT VALUE
199/0	4¼''	FB	180-250.00
199/0	4¼''	Sty.Bee ⎞	
199/0	4¼''	3-line ⎬	135-150.00
199/0	4¼''	LB ⎠	
199.	5¾''	CM	600-750.00
199/I	5¾''	FB	300-350.00
199/I	5¾''	Sty.Bee ⎞	
199/I	5¾''	3-line ⎬	160-180.00
199/I	5¾''	LB ⎠	

LITTLE GOAT HERDER
Hum 200

Hum No.	BASIC SIZE	TRADE MARK	CURRENT VALUE
200/0	4¾''	FB	180-250.00
200/0	4¾''	Sty.Bee ⎫	
200/0	4¾''	3-line ⎬	135-150.00
200/0	4¾''	LB ⎭	
200.	5½''	CM	500-650.00
200/I	5½''	FB	300-350.00
200/I	5½''	Sty.Bee ⎫	
200/I	5¼''	3-line ⎬	160-175.00
200/I	5¼''	LB ⎭	

RETREAT TO SAFETY
Hum 201

Has occurred occasionally with the decimal point size designator.

Hum No.	BASIC SIZE	TRADE MARK	CURRENT VALUE
201/2/0	4''	FB	160-205.00
201/2/0	4''	Sty.Bee	
201/2/0	4''	3-line	115-135.00
201/2/0	4''	LB	
201/2/0	4''	LB	80.00
201.	5½''	CM	800-900.00
201/I	5½''	FB	300-350.00
201/I	5½''	Sty.Bee	
201/I	5½''	3-line	200-225.00
201/I	5½''	LB	

OLD MAN READING NEWSPAPER
Table Lamp
Hum 202
Closed Number Designation

SIGNS OF SPRING
Hum 203

Left: Full Bee, both shoes, both feet down. Right: Full Bee, right foot no shoe and raised.

There is a variation of this figure where the girl has both shoes on. They normally appear with one shoe off (right foot). The value of this variation, found in the smaller size only: $500.00 minimum. Both sizes of this figure were retired as of December 31, 1989. During that year, all pieces produced bore a special "Final Issue" backstamp beneath the base and a small gold-colored medallion attached with a cord. See page 32.

Hum No.	BASIC SIZE	TRADE MARK	CURRENT VALUE
203/2/0	4''	CM	360-430.00
203/2/0	4''	FB	160-220.00
203/2/0	4''	Sty.Bee	
203/2/0	4''	3-line	115-125.00
203/2/0	4''	LB	
203/I	5''	CM	550-650.00
203/I	5''	FB	225-300.00
203/I	5''	Sty.Bee	
203/I	5''	3-line	150-165.00
203/I	5''	LB	

WEARY WANDERER
Hum 204

Hum 204, 5⅞'',
Full Bee

There is a major variation associated with this figure. The normal figure has eyes painted with no color. The variation has blue eyes. There are only four blue-eyed pieces presently known to be in collectors' hands. These are valued at about $5000.00 each. (See color section.)

Hum No.	BASIC SIZE	TRADE MARK	CURRENT VALUE
204	6''	CM	475-550.00
204	6''	FB	225-300.00
204	6''	Sty.Bee	
204	6''	3-line	150-170.00
204	6''	LB	

STORE PLAQUES

First row, top to bottom: Hum 205, Hum 208. Second Row, top to bottom: Hum 187/C, Hum 187, Hum 209. Third row, top to bottom: Hum 187/A, Hum 210.

(cont.)

The following list is of merchant display plaques used by dealers. Each has a large bumblebee perched atop the plaque and a MERRY WANDERER figure attached to the right side. All are 5¼" x 4¼" in basic size. Variations are noted at each listing. See also Hum 187.

Hum 205 (German Language) Occurs in the Crown, Full Bee, Stylized Bee and 3-Line trademarks. Valued at $1000.00 to $1200.00.

Hum 208 (French Language) Occurs in the Crown, Full Bee and Stylized Bee trademarks. Valued at about $3500 to 5000.00.

Hum 209 (Swedish Language) Occurs in the Crown, Full Bee and Stylized Bee trademarks. Valued at about $3500 to 5000.00. Two distinctly different lettering designs have been found.

Hum 210 (English Language) This is the "Schmid Brothers" display plaques. Made for this distributor, "Schmid Bros, Boston" is found molded in bas relief on the suitcase. There are only four known to exist presently. If found this significant piece would likely bring about $12,000.00.

Hum 211 (English Language) There are only two presently known to exist in collectors hands. One in white overglaze, no color and one in full color. This is the only dealer plaque to use the word "Oeslau" as the location of Goebel in Bavaria. Name has since been changed to Rodental, but this is not found on any plaques.

Hum 213 (Spanish Language) Occurs in the Crown, Full Bee and Stylized Bee trademark. Valued at $10,000-12,000.00.

ANGEL CLOUD
Font
Hum 206

One of the original releases in 1934-35, it has been redesigned several times since. It has been in and out of production since but apparently in very limited quantities each time. It has always been in short supply.

Hum No.	BASIC SIZE	TRADE MARK	CURRENT VALUE
206	2¼''x4¾''	CM	300-500.00
206	2¼''x4¾''	FB	300-400.00
206	2¼''x4¾''	Sty.Bee	200-300.00
206	2¼''x4¾''	3-line }	
206	2¼''x4¾''	LB }	30-40.00

HEAVENLY ANGEL
Font
Hum 207

This font, in current production, utilizes the Hum 21 HEAVENLY ANGEL figure in its design.

Hum No.	BASIC SIZE	TRADE MARK	CURRENT VALUE
207	2''x4¾''	CM	115.00
207	2''x4¾''	FB	50-70.00
207	2''x4¾''	Sty.Bee ⎫	
207	2''x4¾''	3-line ⎬	30-40.00
207	2''x4¾''	LB ⎭	

UNKNOWN
Hum 212
Closed Number Designation

This was previously suspected to be another dealer plaque. Then it was thought for a while that this number was intended to be utilized with the letters A through F as mold numbers for a set of musician pieces called ORCHESTRA. It is now known that this was used for a short time merely as an inventory designation for the Band Leader (Hum 129) and several of the musical figurines. The number was not incised on the figures.

NATIVITY SET
Hum 214

In the early 214 sets the Madonna and infant Jesus were molded as one piece. The later ones are found as two separate pieces. Hum 366 the Flying Angel is frequently used with this set. One old model camel and two recently issued new camels are also frequently used with the set but they are not Hummel pieces.

Collectors may note the omission of 214/I in the listing below. It has long been assumed that the mold number was never used because of the possible confusion that might result from the similarity of the "I" and the "1" when incised as a mold number. The existence of a Hum 214/I has now been substantiated. The piece found is in white overglaze and is of two connected geese similar to the geese in the Goose Girl figure. It has the icised M.I. Hummel signature.

HUM NO.	BASIC SIZE	FIGURE	FULL BEE	STYLIZED BEE	THREE LINE	LAST BEE
214/A	6½"	MADONNA WITH INFANT JESUS (1½"x3¾")	415-500.00 65.00	100-140.00 35-45.00	110-140.00 35-45.00	110-140.00 35-45.00
214/B	7½"	JOSEPH	150.00	115-145.00	115-145.00	115-145.00
214/C	3½"	GOODNIGHT (Angel Standing)	70-100.00	55-70.00	55-70.00	55-70.00
214/D	3"	ANGEL SERENADE (Angel Standing)	60-85.00	40-55.00	40-55.00	40-55.00
214/E	3¼"	WE CONGRATULATE (See Hum 220)	115-165.00	90-115.00	90-115.00	90-115.00
214/F	7½"	SHEPHERD WITH SHEEP	155-220.00	120-150.00	120-150.00	120-150.00
214/G	3¾"	SHEPHERD BOY (kneeling)	105-150.00	80-105.00	80-105.00	80-105.00
214/H	3¾"	LITTLE TOOTER	85-125.00	70-90.00	70-90.00	70-90.00
214/J	5¼"	DONKEY	50-75.00	40-55.00	40-55.00	40-55.00
214/K	6½"	COW	50-75.00	40-55.00	40-55.00	40-55.00
214/L	8½"	MOOR KING	150.00	115-145.00	115-145.00	115-145.00
214/M	5¾"	KING (kneeling on one knee)	150.00	115-145.00	115-145.00	115-145.00
214/N	5½"	KING (kneeling on both knees)	135-170.00	110-140.00	110-140.00	110-140.00
214/O	2¼"	LAMB	25.00	10-15.00	10-15.00	10-15.00

Nativity Set (cont.)

In 1988 Goebel began a three-year program to introduce a smaller, third size Nativity Set. They are offered as three or four piece sets as sets in the initial years of the offer and as separate pieces subsequently. They are offered as follows:

1988

214/A/M/0	5¼''	Madonna	110.00
214/B/0	6⅛''	Joseph	110.00
214/AK/0	2⅞''	Jesus	35.00

1989

366/0	2¾''	Flying Angel	85.00
214/J/0	3⅞''	Donkey	45.00
214/K/0	2¾''	Ox	45.00
214/O/0	1½''	Lamb	15.00

1990

214/L/0	6½''	King (standing)	130.00
214/M/0	4''	King (on one knee)	120.00
214/N/0	4½''	King (on both knees)	115.00

1991

214/F/0	5¾''	Shepherd (w/sheep)	135.00
214/G/0	4''	Shepherd Boy	100.00
214/H/0	3''	Little Tooter	100.00

Values quoted above are taken directly from Goebel's Suggested Retail Price List.

Joseph. Hum 214/B, Three Line Mark.

Good Night (Angel Standing). Hum 214/C, 3¼'', 1951 MID. Three Line mark.

Angel Serenade. Hum 214/D. Last Bee mark.

We Congratulate. Hum 214/E, 3½'', Last Bee mark.

Shepherd (with sheep) Hum 214/F, Three Line mark.

Shepherd (kneeling). Hum 214/G. Three Line mark.

Donkey. Hum 214/J. Three Line mark.

Little Tooter. Hum 214/H. Last Bee mark.

Cow. Hum 214/K. Three Line mark.

Moor King. Hum 214/L. Three Line mark.

King (on one knee). Hum 214/M. Three Line mark.

King (on both knees). Hum 214/N. Last Bee mark.

Lamb. Hum 214/0. Three Line mark.

Madonna and Child. Hum 214/A, Madonna 6¼'', Child 3'', Three Line mark.

Christ Child (close up), Hum 214/A. Three Line mark.

UNKNOWN
Hum 215
Closed Number Designation
Not likely to be found. No known examples anywhere. Records indicate it could possibly be a standing child Jesus holding a lamb in his arms.

UNKNOWN
Hum 216
Closed Number Designation
Not likely to be found. No known examples anywhere. Records indicate it might be a Joyful (Hum 53) ashtray if it exists.

BOY WITH TOOTHACHE
Hum 217

Hum No.	BASIC SIZE	TRADE MARK	CURRENT VALUE
217	5½″	FB	210-275.00
217	5½″	Sty.Bee	
217	5½″	3-line	125-165.00
217	5½″	LB	

BIRTHDAY SERENADE
Hum 218

The most significant variation found is the "reverse mold variation." In the older versions of this double figure piece the girl plays the concertina and the boy plays the flute. In the newer models the instruments are the other way around. The 218/O size is listed as reinstated. The "reverse mold" in either size will generally bring about twice the value listed for the non-variation pieces listed below.

Hum 218/0, Last Bee   Hum 218, Full Bee trademark

Hum No.	BASIC SIZE	TRADE MARK	CURRENT VALUE
218/2/0	4¼''	FB	600-700.00
218/2/0	4¼''	Sty.Bee	400-450.00
218/2/0 (rev. mold)	4¼''	3-line	380-400.00
218/2/0	4¼''	3-line	115-140.00
218/2/0	4¼''	LB	
218.	5¼''	FB	700-750.00
218/0	5¼''	FB	600-700.00
218/0	5¼''	Sty.Bee	500-600.00
218/0 (rev. mold)	5¼''	3-line	400-500.00
218/0	5¼''	LB	190-225.00

LITTLE VELMA
Hum 219

This figure bears a number with the ''Closed Number'' designation, supposedly meaning a number which never has been and never will be used to designate the Hummel figurine. It is a girl sitting on a fence, looking down at a frog on the ground. It was never officially released by the factory, although it has turned up due to a no-longer practical policy of distributing pre-production samples. It was never placed in production due to its similarity to Hum 195 and Hum 201. The owner of the first example of this figure to be uncovered has named it "LITTLE VELMA". It was designed in 1952. At least nine examples have been found to date.

Little Velma. Hum 219/2/0

Hum No.	BASIC SIZE	TRADE MARK	CURRENT VALUE
219/2/0	4⅛''	FB	4000-5000.00

WE CONGRATULATE
Hum 220

A very similar figure to Hum 214/E (Nativity Set piece) except this figure is on a base and 214/E is not, and the girl has no wreath of flowers in her hair. (cont.)

Hum No.	BASIC SIZE	TRADE MARK	CURRENT VALUE
220/2/0	4''	FB	400-500.00
220	4''	Sty.Bee	
220	4''	3-line	100-125.00
220	4''	LB	

HAPPY PASTIME
Candy Box
Hum 221
Closed Number Designation

Previously listed as unknown, it is now known that this is a pre-production sample never released. No known examples outside the company archives.

MADONNA
Plaque
Hum 222

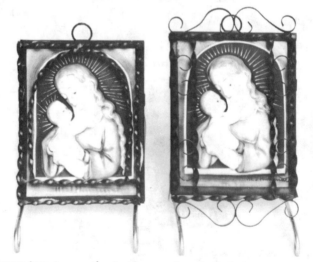

Shows two types of wire frames found. Both have Full Bee trademark. Note that they are slightly different mold designs.

An extremely rare, out of current production piece. It is unique in that there is a metal frame surrounding it. Basic size is 4'' x 5''. Has been found with several different designs of wire frame around it. Most were originally made with a felt backing. Each may be found with any design of the wire frame or, no frame at all.

Hum No.	BASIC SIZE	TRADE MARK	CURRENT VALUE
222	4''x5''	FB	600-1000.00
222	4''x5''	Sty.Bee	

TO MARKET
Table Lamp
Hum 223

A lamp base utilizing Hum 49 as part of the design. In current production, but no pricing information was found in old piece price listings. (See Hum 101.)

Hum No.	BASIC SIZE	TRADE MARK	CURRENT VALUE
223	9½''	FB	350-450.00
223	9½''	Sty.Bee	275-295.00
223	9½''	3-line	260-275.00
223	9½''	LB	250-260.00

WAYSIDE HARMONY
Table Lamp
Hum 224 (also briefly Hum II/111 & Hum II/112)**

A lamp base utilizing Hum 111 as part of the design. In current production. (See page 192.)

Hum No.	BASIC SIZE	TRADE MARK	CURRENT VALUE
224/I	7½''	FB	335-440.00
224/I	7½''	Sty.Bee	260-285.00
224/I	7½''	3-line	250-260.00
224/II	9½''	CM	*
224/II	9½''	FB	350-450.00
224/II	9½''	Sty.Bee	275-295.00
224/II	9½''	3-line	260-275.00
224/II	9½''	LB	250-260.00

*Insufficient data to establish value or substantiate existence of earlier trademarks.
**These two odd marks will bring premium prices when found on the Hum 224 lamp.

JUST RESTING
Table Lamp
Hum 225

A lamp base utilizing Hum 112 as a part of the design. In current production.

Hum No.	BASIC SIZE	TRADE MARK	CURRENT VALUE
225/I	7½''	FB	335-440.00
225/I	7½''	Sty.Bee	260-285.00
225/I	7½''	3-line	250-260.00
225/II	9½''	FB	350-450.00
225/II	9½''	Sty.Bee	275-295.00
225/II	9½''	3-line	260-275.00
225/II	9½''	LB	250-260.00

THE MAIL IS HERE
OR
MAIL COACH
Hum 226

This piece is also known as MAIL COACH. (See Hum 140).

Hum No.	BASIC SIZE	TRADE MARK	CURRENT VALUE
226	4¼''x6¼''	FB	600-750.00
226	4¼''x6¼''	Sty.Bee	
226	4¼''x6¼''	3-line	360-450.00
226	4¼''x6¼''	LB	

SHE LOVES ME, SHE LOVES ME NOT
Table Lamp
Hum 227

A 7½'' lamp base utilizing Hum 174 as part of the design. In current production.

Hum No.	BASIC SIZE	TRADE MARK	CURRENT VALUE
227	7½''	FB	295-420.00
227	7½''	Sty.Bee	
227	7½''	3-line	230-290.00
227	7½''	LB	

GOOD FRIENDS
Table Lamp
Hum 228

A 7½'' lamp base utilizing Hum 182 as part of the design. In current production.

Hum No.	BASIC SIZE	TRADE MARK	CURRENT VALUE
228	7½''	FB	295-420.00
228	7½''	Sty.Bee	
228	7½''	3-line	230-290.00
228	7½''	LB	

APPLE TREE GIRL
Table Lamp
Hum 229

A 7½'' lamp base utilizing Hum 141 as part of the design. In current production.

Hum No.	BASIC SIZE	TRADE MARK	CURRENT VALUE
229	7½''	FB	295-420.00
229	7½''	Sty.Bee	
229	7½''	3-line	230-290.00
229	7½''	LB	

APPLE TREE BOY
Table Lamp
Hum 230

A 7½'' lamp base utilizing Hum 142 as part of the design. In current production.

Hum No.	BASIC SIZE	TRADE MARK	CURRENT VALUE
230	7½''	FB	700-750.00
230	7½''	Sty.Bee ⎫	
230	7½''	3-line ⎬	230-290.00
230	7½''	LB ⎭	

BIRTHDAY SERENADE
Table Lamp
Hum 231

This particular lamp was out of production for many years. It utilizes the Hum 218, Birthday Serenade as its design. The old model is found in the Full Bee trademark and reflects the same old mold girl with accordian/boy with flute design. These old mold design lamps measure about 9¾'' tall and are fairly scarce. Value range: $1000 to $1500. The Hum 231 was reissued in the late 1970's with the instruments reversed. Now the girl plays the flute and the boy, the accordian. The newer pieces are found with the Last Bee (TMK-5) and the Missing Bee (TMK-6) trademarks at about $300-350.00. In current production. See Hum 234.

HAPPY DAYS
Table Lamp
Hum 232

The 9¾'' Happy Days table lamp was placed in production in the 1950's, inexplicably removed from the line after a short period of time. It was reissued in the late 1970's in a remodeled design. The early pieces bear the Full Bee trademark and are valued at between $1000 and $1500. The newer model pieces are found in the Last Bee (TMK-5) and the Missing Bee (TMK-6) trademarks at about $300-350.00. In current production.

UNKNOWN
Hum 233
Closed Number Designation

Unlikely to be found. There is evidence to suggest that this is a preliminary design for Bird Watcher (Hum 300). No known examples anywhere.

BIRTHDAY SERENADE
Table Lamp
Hum 234

This lamp like the larger Hum 231, was also removed from production for a time. Unlike the Hum 231 lamp, however, it can be found in all trademarks beginning with the Full Bee. It was redesigned in the late 1970's with the instruments reversed just as the Hum 231 was. It can be found in the old or new styles in the Full Bee.

234	7¾''	FB	1000-1500.00
234	7¾''	Sty.Bee	750-900.00
234	7¾''	3-line	300-700.00
234	7¾''	LB	285-300.00

HAPPY DAYS
Table Lamp
Hum 235

This is a smaller size (7¾'') of the Hum 232 lamp. It too was placed in production in the 1950's and removed shortly thereafter. It was reissued in a new design in the late 1970's as was the larger lamp. Unlike the larger lamp, however, this one can be found in all trademarks starting with the Full Bee.

Hum No.	BASIC SIZE	TRADE MARK	CURRENT VALUE
235	7¾''	FB	500-750.00
235	7¾''	Sty.Bee	400-450.00
235	7¾''	3-line	300-400.00
235	7¾''	LB	280-300.00

NO NAME
Hum 236A and Hum 236B

Only one example of each of these is known to exist at this time. The figures are two angels, one at the base of a tree and the other seated on a tree limb. Hum 236A has one angel playing a harp at the base of a tree and the other seated on a tree limb above singing. The Hum 236B has the tree angel blowing a horn and the seated angel playing a lute. No known examples outside the factory archives. Too unique to place a value on.

Hum 237
CLOSED NUMBER DESIGNATION

This piece is a plaque using ''Star Gazer'' as its design. None known to be in private collection. Factory Archives only.

ANGEL TRIO SET
Hum 238/A ANGEL WITH LUTE
Hum 238/B ANGEL WITH ACCORDION
Hum 238/C ANGEL WITH HORN

These three pieces are usually sold as a set. In current production, they can be found in the current-use Missing Bee (TMK-6), Last Bee (TMK-5) and the 3-line (TMK-4) trademarks. Each is 2-2½'' high and are valued at $80-100.00 as a set. They are essentially the same set as the Angel Trio, Hum 38, 39 and 40, but these (Hum 238) are not candleholders. See photos of Angel Trio on page 134 for the design.

CHILDREN TRIO SET
Hum 239/A GIRL WITH NOSEGAY
Hum 239/B GIRL WITH DOLL
Hum 239/C BOY WITH HORSE

Left to Right: Hum 239/C, 239/B, 239/A

Hum No.	BASIC SIZE	TRADE MARK	CURRENT VALUE
239/A,B,C	3½''	3-line ⎫	
239/A,B,C	3½''	LB ⎬	105-125.00

LITTLE DRUMMER
Hum 240

Hum No.	BASIC SIZE	TRADE MARK	CURRENT VALUE
240	4¼''	FB	140-190.00
240	4¼''	Sty.Bee ⎞	
240	4¼''	3-line ⎬	85-100.00
240	4¼''	LB ⎠	

Crown	CM	TMK-1	1934-1950
Full Bee	FB	TMK-2	1940-1959
Stylized Bee	Sty Bee	TMK-3	1958-1972
Three Line Mark	3-Line	TMK-4	1964-1972
Last Bee Mark	LB	TMK-5	1970-1980
Missing Bee Mark	MB	TMK-6	1979-1991
Hummel Mark (Current)	HM	TMK-7	1991-Present

ANGEL LIGHTS
Candleholder
Hum 241

The photo shows the arch only. The plate comes with the piece at purchase.

This was a new release in 1978. It is in the form of an arch which is placed on a plate. A figure sits attached to the top of the arch, with candle receptacles down each side of the arch. The arch is not attached to the plate base.

Occurs earliest in the Last Bee trademark only. Has been observed as available at $180.00 to $200.00 usually. Suspended from production on January 1, 1990.

ANGEL JOYOUS NEWS WITH LUTE
Holy Water Font
Hum 241
Closed Number Designation

This is an interesting piece in that it bears the same mold number as the Angel Lights. Produced as a sample only and never put into the line. It is not likely that it will ever be found by collectors. As far as is known, the only example is in the Goebel archives.

ANGEL JOYOUS NEWS WITH TRUMPET
Holy Water Font
Hum 242
Closed Number Designation

This piece was produced as a sample only and never put into the line. It is not likely to ever find its way into a private collection. As far as is known, the only example is in the Goebel archives.

MADONNA and CHILD
Font
Hum 243

Hum No.	BASIC SIZE	TRADE MARK	CURRENT VALUE
243	3¼''x4''	FB	45-60.00
243	3¼''x4''	Sty.Bee	
243	3¼''x4''	3-line	30-40.00
243	3¼''x4''	LB	

UNKNOWN
Hum 244
Open Number Designation

UNKNOWN
Hum 245
Open Number Designation

HOLY FAMILY
Font
Hum 246

Hum No.	BASIC SIZE	TRADE MARK	CURRENT VALUE
246	3"x4"	FB	100-125.00
246	3"x4"	Sty.Bee	50-60.00
246	3"x4"	3-line ⎱	
246	3"x4"	LB ⎰	30-35.00

Crown	CM	TMK-1	1934-1950
Full Bee	FB	TMK-2	1940-1959
Stylized Bee	Sty Bee	TMK-3	1958-1972
Three Line Mark	3-Line	TMK-4	1964-1972
Last Bee Mark	LB	TMK-5	1970-1980
Missing Bee Mark	MB	TMK-6	1979-1991
Hummel Mark (Current)	HM	TMK-7	1991-Present

STANDING MADONNA WITH CHILD
Hum 247
Closed Number Designation

As you can see by the photo here, this is a beautiful piece. It was produced in sample only and never put into production. Too unique to value.

GUARDIAN ANGEL
Font
Hum 248

This piece is a redesigned version of Hum 29 which is no longer in production.

Hum No.	BASIC SIZE	TRADE MARK	CURRENT VALUE
248	2¼″x5½″	FB	100-125.00
248	2¼″x5½″	Sty.Bee	50-60.00
248	2¼″x5½″	3-line ⎫	
248	2¼″x5½″	LB ⎭	30-35.00

MADONNA and CHILD
Plaque in Relief
Hum 249
Closed Number Designation

Molded as a sample only, this plaque was never put in the line. It is essentially the same design as the Hum 48 Madonna Plaque with the background cut away. No known examples outside the Goebel archives.

LITTLE GOAT HERDER and FEEDING TIME
Book Ends
Hum 250/A,   250/B

If these are removed from the wooden bookend bases, they are indistinguishable from the regular figures.

Hum No.	BASIC SIZE	TRADE MARK	CURRENT VALUE
250/A&B	5½″	Sty.Bee ⎫	
250/A&B	5½″	3-line ⎬	230-290.00
250/A&B	5½″	LB ⎭	

GOOD FRIENDS
and
SHE LOVES ME, SHE LOVES ME NOT
Book Ends
Hum 251/A   Hum 251/B

If these are removed from the wooden bookend bases, they are indistinguishable from the regular figures.

APPLE TREE BOY and APPLE TREE GIRL
Book Ends
Hum 252/A   Hum 252/B

If these figures are removed from the bookend base, they are indistinguishable from the regular single figures.

Hum No.	BASIC SIZE	TRADE MARK	CURRENT VALUE
252/A&B	5¼''	Sty.Bee ⎫	
252/A&B	5¼''	3-line ⎬	230-290.00
252/A&B	5¼''	LB ⎭	

UNKNOWN
Hum 253
Closed Number Designation
Goebel records indicate that this piece was a design much like the girl in Hum 52, Going to Grandma's. There is no evidence that it was ever produced and there are no known examples in the archives or anywhere else.

UNKNOWN
Hum 254
Closed Number Designation
Goebel records indicate that this piece was a design much like the girl figure in Hum 150, Happy Days. There is no evidence that it was ever produced and there are no examples in the archives or anywhere else.

A STITCH IN TIME
Hum 255

Hum No.	BASIC SIZE	TRADE MARK	CURRENT VALUE
255	6¾''	Sty.Bee	250.00
255	6¾''	3-line	150-170.00
255	6¾''	LB	
255/4/0	3''	Current	80.00

KNITTING LESSON
Hum 256

Hum No.	BASIC SIZE	TRADE MARK	CURRENT VALUE
256	7½''	Sty.Bee	500.00
256	7½''	3-line }	300-375.00
256	7½''	LB	

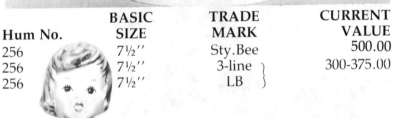

FOR MOTHER
Hum 257

(cont.)

Hum No.	BASIC SIZE	TRADE MARK	CURRENT VALUE
257	5¼''	Sty.Bee	350.00
257	5¼''	3-line	180-205.00
257	5¼''	LB	
257/2/0	3''	Current	105.00

WHICH HAND?
Hum 258

Hum No.	BASIC SIZE	TRADE MARK	CURRENT VALUE
258	5¼''	Sty.Bee	350.00
258	5¼''	3-line	100-165.00
258	5¼''	LB	

GIRL WITH ACCORDION
Hum 259

This piece is a closed number. It is a prototype piece and has never been released. Exists in factory archives only. It is the same as the girl figure in Hum 218, Birthday Serenade.

NATIVITY SET
(large)
Hum 260

There was only sketchy information found concerning complete Nativity Sets and little more about the individual pieces in any of the many price lists utilized. Below is a listing of each piece in the Hum 260 Nativity Set. The set currently carries a retail price of about $3000-4000.00. They are found in 3-line and Last Bee trademarks as well as the current-use Missing Bee mark. The older marks bring slightly more than current retail.

Hum No.	BASIC SIZE	FIGURE
260/A	9¾''	MADONNA
260/B	11¾''	JOSEPH
260/C	5¾''	INFANT JESUS
260/D	5¼''	GOODNIGHT (Angel Standing)
260/E	4¼''	ANGEL SERENADE (Kneeling)
260/F	6¼''	WE CONGRATULATE
260/G	11¾''	SHEPHERD
260/H	3¾''	SHEEP AND LAMB
260/J	7''	SHEPHERD BOY (Kneeling)
260/K	7½''	LITTLE TOOTER
260/L	7½''	DONKEY
260/M	6''x11''	COW
260/N	12¾''	MOOR KING
260/O	12''	KING (Standing)
260/P	9''	KING (Kneeling)
260/R	3¼''x4''	SHEEP

Pieces listed chronologically by Mold Number...
Alphabetical Cross Referencing starting page 83.

ANGEL DUET
Hum 261

This figure, essentially is the same design as Hum 193 but does not have a provision for a candle. It is apparently produced in very limited quantities, for they are very difficult to locate.

There are two major variations to be found. The older variation is, in rear view, the angel that is not holding the song book has an arm around the waist of the other. The newer version shows no arm in the rear view.

Hum No.	BASIC SIZE	TRADE MARK	CURRENT VALUE
261	5½''	3-line	140-180.00
261	5½''	LB	

HEAVENLY LULLABY
Hum 262

This figure is the same design as Hum 24 but does not have a provision for a candle. It is apparently produced in very limited quantities, for they are very difficult to locate. Current production piece sells for about $155.00 but earlier trademarked pieces are valued at $250-350.

Hum No.	BASIC SIZE	TRADE MARK	CURRENT VALUE
262	3½''x5''	Sty.Bee	200-300.00
262	3½''x5''	3-line	130-140.00
262	3½''x5''	LB	120-130.00

MERRY WANDERER
Plaque in Relief
Hum 263

A very rare plaque of the familiar MERRY WANDERER motif. There is only one known outside the factory collection and in a private collection as can be determined there are no more on the collector market. One is known to bear the Three Line trademark. Too unique to price.

ANNUAL PLATES

In 1971 the factory produced its first annual plate. This plate called the HEAVENLY ANGEL (Hum 21) design and was released to the Goebel factory workers to commemorate the 100th anniversary of the W. Goebel firm. The plate was subsequently produced without the inscription and was received so well in the United States it was decided that a similar plate would be released annually from then on. The 1971 plate was not released to European dealers.

Since 1971 the firm has released one new design per year, each bearing a traditional Hummel figurine motif. The plates and their current market value are listed on the following pages.

1971 HUMMEL ANNUAL PLATE
Hum 264

There are three versions of this plate. The first is the "normal version." The second differs from the first only in that it has no holes for hanging. It was exported to England where tariff laws in 1971 placed a higher duty on the plate if it had holes than if not. The law states that holes make it a decorative object, subject to a higher duty rate. The third variation is the special original edition produced only for the Goebel firm factory workers. There is an inscription on the back side of the lower rim. It reads in German as follows: "Gewidmet Aller Mitarbeitern Im Jubilaumsjahr. Wirdanken ihnen fur ihre mitarbeit". Roughly translated it is thanks to the workers for their fine service. This is the least common of the three, hence the most sought after.

1971 through 1975 Hummel Annual Plates

1972 GOEBEL ANNUAL PLATE
Hum 265

There are three known versions of the 1972 plate. The first is the "normal" one with the regular back stamp and the current Goebel trademark. The second has the same back stamp but bears the 3-line mark instead of the current mark. The third is exactly the same as the second but does not bear the inscription "Hand Painted" and the "2nd" is omitted from the identification of the plate as an annual plate.

1976 through 1980 Hummel Annual Plates

1981 Hummel Annual Plate

1982
Hummel Annual Plate

1983
Hummel Annual Plate

1984
Hummel Annual Plate

1985
Hummel Annual Plate

1986
Hummel Annual Plate

1987
Hummel Annual Plate

Hum No.	SIZE	PLATE DESIGN	YEAR	Current Value
264	7½''	Heavenly Angel	1971	450-650.00
265	7½''	Hear Ye, Hear Ye	1972	30-50.00
*265	7½''	Hear Ye, Hear Ye 3-line mark	1972	45-60.00
266	7½''	Globe Trotter	1973	80-135.00
267	7½''	Goose Girl	1974	30-60.00
**268	7½''	Ride Into Christmas	1975	30-60.00
***269	7½''	Apple Tree Girl	1976	25-60.00
270	7½''	Apple Tree Boy	1977	40-70.00
271	7½''	Happy Pastime	1978	35-50.00
272	7½''	Singing Lesson	1979	20-40.00
273	7½''	School Girl	1980	30-50.00
274	7½''	Umbrella Boy	1981	40-55.00
275	7½''	Umbrella Girl	1982	80-100.00
276	7½''	Postman	1983	140-150.00
277	7½''	Little Helper	1984	40-60.00
278	7½''	Chick Girl	1985	60-75.00
279	7½''	Playmates	1986	90-110.00
283	7½''	Feeding Time	1987	125-200.00
284	7½''	Little Goat Herder	1988	80-100.00
285	7½''	Farm Boy	1989	75-120.00
286	7½''	Shepherd's Boy	1990	110-140.00
287	7½''	Just Resting	1991	125-140.00
288	7½''	Wayside Harmony	1992	130-200.00

*Made at the same time as the Last bee marked plate and represents a transition. Not appreciably more valuable.
**Late in 1983 an unusual plate was found in Germany. It was a 1975 Annual Plate but instead of the Ride Into Christmas motif it was a Little Fiddler. No doubt that this was a prototype plate considered for 1975 but obviously not selected. How it managed to find its way out of the factory is anybody's guess. It may have been the only one.
***Somehow a number of the 1976 Annual Plates were inadvertently given the incorrect backstamp "Wildlife Third Edition, Barn Owl" and they were released. How many got out is anybody's guess. It has no value significance.

FUTURE ANNUAL PLATE RELEASES
The 1995 plate will be the final plate issued in this twenty-five plate series.

1988
Hummel Annual Plate

1989
Hummel Annual Plate

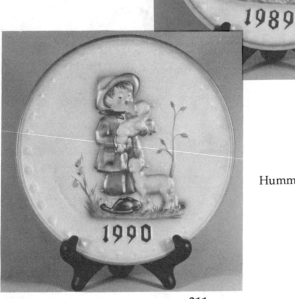

1990
Hummel Annual Plate

1991
Hummel Annual Plate

1992
Hummel Annual Plate

1975 ANNIVERSARY PLATE
Hum 280

This larger plate (10") utilizes the STORMY WEATHER (Hum 71) design. Presently valued at between $60 and $100.00. New anniversary plate is planned for release at five-year intervals.

1980 ANNIVERSARY PLATE
Hum 281

This plate is called "SPRING DANCE" but utilizes only one figure from the Spring Dance piece and the second girl in the plate design is taken from the "RING AROUND THE ROSIE" figurine. It presently sells for $55-60.00.

1975 Anniversary Plate   1980 Anniversary Plate

1985 ANNIVERSARY PLATE
Hum 282

As are the previous Anniversary Plates the latest one is 10″ in diameter. It uses as its design the figurine Auf Wiedersehn (Hum 153). It was released at the factory recommended retail price of $225.00 and is presently selling at $90-135.00.

Hum 289 Through Hum 291
"OPEN NUMBER designation." Number reserved for future release. Because of the sequence of mold numbers it is probable that some or all of these will be future Annual and Anniversary Plates.

FRIENDS FOREVER PLATE SERIES
This is a four plate series of seven inch plates begun in 1992.

MEDITATION
Hum 292
First in the series. The release price was $180.00. The remaining plates to be released are as follows:

1993	Hum 293	For Father
1994	Hum 294	Sweet Greetings
1995	Hum 295	Surprise

BIRDWATCHER
Hum 300

Originally known as Tenderness, this figurine was released in 1979. It is likely that the two trademarks it may be found in are the last two (Last Bee and Missing Bee). The figure is 5″ in height and commonly has an incised 1956 mold induction date. There is evidence to suspect the existence of a piece bearing a 1954 MID and the Full Bee trademark. Current selling range: $135-275.00.

CHRISTMAS ANGEL
Hum 301

A new figurine for 1989, this piece is presently selling at about $150-200.00

CONCENTRATION
Hum 302
Possible Future Edition
Designed much like Hum 256, Knitting Lesson except that there is a boy watching instead of a girl.

ARITHMETIC LESSON
Hum 303
Possible Future Edition
This new design appears to be a combination of one boy and one girl from Hum 170, School Boys and Hum 177, School Girls. The boy in this figure is also much like the boy in the new 1986 Dealer Plaque, Hum 460.

THE ARTIST
Hum 304

Hum No.	BASIC SIZE	TRADE MARK	CURRENT VALUE
304	5¼''	FB	5000-6000.00
304	5¼''	3-line	350.00
304	5¼''	LB	150-175.00

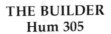

THE BUILDER
Hum 305

Hum No.	BASIC SIZE	TRADE MARK	CURRENT VALUE
305	5½''	Sty.Bee	5000-6000.00
305	5½''	3-line	150-175.00
305	5½''	LB	

LITTLE BOOKKEEPER
Hum 306

Hum No.	BASIC SIZE	TRADE MARK	CURRENT VALUE
306	4¾''	FB	5000-6000.00
306	4¾''	Sty.Bee	1000-1500.00
306	4¾''	3-line	170-200.00
306	4¾''	LB	

GOOD HUNTING
Hum 307

(cont.)

In older versions of this piece the boy holds the binoculars significantly lower than they are held in the photo of Good Hunting on previous page.

Hum No.	BASIC SIZE	TRADE MARK	CURRENT VALUE
307	5¼''	FB	5000-6000.00
307	5¼''	Sty.Bee	1000-1500.00
307	5¼''	3-line	170-200.00
307	5¼''	LB	155-160.00

LITTLE TAILOR
Hum 308

Both have the Last Bee trademark. Left figure bears a 1955 MID and the right figure, 1972 MID. The older MID pieces command premium prices.

Hum No.	BASIC SIZE	TRADE MARK	CURRENT VALUE
308	5½''	FB	5000-6000.00
308	5½''	Sty. Bee	1000-1500.00
308	5½''	3-line }	130-150.00
308	5½''	LB }	

WITH LOVING GREETINGS
Hum 309

When first released in 1983 the suggested retail price was $80.00. It now sells for about $120-130.00 and the basic size is 3½''. Note the two photos here. The one with the line around the base is an early factory sample. When you compare it to the other, the production piece, you will see that the prototype is a good bit more complex. This is a good illustration of how a figure evolves from prototype to production. Obviously the paint brush under the boy's arm was judged too vulnerable to breakage and was removed from the production model.

When first introduced into the line in 1983, the ink pot was colored blue with turquoise being the color of the writing on the tablet. In late 1987 the color of the ink pot was changed to brown and the color of the writing to blue. There has been no explanation for this but, it is of great interest to collectors as this change may make a significant difference in the future. Only time will tell.

SEARCHING ANGEL
Wall Plaque
Hum 310

This figure is a wall plaque and was released as a new design in 1979. The size is 4x2½'', occurs in the Last Bee and Missing Bee. The value of them are $90-110.00 each. There is evidence that there may be an earlier vintage piece bearing the Full Bee trademark.

KISS ME
Hum 311

The older models of this figure show socks on the doll, newer ones have no socks.

Hum No.	BASIC SIZE	TRADE MARK	CURRENT VALUE
311	6''	FB	5000-6000.00
311	6''	Sty.Bee	750-1000.00
311 (socks)	6''	3-line	450-550.00
311 (no socks)	6''	3-line	140.00
311	6''	LB	130-140.00

(See illustration next page)

KISS ME   HUM 311
Left: Three-line mark, no socks, 1955 MID.
Right: Stylized Bee mark, socks, 1955 MID.

HONEY LOVER
Hum 312

This piece was first found illustrated in the *Golden Anniversary Album* as a Possible Future Edition (PFE) when the book was released in 1984. At that point in time, a few had somehow already made their way into collectors hands. It is now out, having been released as a special M.I. Hummel Club exclusive offering. Released at $190.00, it is available to members, only upon after the fifteenth anniversary of their club membership.

Baby in a crib in front of a picket fence. There is a bird perched on fence to left and a large sunflower growing behind the fence drooping over the baby.

CONFIDENTIALLY
Hum 314

Left: 1972 MID. Note bow tie and heavier pedestal.
Right: 1955 MID. No bow tie. Smaller pedestal.
Both bear the Last Bee trademark.

This figure was first produced with a smaller base than the newer model. The new model, redesigned around 1972, has a larger base and a bow tie. The older ones have no bow tie; command premium prices when available.

Hum No.	BASIC SIZE	TRADE MARK	CURRENT VALUE
314	5½''	FB	5000-6000.00
314	5½''	Sty. Bee	1000-1500.00
314	5½''	3-line	} 130-160.00
314	5½''	LB	

MOUNTAINEER
Hum 315

Hum No.	BASIC SIZE	TRADE MARK	CURRENT VALUE
315	5¼''	FB	5000-6000.00
315	5¼''	Sty.Bee	up to 2500.00
315	5¼''	3-line ⎫	130-160.00
315	5¼''	LB ⎭	

RELAXATION
Hum 316
Possible Future Edition

Little boy in large wooden wash tub. There is a banner on the tub that reads Sommerfrische in German script. Sunflower grows next to tub.

NOT FOR YOU
Hum 317

Hum No.	BASIC SIZE	TRADE MARK	CURRENT VALUE
317	6''	FB	5000-6000.00
317	6''	Sty.Bee	175.00
317	6''	3-line ⎫	
317	6''	LB ⎬	150-160.00

ART CRITIC
Hum 318

Hum 318 - 5¾ Art Critic

Listed in the last edition of this book as a Possible Future Edition, this figure was released in 1991. The figure is 5¾'' and the release price was $240.00 and remains that on the 1992 Goebel price list.

DOLL BATH
Hum 319

Right piece is older of the two. Left bears a 1956 MID.

Hum No.	BASIC SIZE	TRADE MARK	CURRENT VALUE
319	5¼''	FB	5000-6000.00
319	5¼''	Sty.Bee	750.00 +
319	5¼''	3-line ⎫	
319	5¼''	LB ⎬	160-175.00

THE PROFESSOR
Hum 320

Hum 320/0 The Professor 4¾''.

The Professor first was listed and illustrated in the *Golden Anniversary Album* and in the last edition of this book as a Possible Future Edition. It was officially released in 1992 with the mold number 320/0 in a 4¾'' size. Release price at retail was $180.00.

WASH DAY
Hum 321

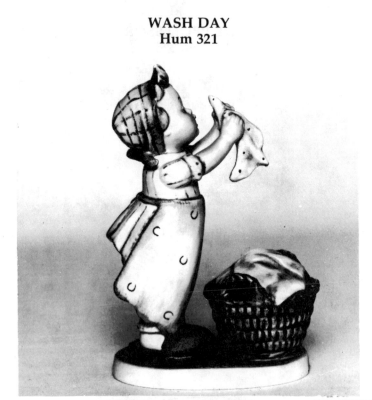

Hum No.	BASIC SIZE	TRADE MARK	CURRENT VALUE
321	5¾''	FB	5000-6000.00
321	5¾''	Sty.Bee	1000-1500.00
321	5¾''	3-line }	160-175.00
321	5¾''	LB }	
321/4/0	3''	Current	60.00

LITTLE PHARMACIST
Hum 322

Both are Three-line mark pieces. German and English language labels.

There are several variations in the labeling of the medicine bottle at the figure's feet. The version written in German (left in photo above) has been temporarily withdrawn from production as of December 31, 1984. One of the most difficult to find is the version with "Castor Oil" on the bottle. It brings a premium price when sold.

In 1988 Little Pharmacist was redesigned and all subsequent production of the figure will reflect the following changes: The base has been made more shallow with rounded corners. This renders the figure shorter than its former 6" size to 5¾". The coat is now curved in front at the button line. A breast pocket has been added and the strap (in back) has been made wider and a second button has been added. His bow tie has been straightened and now the eyeglass stems disappear into his hair.

Hum No.	BASIC SIZE	TRADE MARK	CURRENT VALUE
322	6"	FB	5000-6000.00
322	6"	Sty.Bee	1000-1500.00
322	6"	3-line ⎫	
322	6"	LB ⎬	160-185.00

MERRY CHRISTMAS
Hum 323

This is a new design wall plaque released in 1979. The size is 5¼"x4". It is found with the Full Bee, Last Bee, and Missing Bee trademarks. Values of them are $85-110.00 for the Last Bee and Missing Bee pieces and about $2500.00 for the rare Full Bee pieces.

AT THE FENCE
Hum 324
Possible Future Edition

Boy and girl behind fence peering over at a small barking dog. Yellow bird perched on one of the fence posts. Only one example known to be in a private collection.

HELPING MOTHER
Hum 325
Possible Future Edition

This is a new design possibly slated for production some time in the future. The figurine is substantially similar to Mother's Helper, Hum 133 with the addition of a table at the girl's left. The table has a tablecloth and candle on it. Only two examples known to be in private collections.

NAUGHTY BOY
Hum 326
Possible Future Edition

Hum 326 is a new design that has been placed into prototype production only. Availability at this time is unknown, but possibly slated for release in the future.

THE RUN-A-WAY
Hum 327

Major mold differences discussed in text. Right figure is older mold design.

There exist at least two variations of Hum 327. Significantly they have both been found with the current trademark although each variation bears a different mold induction date (MID). The older design (MID 1955) has flowers in the basket, gray jacket, gray hat, and the crook on the cane is turned more sideways. The newer design (MID 1972) has no flowers, a green hat, blue jacket, and the cane is situated with the crook pointing up. The older pieces command premium price.

Hum No.	BASIC SIZE	TRADE MARK	CURRENT VALUE
327	5¼''	FB	5000-6000.00
327	5¼''	3-line	600-750.00
327	5¼''	LB	170-185.00

CARNIVAL
Hum 328

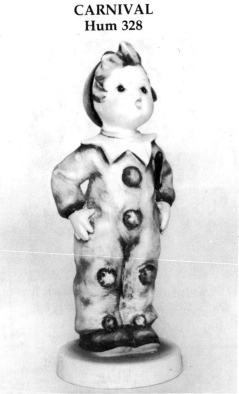

Hum No.	BASIC SIZE	TRADE MARK	CURRENT VALUE
328	6''	FB	5000-6000.00
328	6''	Sty.Bee	1000-1500.00
328	6''	3-line	145-165.00
328	6''	LB	

OFF TO SCHOOL
Hum 329
Possible Future Edition

Boy and girl walking along. The girl has a book satchel in the crook of her left arm. The boy figure is substantially similar to Hum 82, School Boy.

BAKING DAY
Hum 330

This figure was introduced new in early 1985. It has a basic size of 5¼'' and release price was $95.00 suggested retail. It presently sells at about $160-220.00.

CROSSROADS
Hum 331

(cont.)

It has been reported that there is a variation regarding the position of the trombone. It is not terribly obvious in the photo here but if you look closely, you can see the end of the horn protruding above the boy's head. The reported variation is that the horn is reversed so that it points down instead of up as in the one pictured here. This can't really be regarded as a legitimate variation. It is the result of a mistake in the assembly of the parts at the factory and is likely to be the only one in existence.

Hum No.	BASIC SIZE	TRADE MARK	CURRENT VALUE
331	6¾''	FB	5000-6000.00
331	6¾''	Sty.Bee	1500.00
331	6¾''	3-line	300.00
331	6¾''	LB	290-300.00

Hum 331 - Crossroads, Halt sign down, Limited to 20,000 numbered edition 6¾

(See next page)

In 1991 Goebel released a limited edition version of Crossroads with a significant variation. They felt that they needed to recognize the reunification of Germany with a commemorative piece, appropriate to the occasion. They chose to release this piece with the HALT sign on the post laying on the ground at the base, symbolizing the now open borders between the former two Germanys.

The edition is sequentially numbered and is limited to 20,000 pieces. Retail release price was $360.00.

Hum No.	BASIC SIZE	TRADE MARK	CURRENT VALUE
331	6¾''	LB	700.00
331	6¾''	HM	900-1000.00

SOLDIER BOY
Hum 332

Shows cap medallion color variations.

There are known uniform color variations, primarily on the hat medallion. The red cap medallion is found on the older versions.

(cont.)

Hum No.	BASIC SIZE	TRADE MARK	CURRENT VALUE
332	6''	FB	5000-6000.00
332	6''	Sty.Bee	1000-1500.00
322*	6''	3-line }	135-155.00
322*	6''	LB }	

BLESSED EVENT
Hum 333

Hum No.	BASIC SIZE	TRADE MARK	CURRENT VALUE
333	5½''	FB	5000-6000.00
333	5½''	Sty.Bee	1500-2000.00
333	5½''	3-line }	235-260.00
333	5½''	LB }	

*Red cap medallion variation will bring about $100.00 over the value for the regular version.

HOMEWARD BOUND
Hum 334

Older models of this design have a support molded in beneath the goat, the newer versions do not have this support. The older ones command premium prices.

Hum No.	BASIC SIZE	TRADE MARK	CURRENT VALUE
334 with post	5″	FB	5000-6000.00
334 with post	5″	3-line	240-265.00
334 with post	5″	LB	
334 w/o post	5″	LB	210-240.00

LUCKY BOY
Hum 335
Possible Future Edition

This is a standing boy with a piglet under his right arm. He holds an umbrella in left hand. The point of the umbrella rests on the base at his left foot.

Crown	CM	TMK-1	1934-1950
Full Bee	FB	TMK-2	1940-1959
Stylized Bee	Sty Bee	TMK-3	1958-1972
Three Line Mark	3-Line	TMK-4	1964-1972
Last Bee Mark	LB	TMK-5	1970-1980
Missing Bee Mark	MB	TMK-6	1979-1991
Hummel Mark (Current)	HM	TMK-7	1991-Present

CLOSE HARMONY
Hum 336

CLOSE HARMONY   HUM 336
Both have the Three-line trademark but right piece is older mold.
Note the incised dress pattern and higher socks.

Hum No.	BASIC SIZE	TRADE MARK	CURRENT VALUE
336	5½''	FB	5000-6000.00
336	5½''	Sty.Bee	
336	5½''	3-line	195-210.00
336	5½''	LB	

CINDERELLA
Hum 337

Left: Last Bee 1952
MID, eyes closed.

Right: Last Bee, 1958
MID, eyes open.

First versions of this figure have eyes open, newer ones have eyes closed. These variations represent two entirely different molds. Both versions have appeared bearing the Last Bee trademark (TMK-5).

Hum No.	BASIC SIZE	TRADE MARK	CURRENT VALUE
337-eyes open	5½''	FB	5000-6000.00
337-eyes open	5½''	3-line	750-800.00
337-eyes closed	5½''	3-line	175-195.00
337-eyes open	5½''	LB	500-750.00
337-eyes closed	5½''	LB	155-175.00

BIRTHDAY CAKE - CANDLEHOLDER
Hum 338

Birthday Cake was added to the line in the winter of 1988. It measures 3¾" and has a receptacle for your candle as you can see by the photo here. It has an incised mold induction date of 1956. Released at $95.00 it is now listed at $120.00 in the Goebel price list. There are two versions to be found. The differences are with regard to the texture of the top of the cake surface. It is reported that about the first 2000 were produced with a smooth texture. This was changed to a rough texture ostensibly to correspond to the style of today. It has reportedly been found in Stylized Bee mark.

BEHAVE!
Hum 339
Possible Future Edition
Standing girl admonishing dog with pointed finger of right hand. She holds a doll in her left arm.

LETTER TO SANTA CLAUS
Hum 340

Hum No.	BASIC SIZE	TRADE MARK	CURRENT VALUE
340	7″	FB	5000-6000.00
340	7″	Sty.Bee	1500-2500.00
340	7″	3-line ⎤	
340	7″	LB ⎦	200-230.00

BIRTHDAY PRESENT
Hum 341
Possible Future Edition
Standing girl holding potted plant with both hands.

MISCHIEF MAKER
Hum 342

Hum No.	BASIC SIZE	TRADE MARK	CURRENT VALUE
342	4¹⁵⁄₁₆''	FB	5000-6000.00
342	4¹⁵⁄₁₆''	3-line ⎫	170-190.00
342	4¹⁵⁄₁₆''	LB ⎭	

CHRISTMAS SONG
Hum 343

This is one of the six new designs released by Goebel in 1981. There is at least one example of this piece known to exist bearing the Stylized Bee trademark. That particular piece is a prototype and is too unique to place a realistic value on at this time. All others found so far have current-use trademark. Released at $85.00 the present value is about $120-150.00. The basic size is 6¼''.

(See illustration next page)

CHRISTMAS SONG   HUM 343

FEATHERED FRIENDS
Hum 344

Hum No.	BASIC SIZE	TRADE MARK	CURRENT VALUE
344	4¾''	FB	5000-6000.00
344	4¾''	Sty.Bee	1000-1500.00
344	4¾''	3-line	800-1000.00
344	4¾''	LB	165-180.00

(See illustration next page)

FEATHERED FRIENDS   HUM 344

A FAIR MEASURE
Hum 345

Shows major mold differences.
Left: Last Bee mark, eyes down, 1972 MID.   Right: Last Bee mark,
eyes wide open, 1955 MID.

At least two variations of this figure exist and it is important to note that both have been found bearing the current trademark and different mold induction dates (MID). The older design (MID 1956) shows the boy with his eyes wide open; in the newer design (MID 1972) the boy is looking down so that it appears that his eyes are closed. The older Three Line Mark pieces are valued at $500.00 and the old mold Last Bee pieces at $400.00.

Hum No.	BASIC SIZE	TRADE MARK	CURRENT VALUE
345	5½''	FB	5000-6000.00
345	5½''	3-line	
345	5½''	LB	150-195.00

THE SMART LITTLE SISTER
Hum 346

Hum No.	BASIC SIZE	TRADE MARK	CURRENT VALUE
346	4¾	FB	3000-4000.00
346	4¾''	Sty.Bee	1000-1500.00
346	4¾''	3-line	
346	4¾''	LB	130-160.00

ADVENTURE BOUND
THE SEVEN SWABIANS
Hum 347

This multiple figure piece was first released in 1971-72 in limited numbers but is still in production. It is however still released in very small quantities and is difficult to obtain and quite expensive. It is in a private collection and too unique to place a realistic value on.

Hum No.	BASIC SIZE	TRADE MARK	CURRENT VALUE
347	7¼''x8''	FB	$7500-1000.00
347	7¼''x8''	3-line ⎫	2100-2700.00
347	7¼''x8''	LB ⎬	

Pieces listed chronologically by Mold Number ...
Alphabetical Cross Referencing starting page 83.

RING AROUND THE ROSIE
Hum 348

This figure was first released in the 1957. Sizes found in various lists are 6¼'', 6¾'' and 7¼''. (See Hum 353, color section).

Hum No.	BASIC SIZE	TRADE MARK	CURRENT VALUE
348	6¾''	FB	10,000-12,000.00
348	6¾''	Sty.Bee	
348	6¾''	3-line	1750-2000.00
348	6¾''	LB	

FLOWER LOVER or THE FLORIST
Hum 349
Possible Future Edition

Standing boy wearing bib aporn. He holds a flower in left hand and appears to be examining it closely. There are more flowers growing at his feet.

ON HOLIDAY
Hum 350

This 4¼'' figurine was a new release in 1981. There were apparently a few prototypes produced in the Three Line mark era for there have been a few to be uncovered bearing that trademark. These are too unique to price at the present time. The remainder of the figures are found only with the Last Bee (TMK-5), the Missing Bee (TMK-6) and the Hummel Mark (TMK-7) trademarks. Originally released at $85.00 the current price for it is about $145.00.

THE BOTANIST
Hum 351

Basic size of this 1982 new design release is 4''. There is a very rare example of The Botanist known to exist with the Three Line Mark and a 1965 mold induction date. This is apparently a prototype piece and too unique to place a realistic market value on. The new version of the piece bears a 1972 mold induction date. It will be found with the Missing Bee (TMK-6) and the Hummel Mark (TMK-7). It was released at $84.00 and the present price is about $175-185.00.

SWEET GREETINGS
Hum 352

Sweet Greetings was among the six new designs to be released in 1981. Its basic size is 4⅛''. It, like a few others of the new releases, was apparently produced in limited numbers as prototype pieces in the Three Line mark era, for at least one is known to exist that bears that mark. Both the prototype piece and the new release have a mold induction date of 1965. Original release price in 1981 was $85.00 and the present price is about $175-185.00. The earlier piece is too unique to establish a realistic secondary market collector value.

SPRING DANCE
Hum 353

This figure first appeared in the 1960's. The smaller 353/0 with the Three Line Mark is quite rare and the only figure with a higher mold number than 218 on which the "0" designation is used to denote the standard size. This smaller size was released in the Last Bee trademark era.

Hum No.	BASIC SIZE	TRADE MARK	CURRENT VALUE
353/0	4¾''	3-line	3000-4000.00
353/0	4¾''	LB	175-195.00
**353/1	6½''	3-line	500.00
**353/1	6½''	LB	290-365.00

**Not in current production.

HOLY WATER FONTS

Hum 354/A	ANGEL WITH LANTERN
Hum 354/B	ANGEL WITH TRUMPET
Hum 354/C	ANGEL WITH BIRD

Closed Number designation. Three fonts existing in factory prototype, only. Apparently they were never produced.

AUTUMN HARVEST
Hum 355

Hum No.	BASIC SIZE	TRADE MARK	CURRENT VALUE
355	4¾''	3-line	350-400.00
355	4¾''	LB	120-160.00

GAY ADVENTURE
Hum 356

This figure has been known as "Joyful Adventure" also.

Hum No.	BASIC SIZE	TRADE MARK	CURRENT VALUE
356	4¹⁵/₁₆''	3-line	350-400.00
356	4¹⁵/₁₆''	LB	120-150.00

(See illustration next page)

GAY ADVENTURE
Hum 356

GUIDING ANGEL
Hum 357

HUM 357, HUM 358, HUM 359

This figure, Hum 358, and Hum 359 make a charming trio although they are sold separately.

Hum No.	BASIC SIZE	TRADE MARK	CURRENT VALUE
357	2¾''	Sty.Bee	
357	2¾''	3-line	55-70.00
357	2¾''	LB	

SHINING LIGHT
Hum 358

Hum No.	BASIC SIZE	TRADE MARK	CURRENT VALUE
358	2¾''	Sty.Bee	
358	2¾''	3-line	55-70.00
358	2¾''	LB	

TUNEFUL ANGEL
Hum 359

Hum No.	BASIC SIZE	TRADE MARK	CURRENT VALUE
359	2¾''	Sty.Bee	
359	2¾''	3-line	55-70.00
359	2¾''	LB	

WALL VASES (3)
BOY AND GIRL
Hum 360/A
Boy Hum 350/B   Girl 360/C

Stylized Bee trademarked wall vases are considered rare. They were first produced around 1955 and discontinued about 1960. Of the three the BOY AND GIRL (Hum 360/A) seems to be the most easily found. They appear with the STYLIZED BEE mark and as a complete set usually sell for $750.00. Separately they are valued at $200.00 to $250.00 each. Basic size is 4½'' x 6¼''. All three were reissued with the Last Bee and continued in production in the Missing Bee (TMK-6) Mark Status January 1, 1990.

(See illustration next page)

358

FAVORITE PET
Hum 361

Hum No.	BASIC SIZE	TRADE MARK	CURRENT VALUE
361	4¼''	Sty.Bee	750.00
361	4¼''	3-line ⎫	150-250.00
361	4¼''	LB ⎭	

I FORGOT
Hum 362
Possible Future Edition

Girl standing with empty basket in the crook of her left arm. She points at her chin as if trying to remember. She dangles doll from right hand.

BIG HOUSECLEANING
Hum 363

Hum No.	BASIC SIZE	TRADE MARK	CURRENT VALUE
363	$3^{15}\!/_{16}$ ''	3-line	250.00
363	$3^{15}\!/_{16}$ ''	LB	165-225.00

Crown	CM	TMK-1	1934-1950
Full Bee	FB	TMK-2	1940-1959
Stylized Bee	Sty Bee	TMK-3	1958-1972
Three Line Mark	3-Line	TMK-4	1964-1972
Last Bee Mark	LB	TMK-5	1970-1980
Missing Bee Mark	MB	TMK-6	1979-1991
Hummel Mark (Current)	HM	TMK-7	1991-Present

SUPREME PROTECTION
Hum 364

This piece is a 9″, full color madonna and child and is the first limited edition figurine ever offered to the general public by Goebel. Released in 1984, it was scheduled to be produced during that year only, in commemoration and celebration of the anniversary of Sister M.I. Hummel's 75th birthday. It has a special backstamp identifying it as such. As the first figures began to become available it was discovered that some 3000 to 3500 of them were released with a mistake in the stamp. The M.I. Hummel came out as M.**J.**Hummel. The factory tried at first to correct the mistake by modifying the "J" in the decal to appear as an "I". However they attempted to change it by cutting the decal and unfortunately the modification didn't come off too well, the result demonstrating quite obviously what they attempted. As a consequence there are three backstamp versions to be found: The correct backstamp; the poorly modified backstamp; and the "M.J. Hummel" incorrect backstamp spelling. This particular backstamp variation is apparently coming into strong demand. It has reportedly brought as much as $300.00.

361

LITTLEST ANGEL
Hum 365
Possible Future Edition
This design exists in prototype sample only. It is a tiny seated child angel.

FLYING ANGEL
Hum 366

This figure is commonly used with the Nativity Sets and has been produced in painted versions as well as white overglaze. The white ones are rare and command premium prices. It is suspected that the price could be found bearing the Stylized Bee trademark, but it has not yet been uncovered.

Hum No.	BASIC SIZE	TRADE MARK	CURRENT VALUE
366	3½''	3-line ⎫	
366	3½''	LB ⎬	75-95.00
366/0	2¾''	Current	65.00

BUSY STUDENT
Hum 367

(See next page)

Hum No.	BASIC SIZE	TRADE MARK	CURRENT VALUE
367	4¼''	Sty.Bee	500.00
367	4¼''	3-line	100-125.00
367	4¼''	LB	

LUTE SONG
Hum 368
Possible Future Edition

Standing girl playing lute. This design is substantially similar to the girl in Close Harmony, Hum 336.

FOLLOW THE LEADER
Hum 369

Hum No.	BASIC SIZE	TRADE MARK	CURRENT VALUE
369	6¹⁵⁄₁₆''	3-line	600-755.00
369	6¹⁵⁄₁₆''	LB	

COMPANIONS
Hum 370
Possible Future Edition

This design is much like To Market, Hum 49 except that the girl has been replaced with a boy that is remarkably like the boy of Hum 51, Village Boy.

DADDY'S GIRLS
Hum 371

Daddy's Girls was a new addition to the line in 1989. It measures 4⅞'' tall and has an incised mold induction date of 1964 on the underside of the base.

BLESSED MOTHER
Hum 372
Possible Future Edition

This is a standing Madonna and child.

JUST FISHING
Hum 373

This is a new figure released in early 1985 at a suggested retail price of $85.00. It measures 4¼″x4½″. Early Goebel promotional materials referred to this piece as an ash tray. This was in error; probably due to the tray-like base representing the pond. Interestingly it is once more listed as an ashtray in the Goebel price list. Presently selling at about $190.00.

LOST STOCKING
Hum 374

Hum No.	BASIC SIZE	TRADE MARK	CURRENT VALUE
374	4⅜″	3-line	350-400.00
377	4¾″	LB	105-145.00

(See illustration next page)

LOST STOCKING
Hum 374

MORNING STROLL
Hum 375
Possible Future Edition
The design of this piece is a girl pushing a baby carriage with her doll in it.

LITTLE NURSE
Hum 376
This piece is one of the two new designs to be released in 1982. Although most of them are found with the current-use trademark it is known that at least one exists bearing the Last Bee mark (TMK-5) with a 1965 mold induction date. The current-use trademark pieces have a 1972 MID. It was first released in 1982 at $95.00 and is currently valued at about $200.00. The basic size of the figurine is 4″. The earlier vintage piece is too unique to place a realistic market value on.

(See illustration next page)

LITTLE NURSE

BASHFUL
Hum 377

(See next page)

Hum No.	BASIC SIZE	TRADE MARK	CURRENT VALUE
377	4¾''	3-line	350-400.00
377	4¾''	LB	115-155.00

EASTER GREETINGS
Hum 378

Hum No.	BASIC SIZE	TRADE MARK	CURRENT VALUE
378	5½''	3-line	350.00
378	5½''	LB	120-180.00

DON'T BE SHY
Hum 379
Possible Future Edition

Little girl with kerchief on head. She is feeding bird perched on fence post.

DAISIES DON'T TELL
Hum 380

This is the Goebel Collectors' Club Special Edition offered exclusively to club members in 1981. As with all the others it could be purchased by current members with redemption cards for $80.00 in the U.S. and $95.00 in Canada. As of May 31, 1985 it was no longer available except on the secondary market. It's currently valued at about $100. The mold induction date is 1972. There is at least one known to exist bearing the 3-line mark (TMK-4) and one MID of 1966. This latter piece is exceedingly rare and too unique to price.

FLOWER VENDOR
Hum 381

Hum No.	BASIC SIZE	TRADE MARK	CURRENT VALUE
381	5½''	3-line	350-400.00
381	5½''	LB	135-185.00

VISITING AN INVALID
Hum 382

(See next page)

Hum No.	BASIC SIZE	TRADE MARK	CURRENT VALUE
382	4¹⁵⁄₁₆''	3-line*	400-500.00
382	4¹⁵⁄₁₆''	LB	130-150.00

*Very difficult to find.

GOING HOME
Hum 383

   This new piece for 1985 was released at a suggested retail price of $125.00. Basic size is 5''. Now selling at about $170-200.00.

EASTER TIME
or
EASTER PLAYMATES
Hum 384

(cont.)

Hum No.	BASIC SIZE	TRADE MARK	CURRENT VALUE
384	3¹⁵⁄₁₆''	3-line	350.00
384	3¹⁵⁄₁₆''	LB	170-225.00

CHICKEN LICKEN
Hum 385

This is one of the twenty four pieces first released in 1971-72 with the three-line mark. It has a mold induction date (MID) of 1971 and has been in production since. In 1990 Goebel released a smaller size, 3¼'', with the incised mold number 385/4. The recommended retail price at release was $85.00.

Hum No.	BASIC SIZE	TRADE MARK	CURRENT VALUE
385	4¾''	3-line	350.00
385	4¾''	LB	170-240.00
385/4	3¼''	LB	85.00

ON SECRET PATH
Hum 386

Hum No.	BASIC SIZE	TRADE MARK	CURRENT VALUE
386	5⅜''	3-line	350.00
386	5⅜''	LB	150-205.00

VALENTINE GIFT
Hum 387

This rather special figure was the first special edition figurine available only to members of the Goebel Collectors Club, an official organization sponsored by and a division of the Goebel firm. It was originally released in 1977 at $45.00 with a redemption card obtained through membership in the club. The size is 5¾''. The most commonly found piece bears the Last Bee mark (TMK-5) and sells at $250.00-350.00. Older pieces (TMK-4) have brought as much as $1000.00. As of May 31, 1984 it was no longer available except on the secondary market.

(See illustration next page)

VALENTINE GIFT   HUM 387
Stylized Bee and Last Bee trademarks.

LITTLE BAND
Candleholder
Hum 388

This is a three figure piece utilizing Hum 389, 390, and 391 on one base and is provided with a candle receptacle.

Hum No.	BASIC SIZE	TRADE MARK	CURRENT VALUE
388	3''x4¾''	Sty.Bee ⎫	
388	3''x4¾''	3-line ⎬	185-230.00
388	3''x4¾''	LB	175-220.00

LITTLE BAND
Candleholder
Music Box
Hum 388/M

This is the same piece as Hum 388 but is mounted on a wooden base with a music box movement inside. When it plays, the Little Band figure rotates.

Hum No.	BASIC SIZE	TRADE MARK	CURRENT VALUE
388/M	4¾''x5''	Sty.Bee ⎫	
388/M	4¾''x5''	3-line ⎬	275-330.00
388/M	4¾''x5''	LB ⎭	

CHILDREN - TRIO
Hum 389   GIRL WITH SHEET MUSIC
Hum 390   BOY WITH ACCORDION
Hum 391   GIRL WITH HORN

Left to Right: Hum 391, Hum 390, Hum 389

These three pieces are the same figures used on Hum 388, 388/M, 392 and 392/M. They are on current suggested price lists as available in a set of three or separately.

Hum No.	BASIC SIZE	TRADE MARK	CURRENT VALUE
389	2½'' to 2¾''	Sty.Bee ⎫	
389	2½'' to 2¾''	3-line ⎬	40-70.00
389	2½'' to 2¾''	LB ⎭	

Hum No.	BASIC SIZE	TRADE MARK	CURRENT VALUE
390	2½'' to 2¾''	Sty.Bee	
390	2½'' to 2¾''	3-line	40-70.00
390	2½'' to 2¾''	LB	
391	2½'' to 2¾''	Sty.Bee	
391	2½'' to 2¾''	3-line	40-70.00
391	2½'' to 2¾''	LB	

LITTLE BAND
Hum 392

The same as Hum 388 except that this piece has no provision for a candle. Little Band is listed as having been temporarily withdrawn from current production status with no reinstatement date given.

Hum No.	BASIC SIZE	TRADE MARK	CURRENT VALUE
392	4¾''x3''	Sty.Bee	
392	4¾''x3''	3-line	145-180.00
392	4¾''x3''	LB	

Crown	CM	TMK-1	1934-1950
Full Bee	FB	TMK-2	1940-1959
Stylized Bee	Sty Bee	TMK-3	1958-1972
Three Line Mark	3-Line	TMK-4	1964-1972
Last Bee Mark	LB	TMK-5	1970-1980
Missing Bee Mark	MB	TMK-6	1979-1991
Hummel Mark (Current)	HM	TMK-7	1991-Present

LITTLE BAND MUSIC BOX
Hum 392/M

LITTLE BAND MUSIC BOX   Hum 392/M

The same piece as Hum 392 but is placed atop a base with a music box movement inside. When it plays the piece revolves.

Hum No.	BASIC SIZE	TRADE MARK	CURRENT VALUE
392/M	4¼″x5″	Sty.Bee ⎫	
392/M	4¼″x5″	3-line ⎬	275-330.00
392/M	4¼″x5″	LB ⎭	

DOVE
Holy Water Font
Hum 393
Possible Future Edition

The design of this font includes a flying dove and a banner with the inscription " + KOMM + HEILIGER + GEIST + ". This translates in English "Come Holy Spirit." No known examples outside Goebel archives.

TIMID LITTLE SISTER
Hum 394

This two figure piece was a new design released with five others in 1981. It has been found with the Last Bee trademark (TMK-5) but is so rare that no realistic secondary market value can be assigned to it. Both the older vintage piece and the commonly found current-use trademarked pieces bear the 1972 mold induction date. When released in 1981 the price was $190.00 and is presently valued at about $300-360.00.

SHEPHERD BOY
Hum 395
Possible Future Edition

This piece is of a boy and lamb. They are standing by a fence. A bird is perched on a fence post. No known examples outside factory archives.

RIDE INTO CHRISTMAS
Hum 396

This figurine remains quite popular and is in great demand by collectors. Perhaps this is why the company released a smaller version in 1982. The release of the smaller piece necessitated a change in the mold number of the larger one from 396 to 396/1.

Hum No.	BASIC SIZE	TRADE MARK	CURRENT VALUE
396	5¾''	3-line	1200-1600.00
396	5¾''	LB	250-315.00
396/1	5¾''	MB	—
396/2/0	4¼''	LB	135-165.00

THE POET
Hum 397
Possible Future Edition

Standing child reciting from book held in left hand. No known examples outside company archives.

SPRING BOUQUET
Hum 398
Possible Future Edition

Girl picking flowers. She holds bouquet in left arm. No known examples outside the company archives.

VALENTINE JOY
Hum 399

This is the fourth special edition offered exclusively to the members of the Goebel Collectors' Club. Issued in 1980-81 they bear a 1979 mold induction date and measure 5⅝'' and were available for $95.00 with the club redemption card. Although it is known that there are existing examples with the Last Bee trademark (TMK-5) the piece is normally found with the current use trademark (TMK-6). Available only on the secondary market at about $150-250.00.

WELL DONE!
Hum 400
Possible Future Edition

Two standing boys. One, wearing shorts, pats the other, in long pants, on shoulder. No known examples outside the company archives.

FORTY WINKS
Hum 401
Possible Future Edition

Seated girl with small boy next to her. He is asleep with his head on her right shoulder. No known examples outside the company archives.

TRUE FRIENDSHIP
Hum 402
Possible Future Edition

Seated girl eating porridge from bowl held in her left hand. Her right hand holds a spoonful and a bird is perched on her right forearm.

AN APPLE A DAY
Hum 403

An Apple A Day was released in 1988. It is 6½'' tall and carries an incised 1974 mold induction date. The price at the time of release was $195.00. The 1992 Goebel suggested retail price list has it at $240.00.

SAD SONG
Hum 404
Possible Future Edition

Standing boy singing. He looks as if he is about to cry. Holds sheet music at back with right hand. No known examples outside the company archives.

SING WITH ME
Hum 405

First released in 1985. The basic size is 5″. The one in the accompanying photo measures slightly bigger at 5⅛″ tall. A mold induction date of 1974 is found incised on the underside of the base. Found in the Missing Bee (TMK-6) and the Hummel Mark (TMK-7) it is valued at about $180-250.00.

PLEASANT JOURNEY
Hum 406

000-448

Released in 1987, this new piece has a basic size of 6½'' long by 6¼'' high. This piece, like the Chapel Time clock is limited to those produced in 1987. They will not be produced again in the 20th Century. The release price was $500.00 and is valued at about $1200-1500.00 currently.

FLUTE SONG
Hum 407
Possible Future Edition
Seated boy playing flute for lamb standing in front of him. The boy is seated on what appears to be a stump.

SMILING THROUGH
Hum 408

This is the ninth redemption piece available only to members of the Goebel Collectors' Club. It was released in 1985 at $125.00 with redemption card. The mold number incised on the bottom of this figurine is actually 408/0. The reason for this is that a larger model was molded in 1976 but never released. It was made as a sample only and resides in the factory archives now. This larger version was 6'' while the one released to club members is only 4¾.'' As of May 31, 1987 they are available only on the secondary market.

COFFEE BREAK
Hum 409

This is the ninth special edition piece available to members of the Goebel Collectors' Club exclusively. It was available to them, with redemption card until May 31, 1986. The issue price for Coffee Break was $90.00. Now available only on the secondary market at about $150.00.

TRUANT
Hum 410
Possible Future Edition

Walking boy with book satchel on his back. He carries a T-square in his right hand.

DO I DARE?
Hum 411
Possible Future Edition
Standing girl holding flower in her left hand and basket in the crook of her right arm.

IN TUNE
Hum 414

    This figure is one of the six new designs released by Goebel in 1981. Its basic size is 4'' and is a matching figurine to the 1981 Annual Bell. To date it has only been found with the current-use trademark (Missing Bee or TMK-6) or later mark. When released it was priced at $115.00 and is now selling at about $185.00.

BATH TIME
Hum 412

The last edition of this book listed Bath Time as a Possible Future Edition (PFE). It was released in 1990 at $300.00, it is 6¼″. It is listed at $350.00 in the 1992 Goebel retail price list.

WHISTLER'S DUET
Hum 413

    This piece was introduced as "NEW FOR '92" in the fall, 1991 issue of the M.I. Hummel Club newsletter. It is listed as 4" in size and was released at $235.00.

THOUGHTFUL
Hum 415

This is another of the six new designs released by Goebel in 1981. Its basic size is 4½'' and is a matching piece to the 1980 Annual Bell. Thoughtful has a 1980 mold induction date (MID) and has been found only with the current-use trademark (Missing Bee or TMK-6) and the Hummel Mark (TMK-7). The original release price was $105.00 and is now priced at about $190.00.

JUBILEE
Hum 416

Beginning in January of 1985 this very special figurine was made available to collectors and limited to the number of them sold during 1985 only. The figure has a special backstamp reading "50 Years, M.I. Hummel Figurines, 1935-1985, The Love Lives On." It is in celebration of the Golden Anniversary of Hummel figurines. It is 6¼" high and the factory recommended retail price was $200.00. It can bring up to about $300.00 on today's secondary market.

WHERE DID YOU GET THAT?
Hum 417
Possible Future Edition

Standing boy and girl. Boy holds his hat in both hands. It has three apples in it. Girl dangles doll in left hand.

Added to the line in 1990, What's New? is 5¼'' tall. The suggested retail price was $200.00. It can be found with the Missing Bee (TMK-6) and the current use Hummel Mark (TMK-7). The Goebel suggested retail price list places $240.00 on it.

GOOD LUCK!
Hum 419
Possible Future Edition
Standing boy with his left hand in his pocket. He holds an umbrella in his right arm.

IS IT RAINING?
Hum 420

Is it Raining? was added to the line in 1989. The one in the accompanying photo measures 6″ tall. It has a mold induction date of 1981 and the retail price at release was $175.00. 1992 retail in price list is $225.00.

IT'S COLD
Hum 421

This is the sixth in a series of special offers made exclusively to members of the Goebel Collectors' Club. It is available only from them initially requiring a special redemption card issued to members. Each of these special editions have shown themselves to be good candidates for fairly rapid appreciation in collector value. The figurine bears a 1981 mold induction date (MID) and was sold with redemption card for $80.00. It is selling at about $95-120.00 in the secondary market today.

WHAT NOW?
Hum 422

    This is the seventh special edition issued for members of the Goebel Collectors' Club. The usual redemption card was required for purchase of this figurine at $90.00. What Now? stands 5¼'' high and is now selling at about $125.00. Available only on the secondary market as of May 31, 1985.

HORSE TRAINER
Hum 423

Horse Trainer was added to the line in 1990 at 4½'' and a suggested retail price of $155.00. It can be found with the Missing Bee (TMK-6) and the current use Hummel Mark (TMK-7). The collector value is presently about the same as suggested retail at $185.00.

SLEEP TIGHT
Hum 424

A 1990 release, this piece can be found with the Missing Bee (TMK-6) and the current use Hummel Mark (TMK-7). At 4½'' Sleep Tight has a collector value range of $160-185.00 presently.

PLEASANT MOMENT
Hum 425
Possible Future Edition

Two seated girls. One holds flowers in left hand. The other reaches down with right hand toward a yellow butterfly.

PAY ATTENTION
Hum 426
Possible Future Edition

Girl sitting on fence. She holds flowers and basket and is looking away from a crowing black bird perched on the fence post behind her.

WHERE ARE YOU?
Hum 427
Possible Future Edition

Boy sitting on fence. He holds bouquet of flowers. There is a bird perched on a fence post.

I WON'T HURT YOU
Hum 428
Possible Future Edition

Boy with hiking staff in left hand. He is looking down at a ladybug in his right hand.

HELLO WORLD
Hum 429

Released in 1989 as a special edition available to members of the Goebel Collectors' Club with redemption cards of which the expiration date was May 31, 1990. There are already two variations to be found. 1989 is the year of the club's transition from the Goebel Collectors' Club to the M.I. Hummel Club. Apparently a few of these went out with the old special edition backstamp before it was discovered. All those subsequently released will bear the M.I. Hummel Club backstamp. The piece stands 5½'' high and was priced to members at $130.00.

IN D-MAJOR
Hum 430

    This 1988 release is listed at 4⅜'' tall. The one in the photo here measures 4⅛''. It carries a 1981 mold induction date incised beneath the base. It was released at $135.00 and is $170.00 in the 1992 suggested retail price list from Goebel.

THE SURPRISE
Hum 431

This figure, introduced in 1989, is the twelfth special edition for members of the Goebel Collectors' Club (now M.I. Hummel Club) only. The expiration date on the redemption card is May 31, 1990. The Surprise bears the incised mold induction date of 1981 as well as the same date in decal under the current trade mark. This figure is the first to also bear the little bumblebee (see accompanying photo). It is to appear on all future special editions for club members. It is 5⅜'' high and was released to members for $125.00.

KNIT ONE, PURL ONE
Hum 432

One of the newer releases, this piece was first released at a factory recommended retail price of $52.00. Now selling at about $100.00. Basic size is 3''.

SING ALONG
Hum 433

Newly released in 1987 at $145.00 it is at $240.00 in late 1992 Goebel suggested retail price list. It measures 4⅜'' tall and bears an incised mold induction date of 1982.

FRIEND OR FOE
Hum 434
Possible Future Edition

This 4″ figurine was released in 1991 at $195.00 suggested retail. It bears an incised 1982 Mold Induction Date (MID).

DELICIOUS
Hum 435
Possible Future Edition
Standing child about to eat red candy held in left hand.

AN EMERGENCY
Hum 436
Boy with bandage on his head. He is about to push the button on the doctor's gate.

THE TUBA PLAYER
Hum 437

This figurine was released in the winter of 1988. It is listed as 6¼", but the one in the photo here actually measures 6" high. It carries a 1988 mold induction date and the Missing Bee (TMK-6) trademark. It was released at $160.00 and is listed at $225.00 in the 1992 Goebel suggested retail price list. It continues in production in the Hummel Mark (TMK-7).

SOUNDS OF THE MANDOLIN
Hum 438

This 3¾'' figure was released in 1987 as one of three musical angel pieces. The other two are Song of Praise, Hum 454 and The Accompanist, Hum 453. The release price was $65.00 and it is listed at $100.00 in the Goebel suggested retail price list.

A GENTLE GLOW
Candleholder
Hum 439

Newly released in 1987 this piece is a small standing child. The candle receptacle appears to be resting on greenery that the child holds up with both hands. At release the suggested retail price was $110.00. It is listed at $175.00 in the Goebel suggested retail price list of 1992.

BIRTHDAY CANDLE
Candleholder
Hum 440

This 5½" candleholder is the tenth special edition available to members of the Goebel Collectors' Club only. It bears the following inscription on the base: "EXCLUSIVE SPECIAL EDITION NO. 10 FOR MEMBERS OF THE GOEBEL COLLECTORS' CLUB." It was released at $95.00 with a redemption card cut-off date of May 31, 1988. It was released in conjunction with the Tenth Anniversary Celebration of the clubs formation.

CALL TO WORSHIP
Clock
Hum 441

This is only the second clock ever made from a Hummel design. It stands 13" tall and has a musical movement that chimes every hour. There are two tunes to choose from. You can choose either at random by moving a switch beneath. The tunes are Ave Maria or the Westminster Chimes. It is the second offering in what Goebel calls the Century Collection. These are pieces produced in the Twentieth Century limited in production to one year only. This is signified on the base with the addition of the Roman numeral XX. The suggested retail price in the 1988 year of production was $600.00.

CHAPEL TIME
Clock
Hum 442

This is the first clock to be put into production and released by Goebel. It was limited to one year of production (1986) and will not be make again in this century. As part of the artist's mark and date on the bottom is the Roman numeral XX meaning the Twentieth Century. The base also bears the current-use Missing Bee (TMK-6) trademark and a blue M.I. Hummel signature with the inscription "The Love Lives On."

Variation number one: Four belfry windows open. Small round window closed.

Variation number two: Four belfry windows closed. Small round window closed.

There are several variations, mostly having to do with the windows in the chapel building. So far, the most commonly found version is that with all windows closed and painted, except for the four in the belfry. the rarest, as of this writing, is a version with all windows closed and painted. According to

Variation number three: Four belfry
windows open. Small round window open.

Goebel this version was a pre-production run numbering
800-1000. This rare variation is valued at $1500-2000.00. It has
been reported that a few of these have been found with the two
small round windows in the gables open. A third version has
the gable and the belfry windows all open. There are other variations with regard to the base and the size of the hole in the bottom (to replace battery), but these are not presently considered
significant.

The clock is 11½" tall and was released at $500.00 suggested
retail price. It is now valued at $1000-1200.00.

COUNTRY SONG
Clock
Hum 443
Possible Future Edition

Boy blowing horn. He is seated on a flower covered mound.
Blue flowers are used instead of numbers on the clock face.

MORNING CONCERT
Hum 447

This is the eleventh special edition piece made and offered exclusively for members of the Goebel Collectors' Club (now M.I. Hummel Club). They were available to members until the expiration date of May 31, 1989. Morning Concert has a mold induction date of 1984 incised beneath the base and the special edition club back stamp in decal underglaze. It stands 5'' tall and was available to members for $98.00.

CHILDREN'S PRAYER
Hum 448
Possible Future Edition
Boy and girl standing, looking up at roadside shrine of Jesus on the Cross.

THE LITTLE PAIR
Hum 449

In 1990 the M.I. Hummel Club began offering special figures to those members who had passed certain year milestones of membership. This particular piece is made available to only those members who have attained or surpassed their tenth year of membership. Each bears a special backstamp commemorating the occasion. The 10th year club exclusive is available to qualified collectors at $185.00.

UNKNOWN
Hum 450 through Hum 451
Open numbers for possible future editions.

FLYING HIGH
Hum 452

This is the first in a series of hanging ornaments. It is not, however, the first Hummel hanging ornament; the first being the Flying Angel, Hum 366, commonly used with the Nativity Sets. Flying High was introducd in late 1987 as the 1988 (first edition) ornament at $75.00 and is still selling at that price. It measures 3½''x4⅛''.

There are three variations with regard to additional marks. When first released there were no additional markings. The second variation is the appearance of a decal reading ''First Edition'' beneath the skirt. The third is the appearance of the ''First Edition'' mark and ''1988'' painted on the back of the gown.

THE
ACCOMPANIST
Hum 453

This new piece along with Hum 454, Song of Praise and Hum 438, Sounds of the Mandolin, were introduced in 1987 as a trio of angel musicians. It was released at $39.00 and is listed at $80.00 in the 1992 Goebel price list. The figurine measures 3¼" high and has an incised mold induction date of 1984.

SONG OF PRAISE
Hum 454

This piece is one of three angel musician figures introduced in 1987. The others are the preceding Hum 453 and Hum 438, The Accompanist. Song of Praise is listed at $80.00 in the 1992 Goebel price list. It stands 3" high.

413

THE GUARDIAN
Hum 455

A 1991 release, The Guardian 3½'' figure. The suggested retail price at the time of release was $145.00 and is the same on the 1992 Goebel price list.

UNKNOWN
Hum 456

Open number for possible future edition.

SOUND THE TRUMPET
Hum 457

This was a new introduction to the line in 1987. It measures
2¾'' high and has an incised mold induction date of 1984. It
was introduced at $45.00 and is listed at $80.00 in the 1992
Goebel suggested retail price list.

STORYBOOK TIME
Hum 458

    This piece was introduced as new for 1992 in the Fall 1991 issue of *INSIGHTS*, the M.I. Hummel club newsletter, with the name "Story Time". Inexplicably, all references to the piece have subsequently referred to it is "Storybook Time". It is listed as 5" tall and the release price was $330.00.

IN THE MEADOW
Hum 459

This was released in 1987 as one of five 1987 releases. The size is 4″ and the release price was $110.00. It has an incised mold induction date of 1985 beneath the base. It is listed in the 1992 Goebel suggested retail price list at $170.00.

TALLY
Retail Dealer Plaque
Hum 460

Autorisierter
Fachhändler

Goebel

W. Goebel Porzellanfabrik

M.J.Hummel

This dealer plaque was introduced in 1986. It was thought that it was to replace the Hum 187 Merry Wanderer dealer plaque, but in 1990 the Merry Wanderer style was reissued. When Tally was first introduced there was apparently a shortage with dealers limited to only one each, but shortly thereafter the shortage was alleviated. The boy on the plaque is, as you can see, very similar to the center figure in School Boys, Hum 170. The base of the plaque bears an incised mold induction date of 1984.

There are no structural or color variations presently known, but there are variations in the language used on the front of the plaque. There is German as in the photo accompanying, Swedish, French, Spanish, Dutch, a version for British dealers and of course one for the American market for a total of seven. The plaque was released at $85.00 in the U.S. and is presently valued at about $150.00. The foreign language versions are much more rare and can fetch between $600 and $1500 on the secondary market depending upon the language.

UNKNOWN   Hum 461 through Hum 466
Open numbers reserved for possible future editions.

THE KINDERGARTNER
Hum 467

A new release for 1987 this figure stands 5″ high. The release price was $100.00. The actual measurement of the figurine in the photo here is 5¼″ and it bears a mold induction date of 1986 incised beneath the base. It now has a suggested retail price of $170.00 in the Goebel list.

UNKNOWN
Hum 468 through Hum 470
Open numbers for possible future editions.

HARMONY IN FOUR PARTS
Hum 471

This is the 1989 addition to the Century Collection. These pieces are limited to the production year in the Twentieth Century and will not be produced again in this century. They each bear a special back stamp indicating this. The stamp is 1989 underlined with the Roman numeral XX beneath. This is in the center of a circle made up of the M.I. Hummel signature and the words "CENTURY COLLECTION." It measures 9" wide and 10" high. The mold induction date is 1987. The lamp post was originally made of the same fine earthenware that Hummel pieces are rendered in, but it was soon noted that the post was very easily broken. To alleviate this problem Goebel began using a metal post instead. Although there is not presently any difference in the value of these, it is reasonable to project that the earthenware post version may become the more desirable to serious collectors thereby making it more valuable. Only time will tell. Hum 471 was released at $850.00 and is presently valued at about ———.

ON OUR WAY
Hum 472

This unusual piece was introduced as new for 1992 in the Fall, 1991 issue of *INSIGHTS,* the M.I. Hummel Club newsletter. It is the CENTURY COLLECTION piece for 1992. The number available is limited by the number produced during the one year of production. They bear a special identifying backstamp and are accompanied by a certificate of authenticity. Size is 6½″ x 5½″ x 8″ and the release price was $950.00.

UNKNOWN
Hum 473 and Hum 474
Open numbers for possible future editions.

WINTER SONG
Hum 476

This was a 1987 release. It stands 4½'' tall and was priced at $45.00 when introduced and is listed at $95.00 in the 1992 Goebel price list. It bears an incised mold induction date of 1987.

MAKE A WISH
Hum 475

Listed as an UNKNOWN in the last edition of this book it was released in 1989. The figure is 4¼'' and the release price was $135.00. The 1992 Suggested Retail Price list from Goebel lists it at $180.00. It can be found with the Missing Bee (TMK-6) and the new Hummel Mark (TMK-7).

A BUDDING MAESTRO
Hum 477

This figure measures 3⅞'' tall. It was released in 1987 at $45.00 and is listed at $90.00 in the Goebel suggested retail price list of 1992.

I'M HERE
Hum 478

I'm Here was released in 1988 as a new addition to the line. The figure in the photo measures 3'' and is listed in price lists as 2¾''. It carries a 1987 incised mold induction date. Released at $50.00 it is listed at $85.00 in the current Goebel price list.

I BROUGHT YOU A GIFT
Hum 479

Beginning June 1, 1989 the 4" bisque plaque with the Merry Wanderer motif that was given to every new member of the Goebel Collectors' Club is officially retired. At the same date the club became officially the M.I. Hummel Club and a new membership premium, I Brought You a Gift, was introduced. At the time of transition each renewing member was given one. In addition each new member will receive one. It is 4" high and has the incised mold induction date of 1987 on the underside of the base. There are apparently two variations to be found with regard to the club special edition back stamp. If you will look at the accompanying photograph of the base you will note the old club name beneath the bumblebee. The author has not personally seen one with the new name but it stands to reason, as inventory diminishes, Goebel will change the back stamp to reflect the new name if they have not indeed, done so already.

HOSANNA
Hum 480

Released in 1989, this figure stands 4'' tall. It has a 1987 mold induction date incised under the base. The suggested retail price at the time of the release was $68.00 and is now in the Goebel price list at $80.00.

LOVE FROM ABOVE
Ornament
Hum 481

This is the second edition in the hanging ornament series, 1989, that began with the 1988 Flying High, Hum 452. It bears the Missing Bee (TMK-6) trademark and was released at $75.00.

ONE FOR YOU,
ONE FOR ME
Hum 482

This piece was a new release in 1988. It is 3⅛" high and carries a 1987 incised mold induction date. It was originally priced at $50.00 and listed in the 1992 Goebel suggested retail price list at $85.00.

I'LL PROTECT HIM
Hum 483

New in 1989 this figure stands 3¾" high. It bears an incised mold induction date of 1987 on the underside of the base. The release price was $55.00. It is $70.00 in the 1992 Goebel price list.

PEACE ON EARTH
1990 Christmas Ornament
Hum 484

The third in an annual release of M.I. Hummel Christmas ornaments, this one was released at $80.00 suggested retail. The size is 4''.

A GIFT FROM A FRIEND
Hum 485

This little 4⅜'' fellow is offered exclusively to members of the M.I. Hummel club in the club year 1991-92. Its availability to members at $160.00 is subject to the cut-off date of May 31, 1993.

I WONDER
Hum 486

This was a club exclusive offered to member of the M.I. Hummel Club only, during the club of the year of June 1, 1990 to May 31, 1991. They were offered at $140.00. The size is listed as 5¼'' and it bears the Bumble Bee club backstamp.

LET'S TELL THE WORLD
Hum 487

Released in 1990 as part of the CENTURY COLLECTION, Let's Tell the World is 10½''. The production number was limited to the number produced during 1990 and the edition is listed as closed in the 1992 Goebel price list with no price so presumably they are no longer available. The actual number of them produced is not presently known. Each piece bears a special backstamp commemorating the 55th Anniversary of M.I. Hummel figurines. Released at $875.00.

TWO HANDS, ONE TREAT
Hum 493

This special 4″ figure is an M.I. Hummel Club exclusive. It was made available as a renewal premium, a gift, to those members renewing their membership in the club year 1991-92. The club placed a $65.00 valuation on the piece.

EVENING PRAYER
Hum 495

Introduced as "NEW FOR '92" in the fall, 1991 issue of the M.I. Hummel Club newsletter this figure is listed at 3¾″ tall and the release price was $95.00.

LAND IN SIGHT
Hum 530

This large, complicated piece is very special. Land in Sight is a sequentially numbered, limited edition of 30,000 world wide, released in 1992 to commemorate Columbus' discovery of America. It is 9⅛'' x 8⅜'' x 5⅞'' in size. The special backstamp reads: ''1492 - The Quincentennial of America's Discovery.'' There is also a medallion accompanying it. The release price was $1,600.00.

A NAP
Hum 534

This piece was introduced as new for 1991 in the Fall issue of the M.I. Hummel Club newsletter, *INSIGHTS*. It is listed as 2¼″ in size and released at $100.00 and is still listed as that in the 1992 Goebel suggested retail price list.

FLOWER GIRL
Hum 548

This is a special figure available only to members of the M.I. Club and then only upon or after the fifth anniversary of their membership. It is 4½″ high and bears a special backstamp to indicate its unique status. The current price to members is $115.00 with a redemption card.

SCAMP
Hum 553

New in 1992, Scamp is listed as 3½'' in size and was released at $95.00.

GRANDMA'S GIRL
Hum 561

New for 1990, Grandma's Girl is listed at 4'' in size. The initial price was $100.00 and is $125.00 in the current Goebel suggested retail price list. They should be found with both the Missing Bee (TMK-6) and the current use Hummel Mark (TMK-7).

GRANDPA'S BOY
Hum 562

New for 1990, Grandpa's Boy is listed at 4'' size. The initial price was $100.00 and is $125.00 in current Goebel suggested retail price list. They can be found with both the Missing Bee (TMK-6) and the current use Hummel Mark (TMK-7).

WE WISH YOU THE BEST
Hum 600

We Wish You the Best is the CENTURY COLLECTION piece for 1991. Limited in production to the number produced in that year it was released at $1300.00 and is valued at about the same presently. It is listed as 9½'' x 8¼'' in size.

ANGELIC GUIDE
Christmas Ornament
Hum 571

This is the 1991 and fourth issue in an annual series of ornaments. 4'' size, it was issued at $95.00.

LIGHT UP THE NIGHT
Christmas Ornament
Hum 622

The 1992 ornament. This is the fifth in an annual series. 3¼'' in size, it was released at $100.00.

Left ornament is Angelic Guide, Hum 571 and on the right is Hum 622, Light Up the Night.

UNKNOWN
Hum 488 through Hum 492
Open numbers for possible future editions.

FLOWERS FOR MOTHER
Mother's Day Plate
Hum 500
Possible Future Edition
This plate was listed in the index of the M.I. HUMMEL-THE GOLDEN ANNIVERSARY ALBUM. Little else is known at this time. It was not illustrated.

UNKNOWN
The following Hummel mold numbers are called Open Numbers by Goebel signifying that they may be used for Possible Future Editions (PFE).

Hum 495 - 499   Hum 535 - 552   Hum 572 - 599
Hum 501 - 529   Hum 554 - 560   Hum 601 - 621
Hum 531 - 533   Hum 563 - 570   Hum 623 - 712

SMILING THROUGH
Plaque
Hum 690

This is the second special edition produced exclusively for members of the Goebel Collectors Club. It was available through membership in the club only. Members received a redemption certificate upon receipt of their annual dues and they could purchase the piece through dealers who are official representatives of the club for $55.00. It appears bearing the Last Bee trademark only. 5¾" Round. it is presently valued at about $90-100.00. As of May 31, 1984 it was no longer available as a redemption piece.

UNKNOWN
Hum 691 through Hum 699
Open numbers reserved for Possible Future Editions.

1978   1979   1980   1981

1978 ANNUAL BELL
Hum 700

This is the first edition of a bell which the factory has begun producing, one each year. This first bell utilizes the "Let's Sing", Hum 110, motif. It is a first of its kind and like the first edition Annual Plate it experienced quite a rapid rise in value for a while. it was first released at $50.00 and is presently bringing about $30-40.00.

1979 ANNUAL BELL
Hum 701

This is the second edition bell released in 1979. It utilizes the Hum 65 "Farewell" design motif. The suggested retail release price was $70.00. Now selling for about $20-30.00.

1980 ANNUAL BELL
Hum 702

The third edition in the series of annual bells. This bell utilizes the design motif of a boy seated, reading from a large book in his lap. It is somewhat similar to Hum 3 or 8, The Girl Bookworm. The design is named "THOUGHTFUL". Issue price: $85.00. Now selling for about $20-25.00.

1981 ANNUAL BELL
Hum 703

The fourth bell in the series uses the design from Hum 414, IN TUNE. Released at $115 it is now selling for about $30-40.00.

438

1981 Annual Bell
Hum 703

1982 Annual Bell
Hum 704

1983 Annual Bell
Hum 705

1982 ANNUAL BELL
Hum 704
This fifth bell in the series matches the design of Hum 174, SHE LOVES ME, SHE LOVES ME NOT. Released at $85 and now selling at $35-65.00.

1983 ANNUAL BELL
Hum 705
This is the sixth bell in the series. The design is called KNIT ONE. The release price was $90 and it is presently widely advertised at about $40-50.00.

1984 ANNUAL BELL
Hum 706

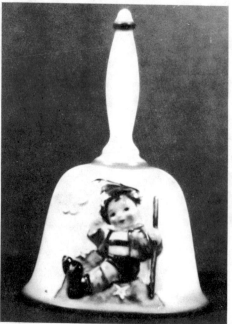

The seventh bell in the annual series derives its design from the figurine Mountaineer. The release price was $90.00 and it is presently selling at $50-60.00.

1985 ANNUAL BELL
Hum 707

The eighth bell in the series matches the design of the figurine Girl with Sheet Music. The release price was $90.00 and it is presently advertised for sale at $35-75.00.

1986 ANNUAL BELL
Hum 708

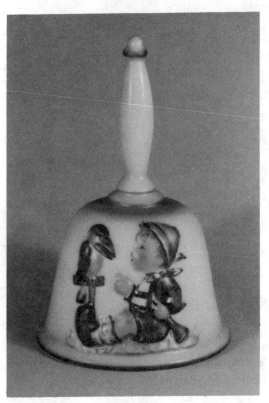

The ninth bell in the series. Uses the figurine Sing Along, Hum 433 as its design. Release price: $100.00. It is presently selling at $65-85.00.

1987 ANNUAL BELL
Hum 709

The tenth bell in the series. Uses With Loving Greeting, Hum 309 as its design. Release price: $110.00. It is presently selling at $100-110.00

1988 ANNUAL BELL
Hum 710

The eleventh bell in the series. Uses Busy Student, Hum 367 as its design. Release price: $120.00. It is presently selling at $70-90.00.

1989 ANNUAL BELL
Hum 711

The twelfth bell in the series. Uses Latest News, Hum 184 as its design. It was released at a suggested retail price of $135.00. A few of these Hum 711 bells were produced with the mold number 710 incised before the mistake was discovered. The present collector value is $90-120.00.

1990 ANNUAL BELL
Hum 712

This is the thirteenth bell in the series. It uses What's New? as its design. The release price was $140.00 and is presently selling at $95-115.00.

443

1991 ANNUAL BELL
Hum 713

The fourteenth bell in the series. It uses Favorite Pet as its design. It is presently selling at $90-115.00.

1992 ANNUAL BELL
Hum 714

The fifteenth bell in the series uses Whistler's Duet as its design motif. Released at $165.00 it is now widely advertised for $100-160.00.

UNKNOWN
Hum 715 through Hum 729
Open Numbers reserved for Possible Future Editions.

ANNIVERSARY BELL
Hum 730

Although this has never been seen nor officially revealed until 1987, it may not come to be. It is listed in the index of the book M.I. HUMMEL-GOLDEN ANNIVERSARY ALBUM. It was not illustrated. The original intention was to release it as a companion piece for a plate in the Anniversary Plate Series, but since the series was cancelled so went the bell.

VALENTINE GIFT
Plate
Hum 738

One of three redemption pieces made available exclusively to members of the Goebel Collectors' Club in 1986. The size is 6'' round and is available to members at $90.00 with redemption card. The cut-off date for purchase of the plate is May 31, 1988. This is the first plate in a series of four; the Celebration Series. The next three are:

1987	Hum 737	Valentine Joy ($98.00 at release)
1988	Hum 736	Daisies Don't Tell ($115.00 at release)
1989	Hum 735	It's Cold ($120.00 at release)

UNKNOWN
Hum 739 and Hum 740

Open Numbers reserved for Possible Future Editions.

MINIATURE PLATES

LITTLE FIDDLER
Hum 744

SOLOIST
Hum 743

BAND LEADER
Hum 742

In 1984 Goebel announced a new series of miniature plates. With the release of the Little Fiddler miniature plate the company also released a list of forthcoming plates in the series. There is no official explanation of the non-sequential mold number in order of release. Each plate is 4'' in diameter and the first was released at $30.00. The list in order of release follows:

(cont.)

CHRISTMAS BELL SERIES

This four bell series began with the 1989 offering and ended with the 1992 bell. They were rendered in a soft blue and each has a clapper fashioned in the shape of a pine cone. They are 3¼'' in height.

The only significant variation to be found is with regard to color. Some 250-300 of the 1990 bell, Ride into Christmas were made in a greenish yellow color and given to company representatives as a Christmas present from Goebel.

1989	Hum 775	Ride into Christmat	35.00
1990	Hum 776	Letter to Santa Claus	37.50
1991	Hum 777	Here Ye, Here Ye	39.50
1992	Hum 778	Harmony in Four Parts	50.00

There has been little or no movement of these pieces on the secondary market so there is insufficient data to establish a secondary market value. The prices reflected above are the initial retail at release.

Hum 776 - 1990 - Chris Bell Letter to Santa Claus red 1989, 2 of 4, 250-300 in greenish yellow, for sales representatives.

Hum 775 - Christmas Bell Ride into Christmas, 1988 Marked -
First Edition - Pine Cone Clapper, 1st in 4

1991 - Christmas Hum Bell Here Ye, Here Ye - 3¼, Hum 777.

1992 - Christmas Hum Bell Harmony in Four Parts 3¼, Hum 778.

(Miniature Plates continued)

1984	Hum 744	Little Fiddler	30.00
1985	Hum 741	Serenade	30.00
1986	Hum 743	Soloist	35.00
1987	Hum 742	Band Leader	40.00

They are known collectively as the "Little Music Makers." Each plate in the series was strictly limited to the number sold in the year of release and the remaining plates were destroyed along with the mold. There has been little or no movement of these on the secondary market, therefore the values listed above are the original release price for the year of release.

LITTLE HOMEMAKERS MINIATURE PLATE SERIES

This is the second series of miniature plates. Each in this series will be accompanied by the release of a smaller, three-inch size of the existing piece from which it draws its motif. Each plate is 4" in diameter. Each plate will be limited to the number sold in the one year of production. There has been little or no movement on the secondary market for these, therefore the values you see here are the original release prices.

1988	Hum 745	Little Sweeper	45.00
1989	Hum 746	Wash Day	50.00
1990	Hum 747	A Stitch in Time	50.00
1991	Hum 748	Chicken Licken	70.00

Hum 745 - Little Sweeper

Hum 746 - Wash Day

(See next page)

Hum 747 - A Stitch in Time

Hum 748 - Chicken Licken

INTRODUCTION TO INDEX

This is a general index for your convenience. It does not include references to the individual pieces, as their location can be readily ascertained by referring to the Master Index for the collection beginning on page 83.